# Contemporary Christologies

# Contemporary Christologies

## A FORTRESS INTRODUCTION

## Don Schweitzer

Fortress Press ◆ Minneapolis

CONTEMPORARY CHRISTOLOGIES
A Fortress Introduction

Scripture quotations from the New Revised Standard Version of the Bible are copyright © 1989 by the Division of Christian Education of the National Council of Churches of Christ in the United States of America and are used by permission.

Cover image: The Art Archive / Haghia Sophia Istanbul / Gianni Dagli Orto / The Picture Desk.
Cover design: Laurie Ingram
Interior photos: Roger Haight: © Ron Hester; Carter Heyward: © Susan B. Sasser; Mark Lewis Taylor: © Kim Schmidt, courtesy of Princeton Theological Seminary.
Book design: PerfecType, Nashville, TN

*Library of Congress Cataloging-in-Publication data*

Schweitzer, Don, 1958-
   Contemporary christologies : a fortress introduction / Don Schweitzer.
      p. cm.
   ISBN 978-0-8006-6463-3 (alk. paper)
   1. Jesus Christ—Person and offices. 2. Theology, Doctrinal—History—20th century. 3. Theology, Doctrinal—History—21st century. I. Title.
   BT203.S252 2010
   232'.809045--dc22
                                    2009053475

The paper used in this publication meets the minimum requirements for American National Standard for Information Sciences—Permanence of Paper for Printed Library Materials, ANSI Z329.48–1984.

Manufactured in the U.S.A.
14 13 12 11 10  1 2 3 4 5 6 7 8 9 10

# CONTENTS

◆ ──────────────────────────────────── ◆

# PREFACE

◆ ─────────────────────────────────────────── ◆

Jesus' question to his disciples, "Who do you say that I am?" (Mark 8:29) continually recurs to those who believe in him as the Christ. Each generation answers it in a variety of ways. This is born out in the Christologies studied in this book. Each reflects something of the context it comes from and how its author experienced this. Yet each also reflects something of Jesus, who first asked this question. These diverse Christologies add new voices to the conversation about Jesus, his saving significance, and the meaning of life that has been ongoing since his ministry began. Each of these new voices is worth listening to.

Each of these Christologies chooses a way or ways of understanding Jesus' saving significance. These choices reflect varying assessments of how Jesus as the Christ relates to the present. This book divides these ways into five types and assesses the strengths and weaknesses of each. A guiding conviction behind this arrangement is that each type primarily addresses a distinct kind of sin or evil. By lifting up the different kinds of sin and evil that different ways of understanding Jesus' saving significance address, this book shows how these can correct and supplement each other. The different atonement models studied here should be seen as unfolding different aspects of Jesus' saving significance rather than as mutually exclusive alternatives.

Many people, places, and institutions played a role in the writing of this book. Melanie Schwanbeck and then Brittany Dove, library technicians at St. Andrew's College library, were a great help in getting books and journals from other libraries in the Saskatoon Theological Union. The interlibrary loans department at the University of Saskatchewan was also tremendously helpful in getting essential materials. Melanie Schwanbeck helped me repeatedly when I had trouble with my computer. St. Andrew's College provided me with a very able and industrious research assistant in Jeff Martens-Koop for the fall of 2008. Ministry at Turtle River Larger Parish and then Wesley United Church in Prince Albert led me to appreciate how different atonement models address different forms of suffering, sin, and evil. Teaching

Christology at Serampore College, Serampore, and Dalit theology at the United Theological College in Bangalore, India, gave me insights for chapter 5. Students in the Christology classes I have taught at St. Andrew's College and St. Stephen's in Edmonton have helped shape my appreciation of the Christologies discussed here. Tatha Wiley, Gord Waldie, and Harold Wells read part or all of the manuscript, offering valuable suggestions, corrections and encouragement. I thank all of the above for their help with this book. Leslie cheered me on to finish it. I dedicate it to her, and to Simon and Ian.

# INTRODUCTION

This book is an introduction to contemporary Christologies. It examines how fifteen theologians from the past forty years have understood Jesus. It is divided into five chapters, each focusing on a particular way of understanding Jesus' saving significance as featured in the Christologies of three theologians. These ways of understanding Jesus' saving significance are sometimes called models of atonement. Each chapter analyzes the form of evil, sin, or suffering that a particular model addresses, how Jesus is seen to overcome this, how salvation is understood in the model, and assesses the model's strengths, and weakness. The aim is to help students grasp the dynamics of different atonement models, their limitations, strengths, and versatility, and to provide samples of contemporary christological thought. The focus of the book is on the exposition of the Christologies studied. But questions, observations, and critical comments on these and the models of atonement they employ are scattered throughout, as critical debate belongs to the substance of theology. An introduction should give some assessment as well as an overview.

The Christologies studied here all belong to the post–World War II era and represent live options in contemporary Christian theology. They continue a tradition of thought going back almost two thousand years. The first Christologies arose in response to Jesus of Nazareth. The dates of his birth and death cannot be determined exactly. He was a Jew born in Palestine, probably in Nazareth, around 7 or 6 BCE.[1] Following in the footsteps of John the Baptist and after being baptized by John, he began an itinerant public ministry in Galilee, preaching the imminent coming of the reign of God, healing the sick, casting out demons, teaching, and gathering a following, at the heart of which were twelve disciples. After traveling to Jerusalem at the time of the Passover celebration, he was crucified by Roman authority, probably in 30 CE. Shortly thereafter, some of his former followers and others claimed that Jesus had risen to new life, proclaimed him to be the Christ, and began to worship God in his name.

Ever since then there have been Christologies reflecting on this. These typically have two foci. One is around Jesus' person. He was a person like others and yet, as the Christ, was distinct in his relation to God.[2] Most contemporary Christologies continue the long tradition of trying to understand what this distinction was and how it came to be. The second focus of Christologies is on Jesus' work, or saving significance. Jesus was understood to be the Christ because he was seen to save or benefit people, delivering them from various forms of sin, evil, and suffering, empowering them to do the good either through his teaching, his example, his death and resurrection, or a combination thereof. Contemporary Christologies seek to articulate what Jesus' saving significance is in the present and how he effects it. These two foci are usually interrelated. Because Jesus is like others and yet distinct in relation to God, he is able to save.

Christologies tend to develop in relation to external factors like the social location of a church, the stability of surrounding society, and socially dominant ideals, assumptions, and practices. They also tend to reflect internal factors like the church tradition a theologian belongs to, theological developments and disputes within it, and the interests of those producing the Christology. These internal and external factors are usually related and yet cannot be collapsed into one another. In time, a combination of external factors like the church's growing presence in the Roman Empire and internal factors like the Arian crisis and later christological debates led to the affirmations of the ecumenical Councils of Nicaea (325) and Chalcedon (451). Their teachings, that Jesus Christ was one with and yet distinct from God (Nicaea), fully human and fully divine, the two natures united without confusion in his one person (Chalcedon), would become basic assumptions for most Christologies up until the time of the Enlightenment (1700s). They continue to be considered normative in the teachings of some churches. In the centuries between the Council of Chalcedon and the rise of the Enlightenment a variety of Christologies were produced that continue to be influential today, such as those of Anselm, Aquinas, Julian of Norwich, Luther, and Calvin.

The Enlightenment was characterized by a critical attitude toward Christian faith, church authority, and teaching. It was accompanied by spectacular developments in forms of knowledge like the natural sciences that often contradicted biblical traditions and church teaching. This helped create an intellectual ethos that challenged the authority of the affirmations of Nicaea and Chalcedon as basic assumptions for Christology and the veracity of biblical traditions about Jesus' birth, miracles, and resurrection. A variety of distinctly modern Christologies developed in response to this, like those of Schleiermacher, Hegel, and Ritschl. Contemporary Christologies have developed in varying ways against this combined background of the biblical witness, the affirmations of Nicaea and Chalcedon, the challenge of the Enlightenment, and theological developments occurring over the course of church history. Contemporary Christologies have also developed in relation to events in the twentieth century.[3] These sometimes influenced Christian theology in contrasting ways. The challenge of the Enlightenment has continued to confront Christian theology with a "crisis of cognitive claims"[4] regarding traditional affirmations about the person and work of Jesus Christ. With this came an increasing secularism in Europe that helped create a sense of the absence of God. The horrors of World War I contributed to this as well, yet also worked in a different direction, helping trigger the theological development of neoorthodoxy, which reaffirmed the transcendence of God and reclaimed a sense of evangelical freedom on the basis of a renewed sense of biblical authority. In the 1960s, Vatican II expressed a new openness to the world and optimism in Roman Catholic thought. In the 1970s, as the oppression of the poor in Latin America and the horror of the Holocaust became focuses of Christian theological reflection, this optimism was criticized. Reflection on the Holocaust led to criticism of anti-Jewish trends in Christology and reflection on the sufferings of victims of "man-made mass death."[5] Reflection on the suffering of the poor and their struggles for justice led to new attention to what can be known historically about Jesus and the connections between his public ministry and death.

Contemporary Christologies have also been influenced by the explosion of difference in the 1960s, as oppressed peoples and social groups began to articulate their specific sufferings and hopes and struggle against their oppression by dominant cultures in Western societies. Theologians in these groups began to develop Christologies in light of these struggles. Some theologians from dominant social groups began to think about Christ in relation to these struggles and in light of their own privilege. Feminist concerns about the impact on women of the way Jesus' maleness and saving significance have been understood have been particularly significant for feminist Christologies. Christian-Marxist dialogues challenged theologians to develop Christologies that would make a difference in the world, particularly in peoples' living conditions. The phenomenon of globalization and the persistence of many religions led some to ponder Christ's meaning in relation to religious pluralism. Late in the twentieth century, the environmental crisis raised new concerns about the saving significance of Jesus for nature and his implications for how nature should be understood. Developments within Christian theology in the twentieth century have also influenced contemporary Christologies. Gustaf Aulén's classic book *Christus Victor*[6] presented an influential typology of three models of atonement that directed attention to the different ways in which Jesus' saving significance has been understood. The quest for the historical Jesus took on renewed life after World War II and became a significant factor for many contemporary Christologies. Karl Barth's emphasis on Jesus Christ as the decisive revelation in terms of which all attributes of God must be understood led to Christologies being developed as a much more integral part of the doctrine of God. A number of the Christologies studied in this book also reflect Dietrich Bonhoeffer's notion of Jesus as the person for others and Paul Tillich's understanding of Christ as addressing the particular alienation or oppressions of a given age. None of the Christologies studied here respond to all these events or incorporate all of these influences, but all are influenced by some of them, and all are developed in contexts that these events and social movements helped shape. Because Christologies tend to develop in relation to external and internal factors, these need to be considered when studying them. For this reason, the overview of each Christology in the chapters that follow begins with a brief biographical sketch of its author, noting influences on and significant developments in their thought.

An attempt has been made to include a diversity of voices in this introduction. But it is unlikely that any book could give an adequate overview of all contemporary Christologies. It would be difficult for any individual to keep up on all the work being done in Christology at present around the globe, or on all the significant Christologies produced in the past forty years. Anyone familiar with contemporary Christology will see that a few of their favorite theologians are missing. The Christologies of significant North Atlantic theologians like Wolfhart Pannenberg, Edward Schillebeeckx, and Elisabeth Schüssler Fiorenza are not included here. There is no representative of African[7] or Australian Christologies. Only two representatives from Asian contexts are included and only one from South America. The choice of Christologies to be studied in this book was dictated by my sense of their significance in contemporary christological thought, a desire to have three examples of each model of atonement being covered, and the limitations of my knowledge. This book is intended to be an introduction. It makes no claim to be comprehensive. It provides a sampling of contemporary Christologies and a discussion of how they understand Jesus. Hopefully readers will find it useful.

## Suggestions for Further Reading

Brondos, David A. *Fortress Introduction to Salvation and the Cross*. Minneapolis: Fortress Press, 2007. An accessible and well-written survey of Western Christologies beginning with biblical traditions and working up to the present.

Macquarrie, John. *Jesus Christ in Modern Thought*. Philadelphia: Trinity Press International, 1990. An overview of twentieth-century Western Christologies.

Schüssler Fiorenza, Elisabeth. *Jesus: Miriam's Child, Sophia's Prophet: Critical Issues in Feminist Christology*. New York: Continuum, 1994. An influential feminist interpretation of New Testament Christology.

Studer, Basil. *Trinity and Incarnation: The Faith of the Early Church*. Edited by Andrew Louth. Collegeville, Minn.: Liturgical, 1993. A good overview of the development of patristic Christology up to the Council of Chalcedon.

Tuckett, Christopher. *Christology and the New Testament: Jesus and His Earliest Followers*. Louisville: Westminster John Knox, 2001. An accessible overview of Christologies found in various New Testament traditions and writings.

Wiley, Tatha, ed. *Thinking of Christ: Proclamation, Explanation, Meaning*. New York: Continuum, 2003. A good introduction to contemporary issues in Christology.

## Discussion Questions

1. What are the criteria for assessing the adequacy of a Christology?
2. Do you consider the teachings of the Councils of Nicaea and Chalcedon on the person of Jesus Christ to be normative?
3. Which of the various events of the twentieth century listed as influences on contemporary Christologies do you consider most important in your context?

CHAPTER 1

◆

# Jesus as Revealer
## Karl Rahner, Dorothee Soelle, Roger Haight

As Western societies became increasingly secularized in the twentieth century, the existence of God ceased to be a basic assumption for many people. Experiences of the absence or "eclipse" of God became an important theme in Western thought.[1] This was partly caused by a major change in the way reality was viewed in Western societies.[2] In the premodern thought of Plato and Aristotle, Augustine, Julian of Norwich, and Aquinas, the world was seen as existing within a transcendent framework of meaning. It was in relation to transcendent reality that human life found its meaning and could find fulfillment. This view of the world came to be replaced in Western societies by another, in which reality is seen in an immanent framework with no intrinsic reference to any transcendent reality. In the dominant ethos of Western modernity, the world and humanity are seen as self-sufficient and comprehensible without reference to God. Here, life is conducted and found meaningful according to what can be calculated and planned. In this modern worldview, religion has an ambivalent place. It can be useful for moral instruction, character formation, and as an aid to social order. But it isn't necessary as such and it can give rise to violence and impede social progress.

This new immanent worldview and the secular societies and life-styles based on it helped give rise to a sense of separation from God that was not addressed by models of the atonement focused on how Jesus relieves one of guilt, strengthens one against moral weakness, or gives hope that counters fear of death. In this context of secular modern societies, the understanding that Jesus saves by revealing the presence and loving nature of God took on renewed relevance.

What follows will examine this as presented in the Christologies of Karl Rahner, Dorothee Soelle, and Roger Haight. The theologies and Christologies that these three produced are very different. Karl Rahner tended to write in a dense style, and was intent on showing how the Christian faith and being Roman Catholic were comprehensible in relation to the dominant forms of knowledge and experience in modern Western societies. He helped stimulate the renewal of trinitarian theology in the twentieth century and was concerned that theology be both continuous with church tradition and meaningful in the present. Dorothee Soelle wrote in a brief, accessible style that focused on the meaningfulness of Jesus in relation to contemporary experiences of the absence of God, injustice, sorrow, joy, and desire. Her theology draws on contemporary drama, literature, art, and her own experiences as much as church tradition. Her thought was immensely popular in peace and justice movements with church affiliations. Roger Haight is a contemporary revisionist Roman Catholic working in the United States, who seeks to show how Christian faith can be understood in what is now a postmodern era. He writes in an accessible style and works in an ecumenical context. Different as their theologies are, they share an emphasis on a particular way of understanding Jesus' saving significance in relation to modern experiences of the absence of God.

The way in which these three see Jesus overcoming the experience of God's absence is illustrated in the musical *The Music Man*. In this drama, a fraudulent traveling salesperson comes into a community and transforms it by revealing something that was present there all along but which its members had been unaware of. Through their encounter with him, the lives of many community members become filled with a new sense of purpose and joy. The potential for this had always been present. But it was not actualized until he disclosed it. A woman in the community describes the salesperson's effect on her in the song entitled "Till There Was You."

There were bells on the hill
But I never heard them ringing,
No, I never heard them at all
Till there was you.

There were birds in the sky
But I never saw them winging
No, I never saw them at all
Till there was you.
. . . . . . . . . . . .
There was love all around
But I never heard it singing
No, I never heard it at all
Till there was you![3]

Rahner, Soelle, and Haight do not see Jesus as a fraudulent traveling salesperson, but each understands him as having saving significance in a similar way. In their Christologies, the main evil that people need to be delivered from is a lack of awareness of God's presence. Jesus saves by making God powerfully present through his life, death, and resurrection. Though God is always present, Jesus gives people a new consciousness of this through the disclosive power of his person. In the encounter with him, a new awareness of God's nearness and love is made available that empowers people to further express God's love in their own lives. Though the Christologies of Rahner, Soelle, and Haight are multifaceted and have significant differences, central to each is a focus on how Jesus is preeminently the revealer of God.

## Karl Rahner

Karl Rahner was born in Freiburg, Germany, on March 5, 1904.[4] He grew up there and in 1922 followed his older brother Hugo in joining the Jesuit religious order. His theological studies began in 1929 in Holland. In 1933 he was sent to study philosophy at Freiburg. The philosopher Martin Heidegger was there, and Rahner participated in his seminar.[5] However, he had to work under Martin Honecker. In some respects, this did not go well. Rahner's thesis attempted a modern reinterpretation of Aquinas's metaphysics of human knowledge.[6] Honecker judged it unacceptable. Rahner published it anyway as *Spirit in the World*.[7] Along with his subsequent *Hearers of the Word*,[8] this provided the theoretical basis for his theology, as he went on to become one of the most influential Roman Catholic theologians of the twentieth century. Rahner taught at the University of Innsbruck from 1937 to 1964. He retired in 1971 but remained active as a theologian until his death in 1984. His theology continues to be influential in Roman Catholic and ecumenical theology.

Rahner's thought was developed primarily in relation to tensions between Roman Catholic teaching and modern Western society. His theological studies occurred when the mood in Roman Catholic and Protestant theology in Europe "was one of reaffirmation in the face of the challenges of modernity."[9] Along with others, he sought to build a bridge between Roman Catholic teaching and forms of thought and experience characteristic of Western modernity by showing how these were compatible when correctly understood. Rahner's thought has a circular dynamic.[10] It began out of his own experience of Jesus mediating the presence of God through the worship of the church and its sacraments. He experienced and accepted church teaching about Jesus Christ as true. The question was, how should this be understood in twentieth-century Western society?[11] His Christology developed in answer to this question.

When Rahner began his theological studies, the dominant view of reality in modern Western thought was that it was a closed nexus of cause and effect. This meant that accounts of miracles, including Jesus' resurrection and much church teaching, seemed to express myths from a bygone age rather than truth one could live by. This conflict between the modern Western worldview and traditional Roman Catholic teaching was creating a pastoral crisis within the Roman Catholic Church in the North Atlantic hemisphere and preventing the church there from effectively communicating its message. Coupled with this, and equally important as challenges to Christian thought, were the explosion of knowledge and the cultural pluralism confronting the Roman Catholic Church as a worldwide institution.[12]

The scholastic approach to theology that preceded Rahner had positioned theology as the queen of the sciences, giving unity to the many different forms of knowledge. Rahner judged that theology could no longer proceed in this way. In the new context of Western modernity, there was simply too much for any one person to know, and the accepted results of various disciplines were now changing too quickly to form a basis from which to interpret the gospel. He responded by instead developing an approach to theology that came to be known as transcendental Thomism.[13] This involved interpreting the truth claims of theology less in relation to *what* people know and more in relation to *how* they know it and *who* they are as people seeking knowledge about themselves and their world.[14]

According to Rahner, when one asks what it means to know something and why one seeks to know it, one transcends the questions characteristic of any one area of study and moves from considering finite or conditioned aspects of existence to contemplating one's relationship to the infinite or unconditioned, which is the final horizon of all human knowing and acting.[15] Moving in this way from asking about aspects of one's being to asking about one's being as a whole, one discovers that an unconditioned mysterious horizon of being—meaning and mystery—is implicitly present in all aspects of life and thought.[16] To be a person is to be positioned between the world of finite realities and an unconditioned horizon of being, and to be oriented toward the latter in search for meaning.[17] According to Rahner, it is only in relation to this that people can gain the unconditioned meaning and affirmation they seek. Salvation is in essence a matter of receiving an affirmation of ultimate meaning from this mysterious horizon, which Christians know as God.[18] This understanding of the person that Rahner developed in his early works laid the basis for his attempt to overcome the conceptual impediments to Christian faith in Western modernity.

Rahner developed his Christology in two stages, though always on the basis of church teaching, particularly as found in the Chalcedonian Definition and the understanding of the person outlined above. For Rahner, Jesus was what the Chalcedonian Definition affirmed him to be, fully human and fully divine, the two natures united in his one person. As such, he is the culmination of God's revelation in history, the irrevocable and unsurpassable expression of God's Word of acceptance to humanity. The revelation of God in history culminates in Jesus, as the Second Person of the Trinity became incarnate in him. In the first part of his career, Rahner developed his Christology along these lines, and this continued to be the basis for his understanding of Jesus' saving significance.

In the 1960s, Rahner began developing a complementary way of understanding Jesus, arguing that in order for Christology to be believable in Western modernity, it must be free of any "mythology impossible to accept nowadays."[19] For Rahner, this meant that the incarnation must be intelligible as an event that did not violate the created order. The Chalcedonian affirmation that Jesus was fully human must be honored as much as the affirmation that he was fully divine. Accordingly, Rahner began to develop a Christology from below to match his previously worked-out Christology from above. In his earlier Logos Christology, or Christology from above, Rahner sought to show how Jesus was God's final Word who disclosed God's gracious presence in a definitive way. In his subsequent Christology from below, he sought to show how this was compatible with a modern understanding of Jesus as a human being.

Rahner did this by arguing that the incarnation occurred through the response of Jesus to the self-communication of the Logos, the Second Person of the Trinity. What is central and redemptive about Jesus is his being the one who fully said yes to God and in whom God said yes to humanity, once and for all. In saying yes to God in this way, Jesus actualized a potential that is in principle present in every person, and he culminated a history of salvation that Rahner argued can be understood as fitting with an evolutionary worldview. Jesus accepted God's self-communication to him supremely by dying in obedience and trust in God. As Jesus did this, God said yes to him in the resurrection, and Jesus became the incarnate expression of God's Word.

For Rahner, the resurrection is not so much subsequent to Jesus' death as included in it as God's affirmation of the trust and obedience that Jesus showed God in his death.[20] The temporal sequence of these events is less important than the intrinsic relationship they exemplify between the initiative of God's Logos and the obedient response of Jesus to this that was constantly taking place in his person. Through this interplay between divine initiative and Jesus' response, Jesus' human nature and the divine Logos became one in his person while retaining their distinctiveness, and Jesus became God's definitive self-communication to the rest of humanity. This becoming one of divine and human natures in Jesus, or incarnation, was an ongoing process that reached its decisive culmination in Jesus' death and resurrection, just as the history of God's self-communication to humanity reached its decisive culmination in Jesus' person. By the divine and human natures becoming one in him while remaining distinct, Jesus effected salvation for all humanity.

This understanding of the hypostatic union that constitutes Jesus' person is the linchpin of Rahner's understanding of Jesus' saving significance. Yet precisely here there is a major tension in his Christology.

In attempting to avoid what he describes as a mythological view of the incarnation, Rahner interpreted the Chalcedonian Definition in such a way that the unity of Jesus' person is found in the interaction between Jesus as a human being and the divine initiative of God's Logos to him. As a result, "there seem to be two free, conscious, subjects in Jesus,"[21] the divine Logos and the human subjectivity of Jesus. Rahner might reply that every person is formed through the interplay of God's self-communication and their response to this. Then the question might be, does this conception of the incarnation do justice to the unity that Chalcedon affirmed between the divine and human natures in Jesus' person?

According to Rahner, this unity does not equal identity.[22] The divine and human natures are united in Jesus' person, but they remain distinct. The Logos of God is united with Jesus' humanity, but it does not become one in the sense of being identical with it. This unity is such that Jesus' humanity becomes God's own by God having accepted it as such.[23] But an element of distinction between the two remains. Rahner sees this unity as bringing something new to God, so that here God, "who is not subject to change in himself," became "subject to change in something else."[24] Yet Rahner's description of this change remained vague.[25] His position seems to be that through a self-communication on God's part and a reciprocal self-giving and emptying on Jesus' part in response, God's Logos became expressed in the person of Jesus in an irrevocable and unsurpassable way.[26] God "became" here in that God's self-communication to the world, which is always God's gift of God's self, reached its definitive expression in Jesus' person. But this change happened in Jesus' person, not in the divine Logos. The Second Person of the Trinity, the divine Logos, "became" in Jesus but not in itself, and so divine immutability remains intact. So Rahner can say that on the cross Jesus' humanity suffered, but the Second Person of the Trinity did not. The divine remains impassible. It can "undergo no such historicity nor any 'obedience unto death.'"[27] Here Rahner wrestles with one of the central and enduring mysteries of the Christian faith.

In developing his position, Rahner attempts to hold together and exploit the soteriological implications of the emphasis in Alexandrian Christology that in the incarnation the divine Logos assumed human nature, and the concern of Antiochean Christology to affirm the integrity of Jesus' humanity and the reality of his human experience. It can be argued from an Alexandrian perspective that there is a significant difference between what Rahner is saying and what Chalcedon affirmed. The understanding of divine nature employed at Chalcedon affirmed God to be impassible, as Rahner does. But the patristic principle that the "unassumed is the unhealed,"[28] which led to the doctrinal developments of Nicaea and Chalcedon and which is essential to Rahner's understanding of Jesus' saving significance, can be seen as requiring a deeper involvement of God in history than Rahner's description of the union of divine and human natures in Jesus' person acknowledges. Following this line of thought, the hypostatic union adopted at Chalcedon states that in Jesus, the Second Person of the Trinity entered history in a way[29] that Rahner was not willing to admit. Rahner would probably describe this way of understanding the incarnation as mythological. There is a tension here in Rahner's thought as he tries to affirm a genuine unity between divine and human natures in Jesus' person, the integrity of each, and the impassibility of the divine.

This tension in Rahner's understanding of the incarnation reflects a constant oscillation running through his thought between the transcendent initiative of God and the finite response of humanity.[30] For Rahner, the former always precedes the latter and makes it possible, while the latter completes the former. For instance, Rahner describes Jesus' resurrection as God's affirmation of Jesus as the Christ, and as such, the irrevocable and unsurpassable expression of God's gracious acceptance of humanity. But for Rahner, the resurrection would be incomplete without its believing reception and continued proclamation by the church. Jesus would not be truly risen without this human response to his resurrection. In turn, this response is always inspired by God's prevenient grace. What makes Jesus the Christ is the perfection of this pattern of initiative and response between God and humanity in Jesus' person. It is through God's initiative and Jesus' response that the hypostatic union in Jesus' person occurs, by which salvation is effected.

How does Jesus effect salvation? As people are oriented toward the divine mystery, seeking and needing a final and definitive validation from it in order to find fulfillment and meaning in life, Jesus saves by disclosing this through his person. Jesus is "the self-revelation of God through who he is."[31] He is the messenger whose person is his message, who brings God's grace-filled self-communication to the world through realizing in himself God's saving will toward humanity. As this happens in him, God's saving will and presence are revealed and made known to people in a new and definitive way. Thus for Rahner, and in this model of the atonement generally, Jesus' person and work are one and the same. By being the person who fully accepts and responds to God's gracious self-communication in trust and obedience, Jesus is the definitive revelation of God. The definitive expression of God's gracious will and presence happens in Jesus' resurrection. Here the final horizon, toward which all life is destined, is revealed.

As the irrevocable and unsurpassable word of God, Jesus completes the history of revelation and the history of human seeking for God simultaneously. Jesus does not change God, God's will, or the structures of human existence. The atonement happens through the coming into being and existence of his person, which culminates in his death and resurrection. Jesus' work, according to Rahner, is simply to reveal God in a new and definitive way. What he reveals was always/already present[32] and accessible to a certain extent through other means. God is the gracious presence, the infinite love from which humanity can never be fully separated. What Jesus changes is the degree to which God's presence is revealed in history.[33] Through his person, he makes God present in a way continuous with God's presence in all times and places, and yet new in its disclosive power. The life, death, and resurrection of Jesus dispel any ambiguity about the nature of God and human destiny. The love of God that he reveals includes by its very nature forgiveness of sin. His resurrection discloses the ultimate power of God's love and thus the hope of eternal life. Through his own response of trust and obedience to God, Jesus gives a new expression to God's nearness and love and so has a transformative effect on human life.

Rahner gives a strong ethical dimension to this. In accepting Jesus as the Christ, God has accepted all humanity into God's life, thus revealing that God is present in every person, as Jesus teaches in Matthew 25. Thus, love for God is love for one's neighbor, and vice versa.[34] This emphasis of Rahner's was particularly important for liberation theology.

Rahner does have a second, related understanding of how Jesus saves. His first, outlined above, depends on people encountering the proclamation of Jesus as the Christ and acknowledging it as such. Here the saving significance of Jesus occurs through his effect on people's consciousness. But following the thought line of Alexandrian Christology, Rahner also argues that, as Jesus' human nature has been accepted by God as God's own in the incarnation, this acceptance by God of one part of the total mass of created reality has a saving significance for the whole, as what happens to any one part affects all of the rest.[35] In accepting the person of Jesus, God symbolically accepts the whole of created reality, thus bestowing salvation on all of it.[36] Rahner repeatedly asserts this without ever explaining how it takes effect. However, this argument reveals an important characteristic of his thought.

In his writings on the new situation of the church signaled by Vatican II, and in his call for theology to divest itself of mythological understandings of Jesus that impede Christian faith in the modern world, Rahner showed attentiveness to historical changes and differences. But when it came to understanding Jesus' saving significance, Rahner preferred to think, as he does in the argument above, in terms of ontological principles and categories, with less regard for historical differences. Rahner tended to analyze societies in organic terms, as wholes, of which each individual is an essentially similar part. The determinative issue for Rahner tended to be not where people are located within the larger whole, or the differences separating them within it, but simply whether they are in some way a part of it or not. He did not balance this organic analysis with equal attention to the location of Jesus in the social conflicts of his time or that of people in the social conflicts of the present. In discussing Jesus' saving significance, he did not attend much to differences in life situation between the rich and the poor, and how Jesus might have a saving significance for one different from his saving significance for the other. As a result, in this regard, Rahner's understanding of Jesus' saving significance tends to be historically abstract.[37]

An important criticism related to this is that, in this abstractness, Rahner's theology related the Christian message primarily to the concerns of relatively privileged people in the North Atlantic hemisphere, those affected by secularism "and the criticisms of the Enlightenment," and paid little attention to the questions and concerns of "nonpersons," the victims of history whose sufferings often result from the former's privilege.[38] Rahner's understanding that through Jesus Christ God is encountered in the neighbor, so that love of God and love of neighbor coalesce, was a great stimulus for liberation and political theologies. But these in turn were sharply critical of the lack of attention to differences in the historical situations of the rich and poor in his thought. In keeping with this, Rahner's Christology shows little attention to Jesus' death as the execution of a prophet who spoke for justice and peace. Rahner's emphasis on how Jesus' resurrection is intrinsic to his death overlooks how it is an interruption of a reign of terror. We find a very different orientation to social divisions, and the location of Jesus within them, in the Christology of Dorothee Soelle, who understood Jesus' saving significance in a similar way.

## Dorothee Soelle

Dorothee Soelle was born in Cologne, Germany, in 1929, to a family that was politically aware, resistant to Nazism, and disengaged from institutional Protestantism. In high school she became fascinated by the Christianity of one of her religion teachers, who helped awaken in her an attraction to Jesus.[39] After studying "philology, German and philosophy in Cologne and Freiburg, and then theology and literature in Göttingen,"[40] she became a school teacher. She and her first husband had four children before divorcing. She later married Fulbert Steffensky, with whom she participated in the political evensong worship services in Cologne from 1968 to 1972.[41] She was never offered a teaching position in theology in Germany, but she taught at Union Theological Seminary in New York from 1975 to 1987. She traveled extensively through Latin America and developed an international reputation through her speaking and writing. She was a leading representative with Jürgen Moltmann and Johann Baptist Metz of German political theology, which she later described as transitional to liberation theology.[42] Soelle died of a heart attack on April 27, 2003.

The initial backdrop for her theology was the economic miracle of post–World War II Germany. Like Rahner, she accepted that the modern Western worldview meant that biblical accounts of miracles could no longer be accepted at face value.[43] However, she never sought to demonstrate that Christian faith is essentially compatible with the guiding ideas and ethos of modern Western societies. Her approach was always much more dialectical in this regard than Rahner's. She acknowledged that modern Western science and technology have benefited humanity in many ways,[44] and she had a lasting love for many aspects of Western culture. But she saw that the disenchanting effects of secularization had been detrimental to human life on a spiritual level, and she came to see the teachings and life of Jesus as deeply antithetical to Western capitalism, militarism, and empire building. She emphasized the critical relationship of Christian faith to the ethos of modern Western societies more than its compatibility.

Soelle's Christology developed in three stages,[45] in step with her growing critique of Western capitalism. The first stage was an early uncritical belief in an omnipotent God, which she abandoned before entering university. In the second stage, which marked the beginning of her work as a productive theologian, she argued that the pervasive influence of modern technology and mass production in Western societies had deadened people to values of community, love, and companionship, and so had reduced human life.[46] Life had become homogenized by modern technologies and bureaucracies, so that people only existed among things, without authentic human relationships. Soelle described this as a kind of spiritual death[47] or inner emptiness,[48] from which people needed to be delivered. In her third stage, beginning in the 1970s, her critique of Western societies deepened as she encountered her guilt as a German citizen in relation to the Holocaust and third-world critiques of Western capitalism. She began to speak of Germany as "a land with a bloody history smelling of gas," and of a "poverty without,"[49] afflicting many, particularly in the third world. For Soelle, the suffering from hunger, poverty, and oppression that the poor of the world endure is a result of greed, callousness, and apathy of the privileged. She judged this suffering to be a continuation of the Holocaust in a different form. The themes of her earlier theology continued in this third stage, so that her mature theology has a twofold focus of struggling against "emptiness within," a life without loving relationships, and "poverty without," resulting from injustice and oppression that robs people of the resources needed to live.[50] For Soelle, the two are related. The "emptiness within" of the privileged and powerful leads to a lack of love for others in need. To turn to one's neighbor in need is to discover Christ in them, and in doing so, to have one's inner emptiness filled.

The wellspring of Soelle's theology was an eros for what she termed "identity"[51] or "fullness of life," a being at peace with God, oneself, and others. She experienced a constant yearning for this and found inspiration and a way toward it in Jesus, in his relationships to his followers, and in the reign of God he proclaimed. She experienced these as concrete utopias that continually attracted her, and she found in Jesus a spiritual resource that empowered her to try to live after his example in her own time. For Soelle, this fullness of life, or "identity" that she believed all people yearn for, is threatened internally and externally. It is threatened externally by oppression, which robs one of the means of sustaining life. For those who have adequate means of living, it is also threatened internally, by despair that a meaningful life is not possible or by fear of losing what we have and the temptation to seek comfort and ease rather than richer relationships with one another. According to Soelle, people need religious language and rituals in order to articulate the value and possibility of a life rich in relationships and to be sustained in seeking it.[52] Jesus saves by providing this kind of language, by disclosing the presence of God and this possibility, which then empowers people to actualize it.

On one level, Soelle's theology is a form of social moralism that seeks to bring "all experience and action under a pressure to change" toward an idealized state.[53] But beneath this, there is a mystical element in her thought, a love for Jesus, not simply for what he did and does, but for the beauty of who he was and what he represents. For Soelle, it is the beauty of Jesus' person, life, and relationships that makes him important for the present. Her theology is filled with a passion to connect with and participate in the love that she saw embodied in him. This passion went beyond moral terms. It found expression in her love of Bach, in her poetry, and in her aesthetic critique of inner emptiness as a sinful state of being.[54] For her, a life without loving relationships is wrong, not because it harms others, but because it wastes the gift, the opportunity to give and receive love, which God has given.

Soelle's Christology is more critical of Western societies than Rahner's. It is also more loosely bound to the church and its traditions.[55] She did not feel bound to produce a Christology consistent with the teaching of ecumenical councils like Nicaea and Chalcedon. Her Christology began with a negation of previous church teaching as outdated and often ethically unproductive. She first developed it as an exercise in theology after the death of God.[56] For her, this meant the death of religious tradition and church teaching as a binding authority. As a child of the Enlightenment, authority for her lay in her own experience and judgments. But Soelle affirmed certain aspects of church teaching and tradition as meaningful and warranting retrieval. She found here a language that helped her articulate what would otherwise be impossible to express.[57] The Bible; figures from church history like Francis of Assisi, Martin Luther King Jr., and Oscar Romero; and religious practices like those of the base communities in Latin America were a source of hope and joy to her. These helped verify Jesus as the Christ, and along with him, provided inspiration essential for struggling against despair brought on by "inner emptiness" or "outer poverty." Her Christology grew out of her own experience of Jesus disclosing to her the presence of God and the possibility of meaning and fulfillment through loving relationships and the struggle for peace and justice.

For Soelle, Jesus is the Christ as he changes people, moving them to express in their own lives the love and commitment to justice that he expressed in his.[58] She never sought to understand how he is able to do this, and so never developed an understanding of his person to undergird her understanding of his saving significance. Quoting Philipp Melanchthon, that "the important thing is to know Christ's benefits, not his nature,"[59] she eschewed any metaphysics or discussions of the Trinity. As a result, her Christology is rather mute on how it is that Jesus is the Christ. For her, Jesus is risen only as he changes peoples' consciousness and moves them to express in their own time and place the love of God that he embodied in his. Otherwise, he remains dead.[60] But while she was not interested in a metaphysical understanding of Jesus' person, she was interested in historical criticism and the "history-like" accounts of Jesus that give concreteness to his teaching and relationships. These are crucial as a guard against idolatrous misappropriations or mystifications of Jesus' message.[61] For her, following Jesus meant entering into the historical conflicts of the present between rich and poor, against the arms race, or around the ecological crisis in a way congruent with the actions of Jesus in his time.

The Christology she developed in her first theological book, *Christ the Representative*, remained basic for all that came after. Here she argued that Jesus is the Christ as he represents God to people and people before God.[62] At this point she used the term *identity* to describe the fulfillment that she believed people innately seek and that she saw represented in the symbol of the reign of God. According to her, a yearning for identity is innate in human nature. People can only experience this in relationships of love,[63] and they need to be empowered by something greater than themselves for this to happen. While a "yearning" for identity "is nourished by an innate knowledge" of it, "however fragmentary," someone else must disclose to people the nature and possibility of the identity they seek.[64] This is the saving work of Jesus. He represents to people the realm or kingdom of identity that they yearn to reach.[65] By revealing its presence and possibility in his person and relationships, he inspires and awakens others to the possibility that they can experience it too. The beauty of what Jesus discloses generates an eros that can energize and move people to seek and experience it in their own lives. In one sense, Jesus does not bring anything new. "The freedom which dawned in him exists, of course, even where it does not appeal to him."[66] Yet in another sense, Jesus is unique in that, for Soelle, this freedom finds its decisive and definitive expression in his person.

Thus, in an era in which "God is dead" or God is experienced as absent, Jesus reveals that God is present by representing God to humanity. At the same time, he represents people to God. Jesus inspires in God a hope in humanity, that they might reach identity, parallel to the hope for identity that he inspires in humanity, so that God does not give up on humanity.[67] All this happens not through any particular act or teaching on Jesus' part but through the sum total of his person and history. By the things he said and did, by his death and resurrection, Jesus reveals to people the possibility and beauty of a life rich in relationships of love. He enables people to see himself, the "Christ," the possibility of such relationships, in the other people; "in the eyes of the street children in Bogota or the forsaken drinkers in our cities."[68]

As for Rahner, so for Soelle, the saving significance of Jesus lies in the new awareness of God's nature and presence that he brings. Jesus changes the human condition in that he makes people aware of their alienation and of the possibility of experiencing something more meaningful.[69] For Soelle, Jesus' saving power lies in the beauty of God's love manifest in him, which moves people more than fear of torture and death or the temptations of apathy and greed. Jesus is risen inasmuch as the beauty of God's love disclosed in him continues to move people after his death. The fulfillment of the possibility that he brings depends upon people's free response to him. Without the human response of faith to the divine initiative in Jesus, Jesus would not be the Christ.[70]

This understanding of Jesus as the Christ, developed in her first book, became more concrete in relation to social conflicts in her later writings. In *Christ the Representative*, apart from a brief discussion of Christian anti-Semitism, Soelle does not relate Jesus' saving significance to justice issues. She simply describes how Jesus enables one to achieve identity in an era of conformity. In subsequent years, as her thought developed into its third stage, she began to locate Jesus concretely within struggles for justice and peace, describing him as "the poor man from Nazareth whom the Romans tortured to death."[71] At the same time the ethical content of her Christology blossomed. What she had earlier termed "identity" became peace and justice, including peace with creation. But Soelle's Christology was never simply about ethics. It continued to have a mystical element of experiencing God in a neighbor, in moments of sorrow and joy, of appreciating the beauty of being, manifest in human relationships and in nature.

There are ambivalences in Soelle's Christology. According to her, Christ discloses the possibility of achieving identity, but its actual achievement lies in the future. Soelle does not describe how this future might be finally achieved. For her, Christ provides a definitive expression of an ever-present reality and possibility. But the New Testament speaks of Christ as bringing more. His resurrection is not just the vindication of his cause and its continuation in the lives of his followers. It is also the establishment of a new reality that gives hope for the final overcoming of sin and death that people are able to participate in now through faith. Soelle does not see Jesus as making this kind of difference or bringing this kind of new reality.[72] As a result, her understanding of the hope Christ brings remains ambiguous.

For Soelle, death is something to be both resisted and accepted.[73] Yet if it is something to be resisted, it must finally be overcome if identity is to be fully achieved.[74] She resists the idea of Christ bringing anything new into history. Yet the meaningfulness she ascribes to loving relationships depends upon the occurrence of a more far-reaching transformation of the human condition than she envisions. In this respect, Soelle's Christology is very romantic. Jesus' meaning as the Christ and the meaning of human life in general lie for her more in the struggle for identity, for peace and justice, than in achieving it. In her theology, the emptiness within or the deprivation and violence that threaten life from without are in some way necessary for life to have meaning, as this is only found in struggling against them. Identity thus becomes something always sought but never fully attained. The eschatological hope that Christ brings functions as a utopia in her thought, but the transcendence of God necessary to sustain the struggle for justice and peace is lacking. She tends to present the radical transcendence of God and genuine immanence as mutually exclusive.[75] Yet in the crucified and risen Christ, both are present. We turn now to the Christology of Roger Haight, who understands Jesus' saving significance in a similar way, only in a postmodern context.

# Roger Haight

Rahner developed his Christology primarily in relation to the crisis of cognitive claims[76] brought on by the accomplishments of modernity.

Soelle developed hers more in relation to the negative aspects of modernity.[77] Haight utilizes the same understanding of Jesus' saving significance as these two, but in relation to the new cultural context of postmodernity.

Haight was born in 1936. He grew up in Caldwell, New Jersey, attending a parochial school run by Dominican Sisters and then Xavier High School in New York City, run by Jesuits. Upon graduating, he joined the Jesuit order. He studied at Berchmans College in the Philippines, then taught high school there for three years. He continued his education at Woodstock College in Maryland and then at the Divinity School of the University of Chicago, where he did a thesis on Roman Catholic Modernism directed by David Tracy. He has since taught at Jesuit graduate schools in Manila, Chicago, Toronto, and Cambridge, Massachusetts, and has been visiting professor in Lima, Nairobi, Paris, and Pune, India.[78] The Board of Trustees of the Baptist Theological Union named him the Chicago Divinity School's alumnus of the year for 2005.[79] He was also singled out for attention by the Vatican. While his book *Jesus, Symbol of God* won the Catholic Press Association's Book Award for Theology in 2000, in December of 2004, the Congregation for the Doctrine of the Faith declared that it contained "erroneous assertions, the dissemination of which is of grave harm to the faithful."[80] He is currently visiting professor of systematic theology at Union Theological Seminary in New York City.

Haight develops his Christology in relation to the ethos, values, and ideas that he sees to be shared by educated people in the new context of postmodernity.[81] He uses the term *postmodern* to refer both to the fragmented nature of the cultures of advanced industrial societies and an intellectual ethos or constellation of values and ideas characterized by the four attributes outlined below that has become predominant in them.[82] He sees this new ethos and social reality of postmodernism presenting both challenge and opportunity to the church. The challenge is that the church must rethink its understanding of Jesus in order to credibly present the Christian message in this context. Haight likens this to the challenge the church faced in moving from being a sect within Judaism to becoming a Gentile religion in the cultural context of Hellenism. The opportunity is that now, as then, this challenge may lead to the development of Christologies that surpass previous formulations in certain respects.[83]

Haight describes the ethos of educated people in postmodernity as shaped by four related characteristics.[84] The first is a sense of the historical nature of reality: Everything is understood to be particular and contingent, to have evolved from something else and to be evolving into something different, though there is no discernible goal to this process. This historical consciousness requires that the legitimacy of christological claims be demonstrated through showing their continuity with what can be known historically about Jesus. It also gives rise to a sense of how ideas and values interact with social structures and how these are changeable through cooperative action. This historical consciousness underlies the second characteristic: a critical social consciousness, an awareness of how ideas and values are socially grounded, reflective of their time and place. This social consciousness is critical in that it is concerned about "massive social evil"[85] and seeks the creation of just social structures. As a result, the ability of a Christology to empower people to resist evil becomes one criteria of its adequacy.[86] This historical and critical social consciousness culminates in an awareness of the irreducible difference between various historical eras and religions, and a refusal to grant privilege to any one era or religion over another. This entails the loss of any sense of an "overarching framework" or perspective that can be claimed as true in opposition to all others.[87] The result is a pluralist consciousness that could give rise to a radical sense of relativism and the absence of any transcendent meaning in life. Haight gives it a slightly different interpretation. The challenge it presents is not to show that there is some transcendent meaning in life, as with Rahner, but rather to show that such a meaning can be discerned without it becoming a source of division and violence to others. Haight sees this to be the central challenge posed by postmodernity to contemporary Christologies.[88]

> Can one interpret Jesus Christ as precisely God's story which is so open to others that it does not coopt their specific identity and does not privilege Christians over against them? Can christology represent a Jesus Christ who is not divisive, but who authorizes the other as other, and hence functions as a principle of unity that respects differences?[89]

A fourth characteristic of this postmodern ethos is a cosmic consciousness, informed by the natural sciences and the environmental crisis, in which humanity is seen to be one small part of an unimaginably large and complex world. This cosmic consciousness creates a new sense of human unity that reinforces the central challenge of postmodernism outlined above.

We constitute a common humanity on this planet, indeed, a community, despite all the differences in religion and culture. We need a christology that will confirm the importance of a common humanity, a human community in a common habitat, and a shared process of nature of which all are a part, and at the same time respects human differences in this postmodern world.[90]

All this renders many premodern and modern Christologies inadequate and ethically problematic. The challenge is to retrieve from them the basis for an understanding of Jesus that is intellectually credible, ethically empowering, and yet open to other faiths in a time when all great religious and moral visions are recognized to be potentially dangerous to others.

Like Rahner and unlike Soelle, Haight writes as a theologian rooted in the church and its teachings. Consequently, he argues that in addressing these contextual challenges, a contemporary Christology must demonstrate its continuity with the message and portrayal of Jesus in the New Testament and the affirmations of the Councils of Nicaea and Chalcedon, as these are part of the church's foundational understanding of Jesus Christ.[91] For Haight, the classical Christologies of the past provide guidelines for the present. While they cannot be simply repeated, they remain important resources and provide internal criteria for contemporary Christologies.

Haight develops his Christology by first searching the New Testament for a commonality underlying its diverse understandings of Jesus as the Christ. He finds that all the Christologies of the New Testament understand Jesus as the bringer or mediator of God's salvation.[92] Through his preaching, teaching, and healing, and through his exorcisms and table fellowship Jesus made God's saving power present in people's lives. In a later publication, he includes Jesus' death on the cross in this, arguing that Jesus' suffering on the cross was paradigmatic of the suffering caused by sin and evil. Jesus' resurrection revealed God's power to save even in relation to the radical evil exemplified here. It also validated his commitment to the reign of God as exemplary and destined to endure in life everlasting,[93] and so validated Jesus as revealing God's nature and presence through his ministry and message.

Haight also searches through the diverse classical Christologies found in the Christian theological tradition and finds that underlying each is the idea that Jesus mediates God's salvation by making God present. By doing so, Jesus is "the concrete symbol of God," and the exemplar of what it means to be fully human.[94] Jesus saves by revealing God's nature and presence, thus overcoming the lack of awareness of this that alienates people from God.

> By being a symbol of God, by mediating an encounter with God, Jesus reveals God as already present and active in human existence. Historically he does this both by being and by making God present in a thematic way through his words, actions, and whole person. Jesus reveals by causing in the persons who come to him in faith an analogous reflective awareness of the presence of God to them.[95]

There are objective and subjective dimensions to this saving work. The objective dimension is Jesus' disclosure of God's gracious presence so that people become explicitly conscious of it. This makes possible the subjective dimension of people consciously participating in God's saving work by expressing in their own lives the same values of God's kingdom that Jesus expressed in his. Becoming more fully aware of God's nature and presence enables people to participate more fully in God's salvific work, so that they "contribute to the material of the final kingdom of God."[96] Jesus continues to be an effective symbol of God in the ongoing course of history through the church bearing witness to his person and work.

As the symbol of God, "Jesus is normative for the Christian imagination."[97] But within a postmodern consciousness of pluralism, this does not invalidate or denigrate other religions. The character of God as Spirit that Jesus reveals "may be conceived as the universal ground of salvation . . . also present in other religions and so normatively revealed in them as well."[98] Jesus as normative demands a recognition of other religions as means of grace, and warrants interreligious dialogue as a means of seeking self-transcendence for Christians and others. Such dialogue does not lead away from Christian faith, but toward an increased recognition of God's grace present in other religions, and to a deeper appreciation of God as revealed in Jesus.

Given that Jesus discloses God's presence and nature in a transforming and normative way, Haight argues that Jesus' person can be understood through either a Logos or a Spirit Christology.[99] A Logos, or descending, Christology stresses the uniqueness and normativeness of Jesus and accounts for this by understanding him as the incarnation of God's Word. A Spirit Christology understands Jesus' saving significance to derive from the inspiration of the Holy Spirit and his response to it. It stresses his consubstantiality with other people, not his distinctiveness. Haight prefers the approach of a Spirit Christology, arguing that Jesus was able to make God present in a transformative way because "God as Spirit was present to Jesus in a superlative degree,"[100] to the extent that one can say, in keeping with the Councils of Nicaea and Chalcedon, that "Jesus was one human person with an integral human nature in whom not less than God, and thus a divine nature, is at work."[101] As such, Jesus is for Christians the normative revelation of the one God, the loving creator of heaven and earth who is active in history in the Holy Spirit.

It is possible to understand Jesus as the Christ in this way, and this is in keeping with the teachings of the ecumenical councils of Nicaea and Chalcedon. This understanding has the merit of intelligibility in relation to the postmodern ethos Haight outlines, in that it does not envisage Jesus' incarnation in what Rahner might call a mythological way. But as with Rahner's Christology, one could argue that Haight's understanding of Jesus' person does not do full justice to the affirmation running through some New Testament traditions that in Jesus' life, death, and resurrection, the Second Person of the Trinity became present in history in a decisively new way. Haight argues that Jesus can only have a credible saving significance today if he is understood as a human being consubstantial with all others.[102] But the New Testament and the Councils of Nicaea and Chalcedon also affirm that God became present in history in a new way in Jesus' person. Haight argues that positing a quantitative difference in the Spirit's inspiration of Jesus can account for this.[103] This additional inspiration of the Spirit enabled Jesus to be the Christ by actualizing the potential present in his human nature as such. But in some traditions of the New Testament, the claim is made that Jesus not only exemplified how human freedom can be fulfilled but, as the incarnation of God, created a new possibility for human fulfillment that did not exist before.[104] The basis for this was seen to lie in a qualitatively new act of God, which included but went beyond Jesus being inspired by the Spirit.[105] In Christ, the Logos, or Second Person of the Trinity, was incarnate in Jesus and experienced death on the cross.

When this way of understanding Jesus as the Christ becomes the starting point for understanding God in light of Jesus, it can lead to dramatic interpretations of the Trinity, as in the theology of Jürgen Moltmann. Haight insists that Jesus must be understood within a trinitarian perspective, as this is necessary to explain the Christian experience of salvation in him.[106] The experience of Jesus Christ is always an experience of Jesus and the Holy Spirit. It has a trinitarian structure. The Holy Spirit both inspires the person Jesus to a superlative degree and inspires the believer to receive him as the Christ. Haight also notes that the doctrine of the Trinity works two ways. It affirms that it is God who is encountered in Jesus and that "God really is in God's self as God is revealed to be in God's self-communication in Jesus and the Spirit."[107] But in keeping with his preference for a Spirit Christology, Haight does not pursue a dramatic rethinking of the doctrine of God on the basis of Christology. He affirms instead a stance of theological humility. The revelation of God in Jesus is real, but it is a gift, primarily the gift of salvation. God remains incomprehensible mystery, genuinely encountered and known in Jesus and the Spirit, but always beyond human comprehension. Haight is concerned with how Jesus' saving significance can be understood in continuity with Roman Catholic Church teaching in an intellectually credible way. Having understood what Jesus means for the Christian and the world in terms of the doctrine of the Trinity, he does not go on to ask, what does all this mean for God? His emphasis on Jesus' saving significance and his sense of the mystery of God direct him away from this.

Haight's Christology seems to support a reformist option in relation to the ills of society.[108] The development of his Christology in relation to the intellectual ethos of an educated postmodern elite reflects, in part, confidence in existing critical movements in society as the best hope for achieving a more just and sustainable society. It affirms many of the same values as Soelle's, but when the two are juxtaposed, one does not find in Haight's Christology the concrete and immediate identifications of Christ with the poor that Soelle insists on. Her Christology related to society in a more radical way, highlighting the gulf between current institutions, social practices and trends, and Jesus of Nazaeth. Like Rahner, Haight interprets the ethical import of Jesus as commensurate with many of the guiding ideals of educated people in North Atlantic countries.

This points to an interesting contrast among the three Christologies studied in this chapter. All employ a similar understanding of Jesus' saving significance, but they differ in where they seek to understand Jesus concretely. Rahner and Haight seek a metaphysical concreteness in their understandings of Jesus. They ask how Jesus is related to God, what enables him to disclose God's presence in the way that he does. These questions lead them to the doctrine of the Trinity. Soelle's Christology lacks this kind of understanding and remains metaphysically vague, but her Christology has a historical concreteness and radical edge in its ethical applications that theirs lack. Can her radical ethical stance be sustained without a sense of divine transcendence that the doctrine of the Trinity conceptualizes to back it up? But conversely, does the cross of Jesus not require a radical understanding of Jesus' presence in relation to contemporary North Atlantic societies?

## Summary

The three authors studied in this chapter see the saving significance of Jesus to lie in the way he reveals God's nature and presence. Each sees the fundamental alienation separating people from God in modern or postmodern Western societies to be a lack of awareness of God. Each argues that this is partly caused by the clash between guiding assumptions of modern or postmodern Western cultures and premodern understandings of the Christian message. In these successive new cultural contexts, traditional notions of Jesus' person and work that have dominated Western Christianity in the past block the reception of the gospel more than they express it. Their meaning can only be retrieved by their message being recast in terms of the transformative power of Jesus' revelation of God.

Rahner, Soelle, and Haight are agreed that the alienation of being unaware of God's presence cannot be overcome by an understanding of his saving significance built around notions of his sacrificial death, his victory over sin and evil, or his moral example. Each sees that this alienation is overcome by the disclosure of God that occurs through his person. Through his ministry, death, and resurrection, Jesus reveals God's gracious presence to people. Like the traveling salesman in *The Music Man*, Jesus reveals something that was there all along, but which people are often unaware of. He makes a new awareness of God's presence and love available to people and so empowers them to express this in their own lives. This can be called the revelatory theory of the atonement. It attends to how Jesus addresses a particular form of

alienation from God that has become prominent in secularized Western societies.

One strength of this understanding of Jesus' saving significance is
that in stressing that Jesus saves by revealing what is already everywhere
present, it enables these Christologies to relate positively to other faiths
in contexts where Christian communities must come to terms with the
challenges of religious pluralism. Another strength of this understanding is that it does not directly clash with other forms of knowledge in
Western cultures. Each of the three Christologies studied here seeks to
show how one can belong to an educated Western elite and still confess
Jesus as the Christ.

But with this apologetic also comes a sharp critique of certain
assumptions about Western secularity. Though Rahner, Soelle, and
Haight each affirms certain aspects of secularism, all reject the notion
that religion is doomed to disappear from Western culture or that faith
in Christ is necessarily intellectually incoherent and morally bankrupt.
Each presents critical faith in Jesus Christ as a defensible position that
can provide a vital contribution to contemporary Western public life.
Each rejects the "immanent frame"[109] of secularized Western societies
as sufficient for understanding and articulating the meaning of human
life.

In the next chapter, we turn to three contemporary versions of the
moral influence theory of the atonement. These also both accept and
challenge the immanent frame of contemporary Western societies. As
they do so, they invoke Christology to unleash a radical critique of the
violence and injustice prevalent in North Atlantic cultures.

## Suggestions for Further Reading

Haight, Roger, S.J. *The Future of Christology*. New York: Continuum,
    2005. Most of Roger Haight's christological thinking is contained in
    his magnum opus, *Jesus, Symbol of God*. This smaller volume con-
    tains a number of essays in which he explores some issues further and
    interacts with the Christologies of others. It also contains a valuable
    chapter in which Roger responds to most of the major critiques and
    reviews of *Jesus, Symbol of God*.
Oliver, Dianne. "Christ in the World: The Christological Vision of
    Dorothee Soelle." In *The Theology of Dorothee Soelle*, ed. Sarah K.

Pinnock. Harrisburg, Penn.: Trinity Press International, 2003. A good overview of Soelle's Christology and its development.

Rahner, Karl. *Foundations of Christian Faith*. New York: Crossroad, 1978. See especially pages 176–321. Rahner's Christology developed over the years. This is his mature statement of it.

———. *The Love of Jesus and the Love of Neighbor*. New York: Crossroad, 1983. This is a late, very brief, yet very insightful and interesting writing of Rahner on Christology.

Sienbenrock, Roman. "Christology." In *The Cambridge Companion to Karl Rahner*, ed. Declan Marmion and Mary Kines. New York: Cambridge University Press, 2005. A succinct overview and assessment of Rahner's Christology and its development.

Soelle, Dorothee. *Stations of the Cross: A Latin American Pilgrimage*. Minneapolis: Fortress Press, 1993.

———. *Theology for Skeptics: Reflections on God*. Minneapolis: Fortress Press, 1995. These two books contain arresting expressions of Soelle's later Christology.

Wong, Joseph. *Logos-Symbol in the Christology of Karl Rahner*. Roma: LAS, 1984. Still the best overview and secondary source on Rahner's Christology.

## Discussion Questions

1. How would you assess Rahner's success in developing a believable Christology for the twentieth century?
2. Is Soelle's socially and politically radical Christology an authentic expression of who Jesus Christ is today?
3. Does Haight's Christology adequately express the meaning of the affirmations of the Councils of Nicaea and Chalcedon in the present postmodern context?
4. Is the revelational understanding of Jesus' saving significance, that he saves by revealing God's loving presence, able to express all dimensions of Jesus' saving significance?

CHAPTER 2

◆

# Jesus as Moral Exemplar

## Rosemary Radford Ruether, Carter Heyward, Mark Lewis Taylor

Peter Abelard (1079–1142) is the name most often associated with what has come to be known as the moral influence theory of atonement. According to Abelard, the atoning significance of Jesus' death should be understood as follows:

> We have been justified by the blood of Christ and reconciled to God in this way: through this unique act of grace manifested to us—in that his Son has taken upon himself our nature and persevered therein in teaching us by word and example even unto death—he has more fully bound us to himself by love; with the result that our hearts should be enkindled

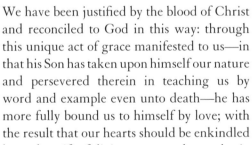

by such a gift of divine grace, and true charity should not now shrink from enduring anything for him.[1]

In this way of understanding Jesus' saving significance, Jesus saves by making people more loving through the transforming power of his example. The beauty of Jesus' life and death moves people to actualize more fully their own potential to love, and his example guides people's action by modeling what love is. Here Jesus saves by his moral influence on people.[2]

In the preceding chapter, we noted how an "immanent frame," or worldview, has come to characterize contemporary Western societies. This view sees the world as shaped by human action and the impersonal forces of nature but has no place for miraculous divine interventions like Jesus' resurrection.[3] This chapter will look at the Christologies of Rosemary Radford Ruether, Carter Heyward, and Mark Lewis Taylor. All three accept this immanent frame and interpret the saving significance of Jesus within it by utilizing versions of Abelard's moral influence theory of the atonement.

The way Jesus is understood to save here can be illustrated with a scene from the movie *How the Grinch Stole Christmas*. As the Grinch is about to dump the Christmas presents he has taken from the residents of Whoville off the top of a mountain, he pauses to hear their cries when they awake to find their presents missing. Instead, he hears them singing and celebrating Christmas as always. The beauty of their unexpected response and their song changes his understanding of Christmas and causes his heart to grow "three sizes" bigger. This change in his "heart" moves and enables him to save their presents through extraordinary effort and then leads him to return them and join the Whos in their celebration. The evil overcome here lay within the Grinch himself. His lack of love and his misunderstanding of Christmas prevented him from fulfilling his potential to love. This lack and misunderstanding were remedied through his being moved to love by the beauty of the Whos' celebration of Christmas even after he has stolen their presents.

Ruether, Heyward, and Taylor each see Jesus as having a similar transformative influence on people. In their theologies, the principal evil that Jesus saves people from is a misapprehension of God and a lack of concern for the victims of society. Each sees Jesus as overcoming this lack of love and moral concern by moving people through his moral influence to act in greater conformity with God's will.

This moral influence theory is a predominantly "subjective"[4] theory of the atonement. It is subjective in that it emphasizes the change Jesus effects in people. Like the revelational model studied in the previous chapter, it sees Jesus overcoming people's alienation from God by changing their apprehension of reality. However, the moral influence theory does not address a lack of awareness of God's presence but a lack of love and a faulty understanding of God. The three authors studied here who employ versions of it do not see secularism or unawareness of God's presence as problematic in the way that the authors in the preceding chapter did. For Ruether, Heyward, and Taylor, the key problem in their historical context is not atheism or a lack of belief, but idolatry.[5] There is also an emphasis on action in the moral influence theory that is not always present in the revelatory theory. The difference is subtle but significant. In the latter, Jesus saves by revealing God's presence to people. The new awareness he gives should find expression in their actions, but it still has a saving significance without this. In the moral influence theory, Jesus only saves as he moves people to act in conformity with God.[6]

## Rosemary Radford Ruether

Rosemary Radford Ruether was born on November 2, 1936, in St. Paul, Minnesota.[7] Her mother's independence and ecumenical Roman Catholicism were a formative influence on her. She went to Scripps College, in Claremont, California, in 1954 and received a B.A. in classics. Here classicist Robert Palmer awakened in her an interest in the historical origins of religions and "the meaning of religious symbols."[8] The civil rights and the Black Power movements, and her own experience working with Delta Ministry in the state of Mississippi in the summer of 1965, taught her to analyze societies in terms of conflicts of power and from the perspective of the oppressed.[9] Vatican II and the changes it brought in the Roman Catholic Church were also significant influences for her. While at Scripps College she met and married Herman Ruether, with whom she had three children. She received an M.A. in classics and Roman history and a Ph.D. in classics and patristics at Claremont School of Theology. She graduated in 1965 with a dissertation on Gregory of Nazianzus.[10] After teaching at Immaculate Heart College in Los Angeles for one year, then Howard University from 1966–76, she became Georgia Harkness Professor of Applied Theology at Garrett-Evangelical Seminary in Evanston, Illinois, until her retirement. She has been visiting professor at numerous schools and remains active at the school of theology at Claremont.

Ruether describes herself as an American Roman Catholic. Her Christology was formulated without sustained engagement with other Christologies developed after the patristic period.[11] She was not trained as a theologian but as "a student of classics and history of religions."[12] Her theological method developed from this training and from her view of history, culture, and religions. Her work has been tremendously influential in contemporary theology, particularly in theology devoted to Jewish-Christian relations in the present, studies of Jewish-Christian relations in the New Testament, feminist theology, social ethics, and ecotheology. She was a pioneer in making gender and power relations along gender lines a significant issue in contemporary theology. She is also very influential as a prophetic woman's voice in Roman Catholicism.

For Ruether, culture is made up of and shaped by traditions, religious and otherwise, almost all of which carry distorting and oppressive ideologies as well as resources for overcoming these.[13] A person is always located within some traditions, and one's location is always a combination of contingency and choice. According to Ruether, within a general acceptance of religious and cultural pluralism that mandates respect for and dialogue with other traditions, one can make relative arguments justifying a preference for one religious tradition over another. But more important than which religious or cultural tradition one locates oneself in is how one does this. For Ruether, everyone must take responsibility for their religious/cultural tradition(s), seeking to overcome its distortions and ideologies on the basis of its own sources.[14] She pursues this through a dialectical historical method. In relation to a series of social injustices to which her inherited religious and cultural traditions have contributed, she traces "the ideological patterns in Christian thought which have served to justify violence and oppression."[15] At the same time she develops a more authentic, liberating reading of the originating event at the source of this tradition. The ideological patterns are judged and negated on the basis of this rereading of the tradition's origin. An alternative understanding of the tradition promoting greater justice and peace is then formulated from this new understanding of its origin.

This methodology reflects what Ruether sees Jesus to have been doing in relation to his own inherited religious traditions and the social injustices of his time. Jesus' death on the cross resulted from his "theoretical struggle against false ideologies of oppression and practical struggle against its social consequences."[16] In taking responsibility for one's own religious-cultural traditions and the world they help form, one takes up one's own cross in imitation of Jesus. Only by going through the struggle and suffering of denouncing injustice and the oppressive elements in one's traditions that give rise to it does one experience resurrection, "a healing word for the present" and a glimpse of "an alternative future."[17] Jesus thus models how one should seek to understand him.

Following this approach, Ruether developed her Christology initially in the late 1960s through her work on Christian anti-Semitism, the first of a series of justice issues that she took up. Her interest in this grew out of her B.A. thesis on "eschatology in the intertestamental Jewish apocalyptic literature" and her critical appropriation of Roman Catholicism.[18] While working on this, she noted a discrepancy between the Christian understanding of Jesus Christ as a divine person who made possible spiritual reconciliation with God and the Jewish understanding of the Messiah as the one who would establish justice within history.[19] She connected this to Christian claims to have received Jesus as the Messiah promised to the Jews, while the Jews had rejected him. For Ruether, this claim was unjust if what Judaism "meant by the Messiah had nothing to do with this Christian concept of the Christ."[20] She set out (1) to demonstrate this through investigating the development of Jewish Messianism and patristic Christology, and (2) to remedy this injustice by proposing a Christology more in keeping with the historical Jesus that was not inherently anti-Semitic. The result was a major work on Christology, finished in 1970, but never published in its entirety.[21] Here she developed her basic understanding of Jesus as the Christ.

In a published excerpt from the conclusion to this work, Ruether argues that the development of patristic Christology, culminating in the Chalcedonian Definition, replaced the historical Jesus with "an archetypal symbol of ideal humanity."[22] Jesus was not the Messiah expected in Judaism, as he did not end injustice in history. Consequently, the Jewish rejection of Jesus was an affirmation of the integrity of their own tradition.[23] The Christian claim that salvation history is fulfilled in Jesus and the church is idolatrous, as it accords ultimate value to a historically relative figure and an imperfect institution, creating a false dualism between the church and the rest of the world, particularly Judaism.[24] This claim to perfection is ethically debilitating, as it prevents the church from acknowledging unredeemed aspects of its own existence[25] and deflects its attention away from demands for justice within history.

Ruether proposes instead that Jesus be understood as the Christ in a paradigmatic and proleptic sense. Paradigmatically, Jesus reveals "the structure of human existence as it stands in that point of tension between what is and what ought to be."[26] His life shows that people have the capacity to struggle against injustice with limited yet real success. The limited realizations of justice that Jesus achieved give a foretaste of the coming reign of God, which still lies in the future. As this happens, the justice that can be realized in history becomes present ahead of time, or proleptically. While injustices continue, Jesus has shown that in principle they can be resisted. In this way, he changes the world by bringing hope for the overcoming of injustice.[27] Ruether presents this understanding of Jesus as the Christ as more authentic to the historical Jesus, more realistic to historical experience, and ethically superior to the Chalcedonian Christology that accorded an ultimate value to the historically relative figure of Jesus, which then became enshrined in much of Western Christianity.

Understood in this paradigmatic and proleptic fashion, Jesus expresses God's word and wisdom for humanity. In her later work on feminist issues, Ruether describes him as the paradigmatic expression of the Logos-Sophia of God.[28] As she applied her dialectical method to emerging justice issues such as racism, feminism, and authoritarianism in the Roman Catholic Church, the details of what Jesus exemplifies became further elaborated and more concrete.

In her groundbreaking book *Faith and Fratricide*,[29] Ruether argues that central to Jesus' teaching "was a proclamation of repentance in relation to the imminent advent of the Reign of God."[30] Three more important features of her Christology come to expression here. The first is Jesus' denunciation of sin and call to repentance. The second, connected to this, is his proclamation of the coming of a more just social order, the reign of God. For Ruether, essential to the paradigmatic nature of Jesus is the way his combined denunciation of sin and announcement of the possibility of a more just future models how people should act in the tension between what is and what ought to be. The third feature is Jesus' use of the symbol of the reign of God as a norm for evaluating the present and depicting the desired future. In Ruether's Christology, this symbol of the reign of God guides the critiques and affirmations that her theology makes of religious traditions and social structures. It symbolizes a "liberated future,"[31] in which the injustices of the present are overcome. The essential difference between this future and the present lies in the social structures of domination and hierarchical authority that need to be transformed into ones of equality and mutual respect.

In the 1970s, as Ruether became increasingly engaged with justice struggles and liberation theologies internationally, her Christology developed further. She began to describe Jesus as an "iconoclastic prophet of God who stands in judgment on social and religious systems that exclude subordinated and marginalized people from divine favor."[32] Part of what makes him paradigmatic for Christians is the way his teaching and preaching express a preferential option for the poor,[33] the principles of which can be applied to issues beyond his own context. By expressing this, he provides a model for people to follow wherever there is oppression or the misuse of power.[34]

However, for Ruether, Jesus is only proleptically the Christ. For her, the Christ establishes justice and liberation within history. This cannot be achieved by one person alone but only by people working together, and so "the Christ" is really a combination of Jesus' influence and the actions of people influenced by him.[35] Jesus has saving significance para- digmatically and proleptically as the Christ insofar as he moves people to follow his example in their own context. The liberated humanity, or "Christ," is glimpsed in Jesus and his relations with others[36] but must be realized through people's own struggles for justice.

What is it that enables Jesus to model a life of love in action so power- fully? Ruether never asks this question. For her, Jesus is fully human, like anyone else. This means there is nothing specifically redemptive about his cross. It is simply "an extreme example of the risk that anyone struggling against oppression takes at the hands of those who want to keep the systems of domination intact."[37] It is the example of his life that is redemptive, not his death. Yet his death does have some redemp- tive significance in her thought. Insofar as Jesus' death results from the power of oppressive forces to destroy the good, his resurrection reveals that this power is not ultimate. For Ruether, the objectivity of Jesus' resurrection cannot be demonstrated and is not important. It was not so much an event that happened to Jesus as "the dramatic influx of a new understanding" that came over his disciples after the initial shock of his death,[38] in which they came to believe that he was risen and spiri- tually present in their midst. For Ruether, Jesus is risen in the "rebirth of protest and new hope" over against unjust death[39] that took place then and that continues wherever people refuse to be silenced by violent oppression.

Ruether's recasting of Christology as the basis of a critical theory[40] that denounces oppression and announces the imperative of seeking a more just future enabled her to take up feminist issues around hierar- chical authority and the oppression of women in the 1970s and 1980s. In doing this, she began to wrestle with patriarchal language for God in Christianity and the maleness of Jesus. For Ruether, the trinitarian language of God as Father and Jesus as only-begotten Son is symbolic and must be deliteralized in terms of its gender and hierarchical parent-child imagery.[41] The development of the doctrine of the Trinity and Chalcedonian Christology involved a spiritualizing and depoliticizing of Jesus and his teaching, partly through a loss of the historical particularity of Jesus as a first-century Galilean Jewish male. Retrieving Jesus' particularity is an important step toward remedying the spiritualizing of his person and teaching.

Ruether argues that there is no intrinsic connection between Jesus' maleness and his liberating power. The challenge of feminism requires that Christian theology reject the hierarchal anthropology of patristic theology in favor of an egalitarian anthropology in which women and men are seen as created equal.[42] Jesus' maleness is ancillary to his being the Christ in paradigmatic and proleptic fashion through his liberating praxis, and his critique of domination and option for the poor enable him to be critically appropriated by feminist Christians in their liberation struggle.

In her engagement with the ecological crisis through the 1980s and 1990s though, Ruether came upon a form of sin, the refusal to accept our place in creation,[43] that her Christology could only partially address. According to Ruether, the environmental crisis arises in part from "exploitive domination of some by others."[44] But it also requires that people embrace the transience and finitude of human life.[45] Her understanding of Jesus as a prophetic figure who denounced oppression addresses the unjust exercise of power by some people over others, which greatly contributes to the ecological crisis. But because her Christology is oriented almost exclusively toward moving people to exercise their power over against evil, it does little to develop the contemplative spirituality[46] that she sees is needed to help people embrace their finitude and accept "natural" death as part of life. Here we touch on a limitation of the moral influence theory that will be discussed more fully in the conclusion to this chapter. We turn now to Carter Heyward's Christology, which was influenced by Ruether's.[47]

## Carter Heyward

Carter Heyward was born on August 22, 1945.[48] She grew up in Charlotte, North Carolina, in a white, liberal, middle-class family, as a "cradle-Christian," who knew "the storybook Jesus" from an early age.[49]

During her youth she was heavily involved with the Episcopal Church and at fourteen gave her life to Christ at a Billy Graham Crusade.[50] She received a B.A. from Randolph-Macon Women's College in Lynchburg, Virginia, in 1967. She then entered Union Theological Seminary in New York City, but after one year returned to Charlotte to work as a lay assistant in her home parish. In 1971, she returned to New York, completing an M.A. in the comparative study of religion at Columbia University and in 1973 an M.Div. from Union Theological Seminary. In 1972, she was accepted as a candidate for the priesthood in the Episcopal Church. After a period of negotiation, she and ten other women were ordained priests in 1974. This was first declared irregular, then sanctioned by the Episcopal Church in 1976.[51] In 1975, she became assistant professor of theology at Episcopal Divinity School in Cambridge, Massachusetts. She received tenure there in 1981 as associate professor after receiving a Ph.D. from Union Theological Seminary in New York in systematic theology in 1980.[52] In 1979, she came out as a lesbian and has been partnered with Beverly Wildung Harrison for many years. In 1998, they and others moved to North Carolina, where she lives for half the year, teaching the other half at Episcopal Divinity School. In 2000, she helped found Free Rein Center for Therapeutic Horseback Riding in Brevard, North Carolina.[53]

After beginning studies at Union Theological Seminary in the fall of 1967, Heyward underwent a profound spiritual and mental crisis, during which the basis for her radical rethinking of Christian beliefs began to emerge.[54] Heyward sees herself as "attempting to build on the best of the old in Christianity,"[55] retrieving and reinterpreting key notions of Christian theology so as to provide a life-giving vision for the present that will undergird struggles for a more inclusive church and greater social justice. This reflects her dialectical assessment of the Christian tradition and traditional Christologies. For Heyward, there has always been something about Jesus that made her "glad simply to be alive and part of something much larger" than herself.[56] But she has also long been troubled by aspects of the classical Christology affirmed at Nicaea and Chalcedon,[57] and by the notion that Jesus died on the cross to obtain from God forgiveness for people's sin. For Heyward, it is essential for Christian feminists to rethink Christology so as to remove these and other aspects that express destructive dualistic ideologies[58] and to retrieve and lift up what is empowering about Jesus for people involved in struggles for justice. This twofold approach is related to her understanding of power, which is central to her theology. Heyward's understanding of Jesus and his saving significance can be interpreted against this background, as for her, "any discussion of Jesus is a discussion of power."[59]

According to Heyward, all persons have the potential to act justly. This power is shared and grows out of people's relationships.[60] It results from the ability and the will to act in a certain way. People's power to act is properly exercised in mutuality with others and in acts that seek to foster mutual well-being among people and creation. This is the state of justice in which life flourishes.[61] The aspect of this power residing in the will is subject to two fundamental perversions. The first is the relinquishing of power that happens when people fail to recognize or fear to exercise their own power. The second is the wrongful exercise of power in the service of narcissism, the unjust elevation of one's own needs and desires above those of others that gives rise to oppression of others.[62]

The failure of some to actualize their own power can contribute to oppression in two ways. First, fear of their own power and responsibility may lead people to seek refuge in authoritarian, hierarchical and "bounded"[63] relationships and social structures. In Heyward's understanding, as these lack mutuality, they are inherently violent and unjust. Second, by not exercising their power to seek mutual relationships, people allow narcissistic aggression to go unchecked. These two perversions of the will affect other people by depriving them of the physical and psychic resources needed for life.

International relations, societies, churches, and personal lives are all sites of struggle between narcissistic expressions of aggression and the power of mutuality that opposes them. This struggle runs along lines of class, race, gender, and sexual preference and has an apocalyptic character. For Heyward, even the natural environment, the basis of life, is threatened by the greed, gluttony, and narcissism of the first world.[64]

Narcissistic aggression, as expressed in class or racial oppression, patriarchy, and American imperialism, is generally "too deeply entrenched in our religious and civil traditions"[65] to be effectively resisted by appeals to reason and good will, or by individuals acting on their own. It can only be effectively countered by public solidarity with the oppressed and collective resistance. This underlies Heyward's critique of theological liberalism as having an inadequate analysis of the realities of power at play in such conflicts,[66] and her approach to Christology.

For Heyward, the person of Jesus is a powerful religious and cultural icon, a crucial site in the struggle for justice between the forces of narcissistic aggression and those who seek to live in mutuality with others. Traditional Christian notions of Jesus as the unique Son of God, fully divine and fully human, dying on the cross to appease the wrath of God feed "twisted psychospiritualities that normalize sadistic and masochistic dynamics, rape and intimate violence, abuse of children, relationships of domination and control, violence against people and all creatures, and wars justified as holy."[67] In opposition to this, Heyward retrieves Jesus as a stimulus and guide toward seeking mutual relationships. The deep entrenchment of narcissistic aggression in contemporary society blinds people to alternatives. The potential costs of confronting it cows people into silence. In order to resist it and seek mutuality, people need moral exemplars and traditions that can open their eyes and bolster their courage. Her Christology seeks to retrieve Jesus as one of these moral exemplars. She understands this retrieval as an act of resistance against the narcissistic aggression expressed in patriarchy, homophobia, authoritarian religious structures, and global capitalism.

At the heart of Heyward's Christology lies her understanding of God as the power and joy arising from relationships of mutuality, and as the erotic desire, the yearning within people, that empowers them to seek these relationships.[68] God is both the yearning for mutual relationships and the spiritual power growing out of these. In her later work, Heyward equates this God with the Holy Spirit[69] and states that this yearning for right relationships, and the power and joy arising from them, has an innate tendency to expand.[70] This happens through people seeking and establishing mutual relations. As people experience the joy of mutuality, they seek more of it. Yet people are also held back from doing this by fear, the temptation to rest,[71] or by their desire for mutual relations becoming perverted into narcissism. Jesus' saving significance lies here, in his effect on the will. Jesus saves through his moral example, by moving and empowering people to seek mutual relations with others, and by modeling this kind of relationship himself.

For Heyward, Jesus had the same relationship to God that every other person has. He has no uniqueness or divine nature that sets him apart.[72] Only as Jesus is like every other person can he have saving significance, for affirmations of Jesus' uniqueness undermine people's power to seek mutual relationships by directing attention toward Jesus

43

and away from their own ability.[73] Jesus' maleness is not intrinsic to his saving significance, and to reject him because of it is to accept the patriarchal ideology, harmful to women, "that biology is destiny."[74] Jesus is an example of what a human life can be. His saving significance lies in what he models, and it is only as he is like others that Jesus can be a model for them.

However, Heyward does not simply dismiss the Chalcedonian Definition of Jesus as fully human and fully divine. Instead, she reinterprets it as Jesus being simultaneously vulnerable and powerful, arguing that Jesus' saving significance results from these two characteristics being indissolubly united in his one person.[75] Jesus is vulnerable in that he is open to others and to the Spirit urging him to seek mutual relations. As he is open to others, he can be hurt by them. Also, his openness to the urging of the Spirit leads him into conflict with unjust social structures and powerful people committed to them. This vulnerability, though, is intrinsic to his saving significance. By being vulnerable, he is able to show others through his example that they too can overcome their fears, tiredness, and narcissistic temptations and, like him, experience the joy of deeper and more extensive mutual relations through seeking justice. For Heyward, as for patristic Christology, Jesus' saving significance lies in God's power being expressed in and through Jesus' vulnerable humanity.

Jesus functions as a guide to others as his relations with other people reveal what is moral. Heyward argues that Jesus exercised a preferential option for the poor and refused to accept hierarchical, authoritarian, or bounded relationships.[76] His example moves people to imitate this by pushing and comforting them.[77] The push comes from the beauty of Jesus' example creating within people a desire to emulate him and from the way his example challenges people to go further in seeking mutual relations. The comfort comes from seeing that Jesus was human and fallible like others and that his praxis expressed how God never gives up on anyone. From this, people can draw the inspiration to recognize and forgive their own failings and those of others. The cross of Jesus shows the cost of seeking mutual relationships. The resurrection is "a statement of faith"[78] that the love of God, the power of mutual relationships, is stronger than the power of sin and death, and rises again after every defeat.

For Heyward, there is a sense in which Jesus as moral exemplar is always ahead of people challenging them to go further. But the relationship of Jesus to his followers, past and present, is dialectical. Jesus moves people to go beyond what they might have been without him. Conversely, people, through their response of faith, as in Heyward's retrieval of him, move Jesus beyond who he would have been without them.[79] Jesus saves people, but people can also save Jesus through their response to him. Through people appropriating Jesus' saving significance in new ways and contexts, the significance of Jesus is extended beyond previous horizons and given new meaning. Jesus is thus able to continue being the Christ in new contexts through people's creative responses to him.

While Heyward powerfully retrieves a sense of Jesus as a moral exemplar for the present, there is a vagueness to her social analysis and her reading of the Gospels. To borrow a term from cultural anthropology, she does not provide a "thick description" of Jesus' context against which to develop a nuanced interpretation of his praxis, nor does she provide a thick description of her own context, or of the nature of mutual relations and narcissistic aggression in it. Heyward did acknowledge a need for a closer analysis of the nature of mutual relationships amid the complexities of her context in her dialogues with Katie Cannon[80] and in her subsequent calls for white feminists to listen to the voices of women of color.[81] But generally, she uses the terms *right* or *mutual relationships* without carefully defining their parameters. Also, while Heyward sees Jesus as a source of empowerment toward right relationship, she never considers that he might be a source of restraint, preventing people's passions from leading them into bad relationships or abusive actions toward others. This may have contributed to a lack of moral discernment in her relationship to her therapist and her reflections on this.[82] We turn now to the Christology of Mark Lewis Taylor, who like Ruether and Heyward, employs a version of the moral theory of the atonement. But unlike Heyward, he engages in a much closer reading of Jesus' context and his own.

## Mark Lewis Taylor

Mark Lewis Taylor was born in Seattle, Washington, in 1951.[83] He grew up near Manhattan, Kansas, in a moderately evangelical Protestant atmosphere, which he has since moved away from. In 1973, he graduated from Seattle Pacific College (now University) and married Anita Kline. They had two daughters before divorcing in 1994. After a trial year at Union Theological Seminary in Richmond, Virginia, he did a Doctor of Ministry degree there, then entered the University of Chicago Divinity School in 1977, graduating with a Ph.D. in 1982. Taylor's father was a cultural anthropologist, and Taylor's Ph.D. dissertation was on the religious dimensions of cultural anthropology.[84] He began teaching at Princeton Theological Seminary in 1982, was tenured in 1989, and became Maxwell M. Upson Professor of Theology and Culture in 2004.

As a child, he spent time in Teotitlan del Valle, a Zapotec village in the province of Oaxaca in southern Mexico.[85] As a professor at Princeton Theological Seminary, he has repeatedly visited Guatemala and Mexico through the 1980s and 1990s, becoming involved there in resistance to American imperialism and right-wing dictatorships, and with anti-death penalty and antiwar/counterimperialism activism in the United States. His Christology reflects his activism and justice concerns.

Following Paul Tillich, Taylor speaks of "Jesus the Christ" or "Jesus as the Christ" rather than of Jesus Christ,[86] as he understands "Christ" to be a symbolic term. In an article published in 1986, he argues that symbols have four related meanings. First, they are privileged images having pervasive importance for a person or group.[87] Second, they are constructed through interpreters interacting with such images. Third, symbols represent the cultural-linguistic world of a privileged image and that of its interpreters. Fourth, a symbol suggests or projects a way of being in the world and invests it with transcendent meaning. In these terms, "Christ" is a symbol denoting the pervasive importance for Christians of Jesus' way of being and relating with others.

Taylor's emphasis on how the symbol of Jesus as the Christ is constructed, how it includes people inspired by Jesus, and how it should move people to certain kinds of action, requires that the Christ symbol be reconstructed so as to bring out its saving significance as its context changes, which gives his Christology a Reformed character. It reflects the Reformed theological tradition's emphasis that theological concepts be continually tested and rethought in light of the witness of the Word and the Holy Spirit in the present.[88]

Taylor's 1986 article argues on the basis of the Gospel narratives that the Christ symbol should be understood as referring to a praxis of recognizing and engaging with the cultures of other peoples and living for the oppressed.[89] These two themes form the axes along which he unfolds the saving significance of Jesus in his subsequent work. Solidarity with the oppressed must include a respectful dialogue with their culture,[90] because Jesus as the Christ works to overcome oppressive ethnocentricity that asserts the values of one's own culture over against those of others. This emphasis on culture as an important dimension of life, a part of people's identities in relation to which the saving significance of Jesus must be realized, is characteristic of all of Taylor's thought.

In 1990, Taylor published *Remembering Esperanza*, a major work in which he developed these insights and proposals more fully. Here he sharpened the idea that symbols are constructed by noting that christological symbols are always developed in "response to contemporary need."[91] In keeping with this, he began here with a social analysis of his North American context, first at a high level of abstraction and then more concretely. At the abstract level, he argued that North American theologies must respond to the demands of a trilemma, involving the need to celebrate cultural pluralism, critique political domination, and appropriate a Christian tradition.[92] New here was the third emphasis, in which Taylor expressed his dialectical understanding of the Christian theological tradition. While it has provided ideological support, directly or indirectly, for abuses and oppressions,[93] it should not be abandoned, because a religious tradition or mythos is necessary to empower and sustain struggles for justice.[94] Consequently theologians must reformulate the symbol of Jesus the Christ so as to rid it of oppressive aspects, such as male-coded language for Christ that perpetuates sexism,[95] and interpret it so that it addresses systemic forms of oppression.

In addition to the three concerns of his trilemma,[96] Taylor also argued that North America is threatened by five systemic evils. The first is an overarching tendency toward " 'abstraction' from material conditions," a turning away "from the sources of human and natural life: matter, bodies, mothers, darkness."[97] In order to oppose this, he set out to name and analyze the "operative patterns and systems of distortion"[98] oppressing people in North America as concretely as possible. This more concrete analysis identified four major forms of oppression that Christology must address. These are *sexism*, the domination of women by men, *heterosexism*, "alienation from intimate companionship with one's own gender and from fully sensual experience of one's own and others' bodies,"[99] *white racism*, the "systemic use and abuse of Africans' bodies and lives"[100] by whites, and *classism*, the domination of one class or classes by others. Of these four, Taylor gave sexism precedence because of its ubiquity and the way it has been paradigmatic for the others.[101]

He also argued that the Christ symbol refers not to Jesus individually but to a sociohistorical dynamic, comprising Jesus and others who followed him. Jesus is a necessary part but not the whole of this dynamic, which is a "freedom-making force that also unifies."[102] According to Taylor, Jesus' role in this dynamic is like that of leaven in bread dough. Jesus is the leaven in the dough of the sociohistorical dynamic that is the Christ.[103] Here there is an ambiguity in Taylor's thought. He writes that Jesus is not the "efficient cause of the Christ dynamic."[104] This efficient cause is the interaction of Jesus with others and with the social, cultural, and political forces of his day. He affirms that Jesus plays a unique role in causing this dynamic to take shape, yet he does not specify what it is about Jesus' interaction with others that causes it and what it is about Jesus' person that enables him to play a unique role in this.

At this point, Taylor was more concerned with the interpersonal nature of the Christ event and its contours as a dynamic in which the oppressed are first liberated, and then oppressors and oppressed are reconciled to form a new unity in which differences are preserved. As the symbol "Christ" denotes this sociohistorical dynamic of reconciliatory emancipation, it must be reconfigured to foster this dynamic in relation to the evils of the present. In this reconfiguration, the liberation of the oppressed is identified with Christ, and so is that aspect of their persons that is devalued. The first identification fosters emancipation. The second fosters admiration and respect toward what was formerly despised, so as to engender reconciliation between victims and their former oppressors. To be in Christ is to work for the liberation of the oppressed and to value their cultural-historical identity that has been denigrated.

Following this logic, he argues that in order to foster a dynamic of reconciliatory emancipation in relation to sexism and the tendency to abstraction, Christ must be reconfigured as "Christus Mater" to foster an emancipation of "women's reproductive powers from matricidal repression"[105] and an overcoming of the tendency to abstract from the body, natural processes, and the material conditions of life. To be "in Christ" then becomes to work for the emancipation of women and to affirm and celebrate their sexuality and reproductive powers.[106] Wherever this is happening, Christ is present. In relation to heterosexism, Christ represents sensualization, an overcoming of heterosexist domination and a sacralization of the body.[107] Similarly, Christ represents the overcoming of white racism and the valuing of blackness. In relation to classism, Christ represents the overcoming of class-based oppression and materialization, the valuing of the natural environment and the material bases of life. It is important to note the connection in all of this to the early church's confession of Jesus as the Christ. It is from the New Testament that Taylor discerns the sociohistorical dynamic of reconciliatory emancipation of which Jesus is the leaven. While Christology is reconfigured so as to foster this dynamic in the present, the shape of this dynamic is derived from the early church's confession of Jesus.

In 2001, Taylor published *The Executed God: The Way of the Cross in Lockdown America*,[108] his second major work on Christology. This work begins with a markedly different social analysis. In the eleven years since *Remembering Esperanza* was published, a brutal form of racist classism had become the predominant evil in the United States. The surging American economy in the 1990s created greater economic disparities, so that an elite class, typically white, became positioned atop an unstable economic pyramid. Accompanying the economic upswing was a massive investment in prisons, which functioned as a system of punishment and a theatrics of terror, to keep the economically deprived—who were frequently African American or Hispanic—in line.[109] This system of punishment and theatrics of terror—the focal point of which was the death penalty—turned the United States into Big House Nation, or Lockdown America, a country where prisons and police functioned to control those outside their walls as well as those within, confining through fear and awe not only the economically deprived, but any in America who might question the justice and sacrificial logic of globalized capitalism at the turn of the millennium. Matching this domestic regime was a global imperial practice sacrificing the lives of surplus populations, including children in Iraq, to maintain the empire of a largely American corporate elite.

The structure of Taylor's Christology remains unchanged in relation to his social analysis in *The Executed God*. "Christ" continues to denote that which is holy, a dynamic of reconciliatory emancipation that is greater than Jesus alone. In this new context of empire, Taylor's reformulation of the Christ symbol focuses on a reappropriation of the Galilean identity of Jesus, as one who resisted empire in its Roman form, particularly through his death and resurrection, and a reappropriation of the notion of following Jesus' way of the cross.[110] Taylor argues that in Lockdown America the crucial dominating power that must be resisted is its theatrics of terror, which keeps people from constructively resisting its injustice.[111] In Jesus' entry into Jerusalem, his death on the cross, and resurrection, Taylor sees a theatrics of counterterror resisting that of the Roman Empire. Christians today must continue this theatrics of counterterror in relation to the empire of the present.

Taylor argues that death by crucifixion was a form of political terror, designed to keep oppressed populations in line. Jesus' death was intended to be a spectacular show to terrorize others. But Jesus stole the show, as his resurrection turned the spectacle of his death into a theatrics of counterterror,[112] inspiring early Christian communities with a counterimperial worldview. The account in Mark's Gospel of Jesus' resistance to empire and his theatrics of counterterror identify his way of resistance with a power greater than that of imperial Rome.[113] Like a great novel, the Gospel accounts have the power to move people to resist the theatrics of terror that shores up Lockdown America with their own theatrics of counterterror, inspired by Jesus.

Taylor developed this further in 2006 in an essay titled "American Torture and the Body of Christ."[114] Here he argues that in the war against terrorism begun by the Bush government after September 9, 2001, the United States had once again become a torture state subverting democracy within its own borders and destabilizing "the rest of the world."[115] In order to reappropriate Christology to resist the American torture state, Taylor suggests that the Eucharist be celebrated with a dramatic identification of Jesus with the victims of torture and with resistance to it.

Like Rosemary Radford Ruether and Carter Heyward, Taylor develops a powerful interpretation of Jesus as the Christ that unleashes the critical potential of the gospel in relation to social evils. Like them, he also sees "Christ" to include the people moved by Jesus, as well as Jesus himself. Unlike Heyward, he employs an extensive and carefully argued social analysis that seeks to be specific about the face of evil in the present. Yet there is a recurring omission in Taylor's thought. As noted, in *Remembering Esperanza*, he does not ask what it is about Jesus' interaction with others that enables him to function as the leaven in the dough that is the Christ dynamic. Similarly, in *The Executed God*, he argues that Jesus stole the show of his death through his resurrection, but he does not inquire into the nature of Jesus' resurrection or what the New Testament traditions claim about Jesus' resurrection. At one point, he suggests that the life Jesus lived "and the way he was remembered made his death a show-stealing act."[116] He also suggests that it is not important "whether the resurrection was a historical event or whether it happened in the way the gospel narratives say it did."[117] What is crucial in his view is that something happened that convinced his former followers that Jesus' way of resistance had not been quashed by his death and moved them to continue it. In one sense, this is true. Exact historical information is not available about Jesus' resurrection. Yet in another sense, Taylor takes here only what he needs from Jesus' resurrection and does not ponder its meaning in depth. What was this "something" that the New Testament calls Jesus' resurrection that caused him to be remembered and venerated in the way that he was? For many in the early church, Jesus' resurrection had implications for his person as well as his cause. The alteration in their faith triggered by Jesus' resurrection ultimately empowered a rethinking of the nature of God. Taylor brilliantly brings out the radical social implications of Jesus' ministry, death, and resurrection and how these can empower the struggle for social justice. Like Ruether and Heyward, Taylor experiences the power of the symbol of Jesus as the Christ without pondering what enabled Jesus to be a source of this power. This leaves a significant aspect of Christology, the understanding of Jesus' person, how he was able to be the Christ, undiscussed.

As a result, for Taylor, Ruether, and Heyward, Jesus as the Christ is a powerful expression of divine power but does not play a special role in defining the source of that power. Throughout Christian history, questions about the nature of Jesus' person, how he was able to be the Christ, have lead to Christian understandings of God or divine power being formed through a dialectic between aspects of Jesus' particularity, such as his humanity or his death on the cross, and cultural understandings of divinity and power, such as the Hellenistic axiom that the divine is immutable.[118] By not pursuing the question of what it is about Jesus' person that enables him to be the Christ, or the leaven in the Christ dynamic, Ruether, Heyward, and Taylor let drop a question that has played a significant role in the development of the understanding of God and the divine power that Jesus reveals.

## Summary

The three authors studied in this chapter all see the saving significance of Jesus to lie in his moral influence. The fundamental sin or evil that Jesus overcomes is lack of moral concern for other or a false image of

God that gives rise to the complicity of churches and the Christian tradition in fostering oppression and injustice. While the sin and evil that must be overcome manifests itself in sinful social structures and organized acts of destruction like the Holocaust, it has its origin in a lack of love and moral concern in people's hearts. Jesus saves both perpetrators and victims from this kind of sin by moving them to seek justice and resist evil and in this way to fulfill their divinely given potential. Jesus does this through his symbolic power. The beauty of his actions and liberating relationships with others moves people by giving them a new sense of values and inspiring them to seek to express these in their own lives. Jesus' power is primarily erotic. He moves people to resist evil and so saves them by creating within them an eros for justice and peace. The salvation Jesus brings in this understanding is not so much a new awareness of God, as in the previous chapter, but a new way of acting and relating to others. The lack of love and moral concern and the sinful social structures that separate people from God are overcome as Jesus moves them to become one with God in their actions and to seek a more just society. In the Christologies studied in this chapter, the atonement Jesus effects is this change in people's lives.

This way of understanding Jesus' saving significance, like that in the previous chapter, avoids the crisis of cognitive claims that traditional notions of God acting in history experienced in relation to the modern worldview shaped by the natural sciences. Removing this intellectual barrier is important for unleashing the critical potential of Jesus in relation to contemporary social issues. However, there is a curious irony in the three Christologies studied here. Each seeks to unleash the critical potential of Jesus and the Gospel traditions in relation to massive and powerfully entrenched social evils, like homophobia, racism, and class domination, that have claimed untold numbers of lives, caused immense suffering, and created immense guilt. Yet each of these Christologies is characterized by a "modesty of soteriological interest."[119] In one sense, their soteriological interest is not modest, in that each seeks to establish justice on earth for all, a never-ending task. Yet their soteriological concern is modest in that there are dimensions of human concern like guilt and the finality and loss of death that they do not address.

In the moral influence theory of atonement, the primary evil Jesus overcomes is an idolatrous concept of God and a lack of moral concern for others. This evil is located primarily in the will, in the failure to love the good and to fulfill one's potential to seek it. Jesus saves by creating within people the will or desire to love others. But as each of the authors studied in this chapter argues, this failure to love leads to massive destruction of other peoples and the environment. This suggests that this theory of atonement alone is not adequate to overcome the evils that these authors address. Can the quest for justice be sustained when the massive destruction caused by sinful social structures is not overcome? According to philosopher Max Horkheimer, the quest for justice is sustained by a belief that executioners will not ultimately triumph over their victims.[120] If so, then the subjective emphasis of the moral influence theory of the atonement needs to be complemented by an "objective"[121] theory of the atonement that unpacks the saving significance of Jesus in terms of the promise he brings of a future for the victims of history. In the next chapter, we turn to three theologians, Jon Sobrino, James Cone, and Elizabeth Johnson, who understand the saving significance of Jesus in this way.

## Suggestions for Further Reading

Jennings, Theodore W., Jr. *Transforming Atonement: A Political Theology of the Cross*. Minneapolis: Fortress Press, 2009. An attempt to recapture the socially transformative meaning of Jesus' cross.

Johnson, Elizabeth A. *Consider Jesus: Waves of Renewal in Christology*. New York: Crossroad, 1990. See especially chapter 7, "Feminist Christology" (pp. 97–113), which provides a succinct overview of feminist Christologies up to the mid-1990s.

Purvis, Sally B. *The Power of the Cross: Foundations for a Christian Feminist Ethic of Community*. Nashville: Abingdon, 1993. A feminist appropriation of the cross as socially transformative.

Rieger, Joerg. *Christ and Empire: From Paul to Postcolonial Times*. Minneapolis: Fortress Press, 2007. Evaluates Christologies from Paul to the present in terms of a social justice perspective congruent with that of Ruether, Heyward, and Taylor.

## Discussion Questions

1. Can Jesus have a saving significance apart from what he moves people to do?
2. Do Ruether, Heyward, and Taylor modify Abelard's understanding of Jesus' saving significance in some ways?

3. Is the socially radical interpretation of Jesus developed by Ruether, Heyward, or Taylor appropriate to the New Testament?
4. What is it about Jesus that continues to inspire radical critiques of social injustice and oppression?

CHAPTER 3

◆

# Jesus as Source of Ultimate Hope

## James Cone, Jon Sobrino, Elizabeth Johnson

Reading through many of the Easter hymns in *Voices United*,[1] a hymnbook of The United Church of Canada, one may notice how often Jesus' resurrection is described in dramatic images of conflict and struggle. Numerous hymns celebrate Jesus' resurrection as a victory, a triumph, an overcoming of sin, evil, and death. Even the hymn "In the Bulb There Is a Flower,"[2] which uses natural images of change such as the turn of the seasons from winter to spring to describe the resurrection, sees it as the basis for the hope that there will be, "at the last, a victory."[3] Like many Easter hymns, this hymn celebrates hope for a radical transformation of reality.

The use of dramatic images of struggle and terms like *victory* to describe Jesus' resurrection reflects the understanding of Jesus' saving significance found in what Gustaf Aulén called the "Christus Victor" or "classic" type of atonement theory.[4] According to Aulén, this was the predominant way of understanding the atonement in the patristic era.[5] It presupposes a dualistic outlook in which reality is seen as a site of conflict between God and evil. Sin here is an objective power, sometimes personified in the figure of Satan, and Jesus' saving significance lies in the victory God achieves over it in Jesus' death and resurrection.[6]

55

This is an "objective" model of the atonement.[7] Jesus' resurrection is understood to effect a change in the structure of reality, bringing the presence of transformed life into the world. In doing so, it promises a final overcoming of evil that empowers people to struggle against sin and evil in the present. What follows will examine how this Christus Victor understanding of the atonement is present in the Christologies of James Cone, Jon Sobrino, and Elizabeth Johnson.

These three theologians address their church communities and link their theologies to justice movements seeking radical social change. Situating themselves at the intersection of these movements and the church, they find in Jesus Christ a source of hope empowering struggles for social justice and an exemplar illuminating where and how the church should be present in these.

The proponents of the atonement models studied in the two previous chapters seek to understand Jesus within the structures of reality presupposed by contemporary Western secularity. Cone, Sobrino, and Johnson relate the two more dialectically. These three are contemporary in their focus on human flourishing and issues like the environmental crisis.[8] Each relates Jesus positively to the values of liberation and justice espoused by contemporary social movements, and to the democratic ideals of contemporary Western cultures. Yet each also sees these cultures as oppressing certain social groups and in need of radical transformation. Each also remains rooted in the biblical traditions and patristic Christology in ways that conflict with secularizing tendencies of Western cultures, which presuppose that humanity has outgrown the kinds of affirmation about Jesus Christ that these theologians make.[9]

## James Cone

James Cone was born on August 5, 1938, in Fordyce, Arkansas.[10] He grew up in the nearby town of Bearden. His mother was a "pillar" of the Macedonia African Methodist Episcopal Church. His father also belonged, and Cone remembers him as having constantly demonstrated courage and resistance to white racism.[11] Cone summarizes the influence of his upbringing on his theology thus:

> Two things happened to me in Bearden: I encountered the harsh realities of white injustice that was inflicted daily upon

the black community; and I was given a faith that sustained my personhood and dignity in spite of white people's brutality.[12]

After graduating from high school, Cone earned a B.A. from Philander Smith College and then a B.D. from Garrett Theological Seminary. He found most of his theology professors at Garrett to be racist in their treatment and expectations of black students. Determined to prove them wrong, he applied himself to earning higher grades, and succeeded. Encouraged by professors William Hordern and Philip Watson, he earned M.A. and Ph.D. degrees in systematic theology at Northwestern University,[13] completing the latter in 1965 with a thesis on Karl Barth's anthropology. He has since received eight honorary degrees, including a doctor of divinity from Garrett-Evangelical Theological Seminary, and is an ordained minister in the African Methodist Episcopal Church.[14]

From 1964 to 1966, Cone taught at Philander Smith College, then moved to Adrian College in Adrian, Michigan. Spurred on by the civil rights struggle, black rioting in American cities in 1967,[15] and the assassination of Martin Luther King Jr. on April 4, 1968, he began to explore the relationship of Christian faith to the Black Power movement, publishing *Black Theology and Black Power* in 1969.[16] Here he argues that "for twentieth-century America the message of Black Power is the message of Christ himself."[17] To be faithful to God's Word in Christ in this context, one had to understand Jesus as black.[18] Next, he wrote *A Black Theology of Liberation*,[19] and in 1969 before it was published became Charles A. Briggs Distinguished Professor of Systematic Theology at Union Theological Seminary in New York, where he remains.

Cone's theology has been written in the context of the United States, with an expanding horizon that has become global through his involvement with third-world theologies.[20] For Cone, the most significant aspect of this context is the conflict between socially dominant white people intent on preserving white privilege and power, and peoples of color, predominantly African Americans, struggling for freedom and dignity, who are the victims of white racist oppression. He continues to see this as a salient issue, which theologians and churches must address.[21] He developed his black theology[22] in response to it.

Against the dismissal of Christianity and the black church by black nationalists, Cone affirmed Jesus Christ as a moral source that could sustain resistance to white racism and prevent this resistance from degenerating into hatred and contempt for whites or blacks who failed to share one's views.[23] He also argued that the failure of white theologians[24] and white churches to denounce white racism and their condemnation of black rioting in response to it made them effectively racist even when not overtly so. The black church in turn had mediated an empowering faith in Jesus Christ and produced leadership and resources for the civil rights struggle but had sometimes fallen into political conservatism tolerant of racism, preaching a gospel of success and disdaining critical theology.[25]

For Cone, a critical theology "based on the Bible and using the tools of the social sciences"[26] is necessary for participation in God's work of redemption. He drew on white theologians, particularly Karl Barth, to develop this. He found in Barth an emphasis on the centrality of Jesus Christ for understanding God, a respect for the Bible as "a primary source for knowledge about Jesus and God," and an emphasis on preaching congruent with black church traditions.[27] Like Barth, Cone affirmed the christological positions of the Councils of Nicaea (325) and Chalcedon (451).[28] He assumed without much discussion that God became incarnate in Jesus, who revealed God's nature and effected salvation. But whereas Barth and patristic Christology were concerned primarily with understanding Jesus' person and meaning in relation to humanity as a whole, Cone was primarily interested in discerning the place of Jesus and thus of God within the racial conflicts of the 1960s. This created a caesura between his Christology and his neoorthodox predecessors. Whereas Barth, Tillich, and Bonhoeffer tended to speak about "the word of man," culture," or "man" generically, Cone argued that Jesus did not have the same meaning for oppressors and the oppressed.[29] He similarly critiqued the Christologies of Nicaea and Chalcedon for their abstractness in relation to Jesus' historical particularity.[30] But he followed Karl Barth in the way he appropriated their affirmations, using the historical particularity of Jesus to reinterpret the doctrine of God.

Cone began his groundbreaking work, *Black Theology and Black Power*, by arguing that the Black Power movement was an affirmation of black freedom and dignity against white racism. Following Barth, others,[31] and the black church tradition, he then argued that Jesus Christ is the starting point for any Christian understanding of reality and thus for any Christian assessment of the Black Power movement. He then characterized Christ's work as "essentially one of liberation,"[32] which empowers the oppressed to struggle against oppression.

In Christ, God enters human affairs and takes sides with the oppressed. Their suffering becomes his; their despair, divine despair. Through Christ the poor man is offered freedom now to rebel against that which makes him other than human.[33]

For Cone, Jesus does this in two ways: first, through his public ministry; and second, through his death and resurrection. First, as a historical figure, Jesus, in his teaching, preaching, miracles, and table fellowship, sided with the oppressed over against their oppressors. Here Cone developed, independent of Latin American liberation theology, an understanding of what became known as God's preferential option for the poor. Second, through Christ's death and resurrection, the power of evil was overcome in principle. This created hope for resistance to it in history, freeing the oppressed from despair and the truth claims of their oppressors. Released in this way from mental and spiritual slavery, they are empowered by Christ to seek their freedom.

According to Cone, white racism is similar to the demonic evil that Christ struggled against in his ministry and overcame in principle through his death and resurrection.[34] As God's definitive Word, Christ brings blacks and whites liberation from its dehumanizing ideology. Christ affirms the worth and dignity of black people against the denigrations of white racism by having sided with them and died for them. In this, there was a profound congruence between Jesus Christ and the Black Power movement.[35] Both affirmed black dignity and demanded that whites recognize it. Because Christ had sided with the oppressed, becoming one with them in his own time, in the context of white racist America, he must be understood as black.[36] Cone maintains that Jesus brings hope for eternal life.[37] But he focuses on understanding the saving significance of Christ in terms of the sociological categories of status and power. In subsequent years, he paid more attention to economic oppression and began to denounce sexism[38] as a sin within the black community. But this initial understanding of Jesus' person and significance continued to provide the essential structure to his Christology, which was further developed in *A Black Theology of Liberation* (1970) and *God of the Oppressed* (1975).

For Cone, the salvific meaning of Jesus is discerned by attending to the past, present, and future dimensions of his person.[39] The past dimension is that of Jesus as a historical person, through whose actions and teachings his being as the Christ became concrete among the social conflicts of his time. Cone derived his understanding of this from the quest for the historical Jesus in the 1960s and a critically informed reading of the Synoptic Gospels. These show that Jesus' person and ministry were focused on his proclamation of the coming kingdom of God, which would end oppression and displace "all false authorities."[40] Drawing on the work of Ernst Käsemann and others, Cone argued that the identity of Jesus Christ in the present must be seen as continuous with the historical Jesus. Jesus' identification with the poor and the continuity of the risen Christ with the historical Jesus mean that differences in social location must be respected when discerning Christ's presence and meaning in contemporary society. This gave Cone a basis in the heart of the Christian tradition for opposing a white Christ supportive of the racist status quo.[41]

The present dimension of Jesus' being results from his resurrection extending his presence to all times and places. As Jesus' person and work bore witness to God's will to liberate the oppressed, he continues to be present wherever such liberating work happens.[42] Cone does not trace how faith in Jesus' resurrection leads to belief in the incarnation. He simply affirms that it reveals Jesus' actions to have "their origin in God's eternal being."[43] Through Jesus' ministry, cross, and resurrection, a joyful exchange took place. God in Christ took on the condition of the poor and oppressed in order to bring them freedom and hope.[44] Jesus' resurrection includes his exaltation as "Lord," which affirms God's revelation in him as the final truth. By taking on the condition of African Americans, Christ brings them a true image of themselves, over against that forced on them by white racism. In effect, he is present as the one Word of God to which the church must at all times listen. This one Word does not obliterate others but illuminates them and receives new meaning from them, particularly through exemplary interpreters like Harriet Tubman or Richard Allen. The continuity of the risen Christ with the historical Jesus means that the Word of God in Christ continues to sound forth through oppressed peoples' cries for freedom and dignity.[45] As Jesus is present today in the struggles of the oppressed for freedom, he is known through participation with them in these struggles.[46] Yet the risen Christ is also transcendent to the oppressed, sustaining them with hope and assurance,[47] functioning as a critical presence "that makes possible the affirmation of black humanity in an inhumane situation."[48]

Faith that Jesus is risen led Cone to adopt an intellectual posture similar to Karl Barth's,[49] described by Paul Ricoeur as a "broken dialectic."[50] Against the argument of William Jones that black suffering reveals God to be a white racist, Cone acknowledged the reality of the former but pointed to Christ as evidence against the latter.[51] Because Jesus' resurrection reveals the truth to be liberating,[52] Cone evaluates ideas and traditions pragmatically. Cone's intellectual posture and pragmatism are evident in his affirmation of Jesus' resurrection over against Western secularity and the demand for demythologization in theology. This demand fails to acknowledge that what the New Testament called powers and principalities continue to be present in transpersonal phenomena like white racism.[53] Pragmatically, this demand functions as a tool of white racism, stripping black communities of an empowering moral source necessary for their liberation. Against the brute force of white racism, the resurrection of Christ affirms the ultimate power of God's love to uphold justice and eventually end racist oppression.

In Gustaf Aulén's Christus Victor typology, sin and death are objective realities, cosmic powers that find expression in earthly realities. Cone used this conceptuality to address the transpersonal nature of racism, to articulate the future dimension of Jesus' person and to show how Christ's death and resurrection provide a transcendent principle of expectation for the liberation of the oppressed. He radicalized it "politically," identifying "Gerald Ford and other government officials, who oppress the poor, humiliate the weak, and make heroes out of rich capitalists," and "police departments and prison officials" responsible for the shooting and killing of blacks because they demand "their right to exist," as contemporary expressions of the powers and principalities behind Christ's death, which had been objectively overcome in principle in his resurrection.[54] This overcoming includes the promise that it will become actual in the future and so empowers the oppressed in their struggle for freedom. Cone's adaptation of the Christus Victor model of atonement is his primary way of interpreting Jesus' saving significance and is found throughout his work.[55]

These past, present, and future aspects of Jesus' being as the Christ inform Cone's notion of Jesus' blackness. Against the backdrop of sometimes strained relations between Jews and African Americans in the United States, Cone argued that Jesus "is black because he was a Jew."[56] As Jesus was Jewish, he must be interpreted in line with Jewish traditions of God as liberator of the oppressed, deriving from the exodus. In his public ministry and death, Jesus fulfilled the role of God's servant, taking on himself the experience of the oppressed. Through his resurrection, he brings them hope and becomes present in and with them. Therefore, as the risen Christ in the present, Jesus is black. "Black" here is a concrete instance of "oppressed"[57] and is understood sacramentally. For Cone, regardless of what his skin color was,[58] Christ is black literally and symbolically,[59] truly present in the black experience of oppression and struggle for freedom, just as he has been understood to be truly present in the Lord's Supper.[60]

While "Cone's version of the Black Christ freed Black people from the shame of worshipping a White Christ," it does not address the oppression of women within the black community by black men.[61] Cone's way of understanding Jesus as black could be extended to understanding Jesus as present in and with women in their suffering from and struggle against sexism.[62] But as Cone's self-acknowledged failure to adequately address sexism[63] indicates guilt, it also points to a need for forgiveness.[64] This is an aspect of Jesus' saving significance that Cone has left largely unexplored.

# Jon Sobrino

Jon Sobrino was born on December 27, 1938, in Barcelona, Spain. He joined the Jesuit order when he was eighteen and went to El Salvador, then to St. Louis University in St. Louis, Missouri, completing a master's degree in engineering in 1965. He returned to El Salvador to teach and was ordained as a priest in 1969. He completed a doctorate in theology at the Hochschule Sankt Georgen in Frankfurt, Germany, in 1975. In 1974, he returned to El Salvador, becoming professor of theology at the Catholic University of Central America in San Salvador. His books, talks, and articles have brought him international recognition as a leading Latin American liberation theologian. On November 16, 1989, Salvadoran troops entered the house where he lived and killed six of his Jesuit colleagues, their housekeeper, and her daughter. Sobrino survived because he was away.[65] In 2007, the Congregation for the Doctrine of the Faith issued a Notification that certain propositions in his later books do not conform to Roman Catholic teaching.[66] He continues to be professor of theology at the Catholic University of Central America and director of the Monsignor Romero Centre there.

Sobrino's Christology is written out of a Latin American context, in which the Roman Catholic Church has been a powerful but politically ambivalent institution and in which deadly poverty combined with murderous repression of the poor makes social change imperative but seemingly impossible.[67] According to Sobrino, this results from global economic forces and the moral indifference of North Atlantic countries to the fate of the poor in Latin America, Africa, and Asia.[68] In Latin America, Jesus had been understood along the lines of the christological teachings of the Councils of Nicaea and Chalcedon, but only in terms of his significance for the salvation of individuals after death. This changed in 1968, when the Second General Conference of Latin American Bishops, meeting at Medellín, Colombia,[69] affirmed that salvation includes deliverance from injustice in history and that Christ's true humanity appeared in his liberating relationships to the poor.[70] In keeping with Vatican II's injunction to interpret the gospel in relation to "signs of the times," Sobrino took the suffering of the poor in Latin America and this new image of Christ as liberator endorsed at Medellín as two such signs and developed his Christology in relation to them.[71] Behind these influences stand others. The Marxist challenge that theory should change society has given his thought a pragmatic bent. European theologians Karl Rahner, Johann Baptist Metz, and Jürgen Moltmann have provided him with many ideas. Finally, questions about the orthodoxy of his Christology have led Sobrino to continually relate it to the affirmations of Nicaea and Chalcedon. The Christology set forth in his first book, *Christology at the Crossroads: A Latin American Approach*, was defended and developed in a second, *Jesus in Latin America*. It then found mature expression in two subsequent volumes, *Jesus the Liberator* and *Christ the Liberator*.[72]

According to Sobrino, the most pressing theological issue in Latin America is the liberation of the poor[73] from economic oppression, violent repression, and a lack of dignity.[74] This means that the theoretical engagement with atheism, and unbelief characteristic of the preceding generation of Roman Catholic theology in Europe has to give way to practical critiques of the false gods that give rise to injustice and deadly poverty, and a rethinking of the traditional Christology of Latin American churches that leaves them untroubled.[75] He characterizes the difference between liberation theology and its European counterparts thus: "in Latin America . . . we are not doing theology after Auschwitz, but during Auschwitz."[76] However, theoretical issues remain. Throughout Sobrino's Christology there are echoes of Karl Barth's insistence that the true nature of God and human liberation can only be known by attending to the concreteness of God's revelation in Jesus Christ.[77] As Christ comes from God, a descending Christology from above is necessary to respect divine mystery and transcendence. But to prevent the notion of Christ from being filled with alien content, a Christology from below,[78] moving from what can be known historically about Jesus must also be employed, so that Jesus' person defines the meaning of the formal terms of a Christology like Chalcedon's.[79] Sobrino values the affirmations of Nicaea and Chalcedon as guides to understanding the person of Jesus Christ in relation to history as a whole. But to understand the nature of God and the place of Jesus Christ within history, their abstract terms must be informed by what can be known about Jesus historically[80] and interpreted in relation to "signs of the times," like the suffering of the poor.

Sobrino sees Jesus to have saving significance in three ways. First, he reveals the nature and will of God through his ministry, death, and resurrection. Second, he exemplifies what it means to follow God's will and be fully human. Third, through his ministry, death, and resurrection, the power of sin and death were overcome in principle, so that he provides a transcendent source of hope for liberation.

Sobrino argues that Jesus' ministry brought the reign of God to people as a free gift, regardless of their social worth. As the coming of God's reign was the focus of Jesus' ministry and the cause for which he died, it must remain the focus of the church's life and mission. Jesus' ministry was fundamentally concerned with liberating the poor from external oppression, and they were its primary recipients.[81] Jesus revealed God to have a preferential option for the poor. The basic values of the kingdom are justice, mercy, and reconciliation—justice understood as the opportunity to live with dignity.[82] The drawing near of God's reign meant liberation to the poor and those categorized as sinners,[83] which brought Jesus into conflict with Jewish religious and Roman political authorities benefiting from their oppression, and led to Jesus' death.[84] In resurrecting Jesus, God vindicated his message as true.[85]

As the focus of Jesus' ministry was the coming of God's reign, so the revelation of God in him achieves its end as people respond by following him and seeking God's reign. The reign of God comes through the liberation of the poor. Jesus not only reveals God, he exemplifies the way to God and how to follow God's will. To be truly human is to embody in one's own life what Jesus embodied in his.[86] This following of Jesus is an expression of faith and at the same time a necessary condition for existential or "inner"[87] mystical knowledge of God and Jesus. The truth of Jesus known cognitively, and that known existentially through following him, mutually inform one another so that seeking the reign of

God after the example of Jesus becomes the way to God. Those who follow this way, like Oscar Romero,[88] may become a source of hope and example for others of what it means to follow the primary exemplar, Jesus Christ. Jesus thus is the "channel,"[89] or way, that leads both to God and to fullness of life, for one's self and others.

The way of Jesus leads inevitably to the cross, this being understood as representative of the violent repression that can result from conflict with oppressive social power. Particularly in his later work, following the martyrdom of Oscar Romero, his Jesuit colleagues, and countless others, Sobrino has stressed the immensity and relentlessness of the violent oppression inflicted on the poor, particularly in the Southern Hemisphere, and speaks of them as the crucified people(s).[90] In their suffering, the crucifixion of Jesus continues. Their suffering and struggle for justice is thus the primary place where God is revealed and encountered. The task of Christians is to help bring the suffering poor down from the cross by seeking the coming of God's reign.

In the face of the long history of cruelty, suffering, and martyrdom inflicted on the poor, following Jesus is made meaningful by the hope and love arising from faith in his resurrection. The resurrection of Jesus reveals the ultimacy of God's love, that it is greater than sin and death.[91] It is the great victory of God's love over the forces of violent oppression that brings an empowering hope for the final overcoming of injustice and oppression in history. But while Jesus' resurrection reveals that God's love is effective and will ultimately triumph, it is the cross that makes it credible to the victims of history, by showing that God shares their suffering and is with them in their struggle. Through Jesus' cross, God draws near to the poor. Through his resurrection, God gives them hope. Both are essential for Jesus and God to be good news to them.[92] As the victory of God's love shines a ray of hope into history, it makes emulating Jesus' example an exigency for his followers.[93] Jesus died not to pay the penalty for sin but out of faithfulness to God's reign, so that sin, injustice, and oppression might be ended.

Sobrino sees in Jesus' own relation to God a dialectic of nearness and distance. In *Christology at the Crossroads*, he argues that in an early stage of his ministry, Jesus' trust in God was vindicated by signs that God's reign was breaking into history.[94] But as the kingdom did not come in fullness, Jesus entered a second stage, in which he had to continue to trust in God even as God became more and more remote during his journey to Jerusalem and then on the cross. In his later work, Sobrino has dropped this chronology but continued to argue that as Jesus' ministry gave rise to persecution culminating in his death, Jesus had to continue to trust in God even as God's presence became more distant from him.[95] Jesus was the Son of God, fully divine, precisely as in his fully human finitude he continued to let God be God and to trust God even to the point of dying on the cross.[96] Precisely by doing this, Jesus let God be transcendent and succeeded in credibly realizing/revealing God's love in history by accepting suffering for God's sake and dying on the cross to bring God near to the poor in an ultimate sense.

This understanding of Jesus' humanity and divinity drew criticism from the Congregation for the Doctrine of the Faith.[97] His use of biblical scholarship in *Christology at the Crossroads* was condemned as academically deficient by noted New Testament scholar John Meier,[98] and his portrayal of the Pharisees and Jewish religious leaders has been criticized as anti-Judaic.[99] Sobrino's Christology does have weaknesses in these areas.[100] Although his later work corrected some problems in his claims about what can be known about Jesus historically, he has not been attentive to how his portrayal of the Pharisees at times perpetuates a Christian tradition of denigrating Judaism. But other readers note what these critics fail to appreciate: how Sobrino develops from Jesus' ministry, death, and resurrection a "comprehensive and uncompromising vision"[101] of how the church must relate to the sufferings of the poor that is in many ways faithful to what the best of New Testament scholarship[102] can discern about Jesus.

## Elizabeth Johnson

Elizabeth Johnson was born on December 6, 1941, in New York City. She grew up there, in a Roman Catholic family, doing a B.S. at Brentwood College, New York, then an M.A. in theology at Manhattan College, and joining the Sisters of Saint Joseph in Brentwood. She "taught religion and science in Catholic elementary and high schools,"[103] then was an adjunct faculty at St. Joseph's College in Brooklyn for four years before entering the doctoral program in systematic theology at the Catholic University of America in Washington, D.C., in 1977. She graduated with a Ph.D. in 1981, doing her doctoral thesis on the theology of Wolfhart Pannenberg. She stayed there to teach for eleven years, then went to Fordham University in New York in 1991, where she continues as Distinguished Professor of Theology. Johnson has authored numerous articles and seven books, several of which have won prestigious awards. She has received twelve honorary doctorates and fourteen academic and teaching awards.[104]

In 1965, Johnson was about to take her final vows to enter the Sisters of Saint Joseph, but she felt conflicted between doing this and participating in the social justice struggles of the 1960s.[105] This conflict was resolved when she sat one afternoon under a favorite pine tree and read a draft of *Gaudium et Spes,* a document of Vatican II, also known as the Pastoral Constitution on the Church in the Modern World.[106] Reading this, her "young, questing spirit . . . found its life-long direction."[107] She completed her vows and entered the religious order, as a place from which to engage in the social justice struggles she felt called to join. There was something distinctive about her joining a religious order to participate in social justice struggles in a time when many were leaving religious orders for precisely this reason. One can see here a particular dynamic, a distinctive approach to social justice that is reflected in her theological methodology.

Early on, Johnson adopted Rosemary Radford Ruether's principle of feminist theology, that what enables the full humanity of women to flourish "is redemptive and of God; whatever damages this is nonredemptive and contrary to God's intent."[108] But Johnson sought a much fuller appropriation of the Christian theological tradition, particularly patristic Christology, than Ruether. Rather than simply return to "the historical Jesus . . . as an iconoclastic prophet," as Ruether did, Johnson sought to "think through a full Christology which is faithful to the hard won insights of the tradition's faith proclamation at the same time that it breaks out of the usual androcentric pattern."[109] In order to engage issues of patriarchal oppression, she did not shed traditional christological doctrine but entered more deeply into it to rethink it so as to unleash its critical potential in relation to present injustices.

Johnson did this through a three-step method[110] of first uncovering bias in the tradition and its practices damaging to the full humanity of women and creation as a whole. After this critique comes a rereading of the sources, "Scripture, tradition, and women's experience,"[111] in search of alternative understandings faithful to the best in the past but liberating for women and creation as a whole. From this search comes a new understanding of Jesus Christ that is then developed to address the evils of sexism and patriarchy while retaining the breadth of soteriological concern of classical christological formulations.[112] Johnson's is a liberation theology that moves from the particular oppression of women to seek an understanding of Christ that will promote justice for all.

Christology has been a central focus of Johnson's career and key to the understanding of God articulated in her award-winning book *She Who Is*.[113] This was the fruit of almost a decade of work addressing the destructive effects of patriarchal understandings of God. Johnson emphasizes that symbols, particularly the symbol of God, function to shape the world in which believers live.[114] In the early 1990s, she argued that "the daily language of preaching, worship, catechesis, and instruction conveys" the message that God is male, which in turn functions "to support an imaginative and structural world that excludes or subordinates women."[115] Having identified this bias in the Christian theological tradition, she turned to Christology to find grounds for overcoming it. In an earlier essay, she noted how a preceding generation of Catholic and Protestant theologians, under the influence of Barth, had been rethinking the doctrine of God in light of Christology.[116] Like Cone and Sobrino, Johnson turned to what can be known historically about Jesus to correct the historical abstractness of classical Christology. She invoked Jesus' preaching of the reign of God to see in him a call to seek justice and enter into solidarity with the poor and oppressed.[117] But the quest for the historical Jesus could not question the connection between Jesus as the image of God and the assumption that God must be imaged as male. Johnson went further, unearthing how "the Jewish figure of personified Wisdom (Hokmah in Hebrew, Sophia in Greek)"[118] a female image, played a pivotal role in the development of the early church's Christology, enabling "the fledgling Christian communities to attribute cosmic significance to the crucified Jesus, relating him to the creation and governance of the world, and was an essential step in the development of incarnational christology."[119] Interpreting Jesus in terms of this female image helped the early church understand Jesus as God incarnate. Unearthing this showed that Jesus' maleness was not intrinsic to his being the Christ. He had been understood as the Christ in feminine terms in the New Testament, and consequently can be represented by women as well as men.

Johnson also argued that the maleness of Jesus became a basis for imaging God as male partly because the dualistic anthropology used by patristic theologians understood women's humanity to be a lesser version of men's. When the latter was assumed by the Word, the former was included. But as Johnson notes, since this dualistic anthropology has given way to a more egalitarian understanding of male and female humanity as equally created in the image of God, then the latter is not subsumed under the former. In this more egalitarian anthropology, sexuality is just one of a number of elements that constitute human nature and identity. Recognizing this allows Jesus' maleness to be acknowledged without becoming theologically determinative and exclusive. Where this anthropology predominates, if the saving significance of Jesus does not lie in his assuming a human nature embracing both genders, then he is not the redeemer of women.[120] The quest for the historical Jesus shows that what was characteristic of Jesus as Sophia/Christ was not his sex but the liberating gestalt of his ministry, which brought liberation from an oppressive status quo to women and men. It was this, not his sexuality, that led to his death and thus to his resurrection/vindication as the Christ.[121] Through his resurrection, Jesus becomes present in all those, male and female, who gather in his name and live out his message in redemptive ways.

Like Cone and Sobrino, Johnson sees Jesus' ministry, death, and resurrection to form an interrelated whole. His ministry provoked conflict, which led to his death. The powers and principalities of sin and evil that his ministry opposed are epitomized and symbolized by his cross. His resurrection represents the decisive victory of God's love over this and becomes a source of hope for a final overcoming of sin, injustice, and evil. Here in Jesus' resurrection, the power of God's love is revealed to be that than which "nothing greater can be conceived."[122] Critically, Johnson demands that God be reimagined in light of Jesus Christ, as relational, as present in and suffering with the victims of history, also as radically transcendent to creation and able to deliver from evil. In doing this, Johnson employs her notion of Jesus as the prophet and child of Sophia. This leads her to begin with the experience of Spirit-Sophia, then to move to Jesus-Sophia as the definitive revelation and saving action of Sophia, and then to Mother-Sophia as the unoriginate First Person of the Trinity.[123] The result is her distinctive understanding of the Trinity as holy mystery in three persons: Spirit-Sophia, Jesus-Sophia, and Mother-Sophia. As such, God as holy mystery is one who loves in freedom and whose suffering love is a virtue, not a necessity.[124] This love does not require the sacrifice of Jesus as an innocent victim to atone for sin—a notion Johnson repeatedly repudiates.[125]

Subsequent to *She Who Is*, Johnson turned her attention to other topics, including the environmental crisis. Here she developed the ecological significance of the Christus Victor model of atonement through a focus on the bodily resurrection of Jesus. Following Rahner, she emphasized that, as Jesus' body was resurrected, a part of the natural world was taken up into the glory of God. This transformation of one piece of nature "pledges a joyful future beyond death" for the rest.[126] From this expectation of future redemption for creation comes a new moral framework for understanding the environmental crisis. It is not simply raw material for human use but was created by God and is destined for glory, and should be respected as such.

# Summary

Jesus' death and resurrection is central to each of the Christologies studied in this chapter. In each, Jesus' ministry is seen to have been oriented toward the liberation of the oppressed and to have provoked violent opposition resulting in his death. What separates his cross from the long line of others in the history of injustices is his resurrection. It is the great interruption, in which the ultimacy of sin and death is broken and the power of God's love is revealed and begins to become newly effective. It is the great dawn that brings hope to a hurting world and assurance that, in the end, justice will prevail. While the justice concerns of these Christologies are similar to those that Ruether, Carter Heyward, and Mark Lewis Taylor focus on, the breadth of expectation here is far greater. Here, as there, Jesus is a moral example, but these theologians draw from Jesus' death and resurrection a hope for the coming of a new creation in which sin and death are no more. This provides a transcendent principle of expectation that the former lack.

The basis of this all-encompassing and ultimate assurance, the resurrection of the crucified Jesus, puts these theologians into conflict with the secularism of contemporary Western societies to a much greater extent than the moral influence theory employed by Ruether, Heyward, and Taylor. In the "immanent frame"[127] characteristic of Western societies, this understanding of Jesus' resurrection can be criticized as an unsupportable superstition, the mythology of a bygone era. Cone, Sobrino, and Johnson challenge central aspects of the metanarrative underlying Western secularism, particularly the notion of progress. But rather than challenge the notion of progress per se, each attends to the nonpersons of Western modernity[128] and sees in their suffering, and in the tyranny and cruelty of Western societies in regard to them, that the claim of these societies having arrived at a more mature, civilized state by repudiating, privatizing, or demythologizing the gospel are false. These theologians read the story of Jesus' ministry, death, and resurrection as the narrative in terms of which Western societies must be critically evaluated.[129] But at present this perspective remains a minority position that frequently struggles to communicate its hope in the public spheres of Western societies.

Each of these Christologies employs a Christus Victor understanding of the atonement to relate the saving significance of Jesus' ministry, death, and resurrection to present injustices. This model harbors the danger of dualistic thinking, in that it locates the source of suffering and evil in the sin of others. It is open to the temptation to seeing the victims of history becoming liberated through the destruction of their oppressors.[130] But the interpretations of Jesus' ministry that Cone, Sobrino, and Johnson provide act as safeguards against this. Each sees Jesus' ministry to express a transcendent principle of justice, the preferential option for the poor.[131] In light of this, the resurrection of Jesus gives rise to hope for the establishment of justice and reconciliation,[132] not the destruction of evildoers.

The previous chapter suggested that something more than the moral influence of Jesus is needed to sustain the life of faith and struggles for justice. The Christologies studied here provide a transcendent principle of expectation for the ultimate overcoming of sin and evil to supplement the moral influence of Jesus with their interpretations of Jesus' death and resurrection. However, in the struggle for justice, mistakes will be made. Ideals are betrayed. Identities are compromised. How do people carry on in light of this? Do struggles for justice not need something more than hope for the overcoming of evil to sustain them? Do people so engaged not also need an assurance of forgiveness and acceptance in spite of their failings? In the next chapter, we turn to three theologians, who each employ a version of Anselm's vicarious substitution theory of atonement to understand how Jesus mediates a sense of God's nearness and acceptance that does not depend on human abilities or accomplishments.

## Suggestions for Further Reading

Baum, Gregory. *Religion and Alienation: A Theological Reading of Society*. New York: Paulist, 1975, 193–226. A sociological perspective on the socially radical interpretation of Jesus Christ found in this chapter and in chapter 2.

Dyke, Doris Jean. *Crucified Woman*. Toronto: United Church Publishing House, 1991. A study of responses to the sculpture *Crucified Woman* by Almuth Lutkenhaus-Lackey.

Fabella, Virginia, M. M., and Mercy Amba Oduyoye, eds. *With Passion and Compassion: Third World Women Doing Theology.* Maryknoll, N.Y.: Orbis, 1988. Has several essays by African and Asian women in which the Christus Victor model of the atonement is adopted to express Jesus' saving significance.

Ray, Darby Kathleen. *Deceiving the Devil: Atonement, Abuse, and Ransom*. Cleveland: Pilgrim, 1998. A more recent attempt to retrieve the Christus Victor understanding of Jesus' saving significance.

Tracy, David. *On Naming the Present: On God, Hermeneutics, and Church*. Maryknoll, N.Y.: Orbis, 1994, 36–46. Addresses some issues concerning the intelligibility of the way Jesus' resurrection is interpreted in the Christologies in this chapter.

## Discussion Questions

1. Are there commonalities in the social contexts from which Cone, Sobrino, and Johnson develop their Christologies?
2. How do Cone, Johnson, and Sobrino relate Jesus' call to seek reconciliation with one's enemies to his proclamation of liberation for the poor?
3. Is the Christus Victor understanding of Jesus' saving significance adequate for the present?
4. How is the ancient principle of patristic Christology, "That which is not assumed is unhealed," present in the Christologies of Cone, Sobrino, and Johnson?

# CHAPTER 4

◆

# Jesus as the Suffering Christ

## Jürgen Moltmann, Douglas John Hall, Marilyn McCord Adams

The Gospels describe Jesus as healing people, casting out demons, and miraculously feeding multitudes. These actions are portrayed as signs of God's salvific power working through Jesus. Instances where Jesus "could do no deed of power"[1] are recorded, but the former greatly outnumber these. Shortly after Jesus' death, his disciples and others came to believe that God had raised him to new life. They saw this as another act of divine power associated with his person. These perceptions of God's saving power in Jesus' ministry before his death and afterward in his resurrection led Christians early on to claim that God's saving power was at work in his death too. Jesus' death became proclaimed as something he underwent for the salvation of others. His execution is portrayed in the New Testament as a sin on par with the murder of prophets yet also as willed by God for the salvation of the world.

Anselm of Canterbury (1033–1109) developed a distinct interpretation of the saving significance of Jesus' suffering and death.[2] According to Anselm, each person, as a result of their sin, owes an infinite debt to God, which they as finite and sinful can never repay. Christ, as fully human and fully divine, is able to pay this penalty by suffering in our place on the cross. As sinless, Christ owes no penalty to God.

Because he is human, he is able to suffer in our place. Because he is divine, his suffering can fulfill the infinite debt that sinners owe God. Thus, through Jesus' suffering and death, sinful humanity is reconciled to God and assured of salvation. Paul Tillich judged Anselm's theory of atonement the most effective in Western Christianity.[3] Tillich disputed Anselm's view that Jesus' sufferings substituted for humanity's, but he affirmed that "the suffering of God, universally and in the Christ, is the power which overcomes creaturely self-destruction by participation and transformation."[4]

Anselm's theory addresses the alienation between people and God that results from peoples' sinful actions and condition. This is experienced as guilt. In Shakespeare's play *Macbeth*, this guilt is represented by an imaginary blood stain that Lady Macbeth sees on her hand and cannot wash away.[5] The guilt she feels for urging her husband to murder the king causes her to see blood on her hand and continually try in vain to wash it away. Guilt is a form of spoiled identity. It arises from actions contrary to what one should have done. It indicates that one's person has become separated from God. According to Anselm, this separation is overcome by God in Christ entering into the guilty person's place. In the New Testament, Jesus' suffering and death destroyed his identity as God's Messiah, until his resurrection. Yet after his resurrection, his death was seen on another level to be part of his work and being as the Christ. Jesus is seen to have overcome sinful humanity's alienation from God through entering into the human condition of guilt and condemnation by suffering death on the cross.

The idea that Jesus' death was required by God for the forgiveness of sin has long been criticized as contrary to the idea of God as love. Late in the twentieth century, a renewed wave of protest against this valorization of Jesus' suffering arose from feminist, womanist, and other theologians. For many, this is summarized in a frequently cited article by Joanne Carlson Brown and Rebecca Parker.[6] They argue that the glorification of Jesus' suffering as salvific encourages women to accept abuse, creates a conflict within children who are being abused, and sustains a culture of abuse. They concludes that if "Christianity is to be liberating for the oppressed, it must itself be liberated from this theology."[7]

Despite this critique, others continue to argue that Jesus' suffering and death have a special saving significance. An Anselm-like emphasis on the efficacy of Jesus' death is central to the Christologies of Jürgen

Moltmann, Douglas John Hall, and Marilyn McCord Adams. None accepts Anselm's theory of atonement entirely, but each sees Jesus' agony on the cross as an expression of God's love, an event in which Jesus accomplished something of decisive saving significance.

## Jürgen Moltmann

Jürgen Moltmann was born on April 8, 1926, the second of five children. He grew up in a settlement near Hamburg.[8] In his childhood, he was an indifferent student, and Christianity was peripheral to him. In 1943, his class at school was conscripted as air force auxiliaries.[9] During an Allied bombing raid on Hamburg that killed a nearby friend, he began to seek God.[10] He was captured by the British and held in a series of prisoner-of-war camps. In one, the inmates were confronted with pictures of Nazi concentration camps. This added shame for the crimes of his people to his depression over the war and captivity.[11] Shortly thereafter, he was given a Bible, began reading it, and gradually became a Christian.

In 1948, he returned to Germany and studied theology at Göttingen. There he met Elisabeth Wendel. They were married on March 17, 1952, and together had four daughters. His professor Otto Weber led him into the Reformed tradition of Christian theology, and he "followed Elisabeth into the United Church of Prussia."[12] In 1952, he completed a doctorate on the theology of Moyse Amyrut. From 1953 to 1958, he was a pastor of the Reformed parish of Bremen-Wasserhorst. During this time, he did a postdoctoral thesis on Christoph Pezel. In 1958, he was invited to join the faculty at Wuppertal and in 1961 published a book on the Reformed doctrine of predestination.[13] In 1960, he read Ernst Bloch's *The Principle of Hope*[14] and began to work on a theological parallel to it.[15] The result was *Theology of Hope*,[16] which brought him international fame and began his career of lecturing around the world. He assumed the chair for systematic theology in the Protestant faculty of Eberhard-Karls University, Tübingen, in 1967, remaining there until retiring in 1994. He has written numerous articles and books. *Theology of Hope*, *The Crucified God*,[17] and *The Church in the Power of the Spirit*[18] form a trilogy in which he tries in each to "look at theology as a whole from one particular standpoint."[19] Moltmann's work to this point was an important influence on liberation theologies developing around the world in the late 1960s and early 1970s. However, in October of

1977, he attended the "Encounter of Theologies" Conference in Mexico City.[20] Here sharp criticism from liberation theologians with whom he thought he was allied solidified the realization that he could no longer sum up the whole from one standpoint and thus speak for everyone. As a result, he changed his approach and embarked on his series of Messianic Theology,[21] which totals six volumes.

For Moltmann, how God is present and the meaning of life in the face of suffering and death form the ultimate horizon in which Jesus must be understood as the Christ.[22] But for Moltmann, this question must not be left abstract. Christian theology must enter into its present context, take up the forms this question has there, and seek to understand the gospel in relation to them.[23] Moltmann pursues this in each of his major books by first outlining the crises of the present in relation to which inherited formulations of Christian doctrine have become indeterminate. Next comes an inward movement in relation to the tradition of Christian theology, in which he returns to the biblical text and other sources of the tradition, rereading them in light of these crises. Finally comes an outward movement, in which he reconceptualizes Christian doctrines on the basis of this rereading, striving to maintain their Christian identity while relating them in an efficacious way to the present.[24] Moltmann gradually developed his thought by repeatedly working it out through this approach.[25]

In the early 1960s, the subject of hope was popular in Western societies. After the golden years of welfare capitalism in the 1950s, the future seemed open and new possibilities seemed to be dawning. Moltmann, influenced by the thought of Ernst Bloch and others,[26] responded to this with his *Theology of Hope*, in which he sought "to give back to Christianity its authentic hope for the world."[27] Here Moltmann's Christology begins by understanding Jesus as a Jew, whose resurrection fulfilled and renewed the traditions promising salvation in the Hebrew Bible.[28] According to Moltmann, in the context of these traditions, Jesus' cross represents god-forsakenness, judgment, and curse, all that negates life and is deadly in death.[29] His resurrection represents the negation of this negation, the coming into history of a new ultimate reality that makes what his cross represents a scandal by creating hope for its overcoming. Jesus' identity lies in "the total contradiction of cross and resurrection."[30] Because what his cross represents continues to be present in history, the contradiction between it and his resurrection remains an open dialectic that will only be resolved in the coming of a new creation in which death and suffering are no more.[31] This creates a sense of all-encompassing mission, in which the church bears witness to Jesus' resurrection through seeking an exodus for all humanity from suffering and oppression. This dialectic makes Christian theology into a critical theory that takes up the Marxist challenge to transform the world rather than simply understand it. Jesus' resurrection cannot be understood within the view of history characteristic of Western modernity,[32] but it can present an alternative and more meaningful understanding of history in which people "can and must live."[33] Here Jesus' saving significance is understood along the lines of the Christus Victor model of atonement. The sin and evil represented by his cross are overcome in principle by his resurrection.

Moltmann's *Theology of Hope* generated much excitement, praise, and critical discussion. While it directed the church in Germany away from its post–World War II insularity toward engagement with the world,[34] in Canada and the United States it sometimes encouraged an uncritical baptizing of 1960s white middle-class Christian optimism.[35] Moltmann's emphasis on eschatology and the future were criticized by Langdon Gilkey for lacking a sense of how God works in the present.[36] Also, some reviewers saw a one-sided emphasis on eschatology in *Theology of Hope* and too little attention to the cross.[37] In fact, Moltmann's *Theology of Hope* interprets Jesus' resurrection in light of his cross. Subsequently, he turned to interpreting Jesus' cross in light of his resurrection. The result was *The Crucified God*, which introduced significant changes into his Christology.

In the mid-1960s, a Christian-Marxist dialogue in Europe helped radicalize Moltmann's thought.[38] Events like the assassination of Martin Luther King Jr. and the crushing of "'socialism with a human face' in Czechoslovakia" deflated 1960s optimism.[39] Through the writings of Elie Wiesel and others, the Holocaust became a major topic in Western Christian theology. Moltmann described the presenting crises of his context in the early 1970s with this question: "What does it mean to recall the God who was crucified in a society whose official creed is optimism, and which is knee-deep in blood?"[40] To answer this question, Moltmann again begins by seeking to understand Jesus within his Jewish context, picking up where he left off in *Theology of Hope*. In *The Crucified God*, he goes back to the historical Jesus, noting the "staggering novelty"[41] of Jesus' claim about himself, which was amplified by his resurrection as the crucified Christ. Here Moltmann argues that, while faith in Jesus Christ began from Jesus' ministry and resurrection, the challenge to understand him comes from his cross.[42] Historically, Jesus' cross resulted from conflicts arising from his ministry. His forgiveness of sin and claim to authority brought him into conflict with Jewish law. To some Jewish contemporaries who did not accept his claim, he appeared as a blasphemer deserving death.[43] But while this played a role in Jesus' death, the threat he posed to Roman rule was an equal or greater cause of it.[44] Jesus was executed as a political rebel. Ultimately though, according to Moltmann, Jesus died because the God in whose name he acted abandoned him.[45] This abandonment opened a rift within God between Jesus the Son and God the Father, in whose name Jesus acted. In this rift, the deity of God as proclaimed by Jesus was at stake.[46] This rift was overcome in eternity in Jesus' resurrection. This overcoming will become universal in the coming of a new creation in which God will be all in all. Moltmann asserts that every Christology is an attempt to understand why God abandoned Jesus in this way.[47]

According to Moltmann, seeking to understand Jesus' cross through the patristic doctrine of the two natures of Christ and the axiom of divine immutability tends to "'evacuate' the cross of deity,"[48] obscuring that here one of the persons of the Trinity suffered and died. Instead of pondering how Jesus' death is related to his divine and human natures, Moltmann assumes their hypostatic unity in Jesus' person and seeks to understand his death in terms of his relationships with the other persons of the Trinity: God the Father and the Holy Spirit.[49] In dying, Jesus is abandoned by God the Father so that he experiences what Moltmann calls the abyss of god-forsakenness. This includes despair, meaningless suffering, and guilt. As Jesus suffers abandonment, God the Father suffers the loss of the Son. Through undergoing this abandonment, Jesus enters into the place of guilty and/or god-forsaken humanity and creation. In doing so, he brings God to where people are, overcoming their alienation from God. Through this overcoming of alienation, God becomes universally present and creates the basis for an all-inclusive community.

Moltmann expanded his trinitarian Christology in subsequent works. For him, Jesus Christ crucified and risen is the entry point to all that Christian theology has to say.[50] He is present as the Son, the Second Person of the Trinity within the Godhead through all eternity. The Son is generated to express the Father's self-diffusive love. The Holy Spirit proceeds from the Father with the Son.[51] As the three persons share the same divine nature, their love is that of like to like. The love of the Father seeks to communicate itself further to that which is Other, and so the Father creates the world through the Son.[52] As the source of the world's salvation, the Son is also the Logos, the reason for its being. The world exists for the further communication and celebration of God's love that Jesus expresses. Jesus became incarnate not simply to redeem from sin but, more fundamentally, to perfect creation. He would have become incarnate even if there had been no sin.[53] As the Logos, Jesus imparts a messianic knowledge of the world as in bondage to transience yet open to the coming of God.[54] The Son is sent to save creation in the Spirit. Jesus appears in history as the Messiah inspired by the Spirit, in continuity with the prophets and as the brother of all who follow him. But his resurrection, an eschatological event shedding light on the whole of his existence, reveals that he has also always been the unique Son. His Sonship is his messianic secret. Jesus grows into it in the course of his public ministry through the inspiration of the Spirit, his relationships with men and women, and his relationships with the poor.[55] Jesus does not simply proclaim the coming of God's reign. As the Son, he brings the kingdom in his person.

Jesus' healings, exorcisms, and prophetic denunciations drive the powers of destruction out of creation.[56] His table fellowship with sinners, his forgiveness of sins, and ultimately his suffering and death bring God near to those whose lives have been ruined by participating in or suffering the effects of these powers. The new reality he brings is established through his death and resurrection and subsequently experienced in and through the Holy Spirit. His Sonship is fully actualized in history through his suffering and death on the cross. God raises and exalts Jesus through the Holy Spirit. Once exalted, Jesus sends the Spirit to actualize the new community that his life, death, and resurrection make possible. As the risen Christ, he is present in the worship and ministry of the church, in the poor and their struggles for justice, and as the exalted Christ whose parousia is yet to come.[57]

Moltmann's Christology does not completely bypass the Chalcedonian Definition. He does not ponder how Jesus' divine and human natures are united in Jesus' person, but he understands Jesus to be divine as the "only-begotten Son" and human as the "firstborn among many brothers."[58] The former is the foundation of the latter. Both are "unique dimensions of the whole being of Jesus Christ,"[59] and cannot be separated. For Moltmann, the question of how the Second Person of the Trinity is united with Jesus' humanity or why there is suffering is less important than the question of where God is in relation to suffering.[60] The soteriological principle behind the development of patristic Christology, that which is not assumed is not healed,[61] guides his thinking about God's relation to suffering. Jesus brings salvation to humanity and creation most profoundly by entering into its condition and undergoing the suffering this brings. Through his incarnation and death, Jesus enters into the situation of the poor, the guilty, those enduring meaningless suffering, those enduring the cruelty of others, those enduring a natural death, and the suffering of the natural environment in the ecological crisis.[62] The love of God overcomes all these forms of alienation in principle by entering through Jesus' suffering and death into the god-forsakenness and/or guilt they express. Through this action on God's part, the love of God "reaches . . . the loveless and the unloved"[63] with an offer of acceptance and communion. This understanding of Jesus' death was a major development in Moltmann's Christology.

*Theology of Hope* presents Jesus' cross and resurrection as contradicting each other, and Jesus' resurrection as bringing the promise of a new future for creation. Langdon Gilkey asked how God works to create this new future.[64] In *The Crucified God*, Moltmann argues that God's salvific activity is paradigmatically revealed in Jesus' cross as God's undergoing and suffering the sin and alienation of the world.[65] This introduced a new dimension to his understanding of the cross. The contradiction between Jesus' cross and resurrection in *Theology of Hope* remains, on one level. But with this new understanding of how the intertrinitarian dynamics involved in Jesus' cross lead to his resurrection, introduced in *The Crucified God*, Jesus' cross on another level becomes the way to his resurrection and so stands in continuity with it. It is through Jesus' death that creation's alienation from God is overcome.[66] This is the beginning of the new creation promised in Jesus' resurrection. Subsequently, Moltmann affirmed that God creates salvation through self-emptying, self-humiliation, and vicarious suffering.[67] In light of this, God is present in history as "the passion for the possible"[68] in the suffering of the oppressed; and in the joyful celebration of liberation, God's presence with the victims, and hope for the coming of God's reign.

This second understanding of the cross generated considerable criticism of the kind frequently made of Anselm's theory of atonement; that it makes God into a bloodthirsty tyrant demanding the death of an innocent victim.[69] Moltmann's critics did not always consider his argument that God suffers the loss of the Son in this abandonment, and that while God the Father abandons Jesus here, they are simultaneously profoundly united in what they will.[70] This is a deeply personal part of his theology,[71] and very controversial. By speaking of God the Father abandoning Jesus the Son in this way, Moltmann attempts to articulate how the triune God participates in human suffering, despair, and guilt while remaining transcendent to it.[72] Yet Moltmann's placing the sufferings of the persons of the Trinity in Jesus' cross at the center of his doctrine of God led him to see suffering as characteristic of all God's creative acts, including creation, in a way that makes suffering of some sort intrinsic to God's being. This undermines God's transcendence.

After Moltmann made Christ's sufferings paradigmatic for how God acts in history, a tension emerged in his theology between divine and human freedom. In *Theology of Hope*, Moltmann noted a "reversal of subjects" developing in relation to the promises of God in the Hebrew Bible, modern Jewish theology, and German idealism, in which the fulfillment of God's promises came to depend on human action rather than God's faithfulness.[73] This development made hope for the coming of God's reign uncertain. In *Theology of Hope*, this hope was based on God's active faithfulness revealed paradigmatically in the resurrection of Jesus. In *The Crucified God*, it was based on God's initiative in Christ and the Holy Spirit, creating the conditions that make possible a free response to God on the part of alienated humanity.[74] But in subsequent works, Moltmann began to speak of how God preserves the world and overcomes human opposition through God's willingness to suffer that opposition and patiently endure until women and men choose to act otherwise.[75] God creates a space for human response by waiting for it.[76] This introduced a tension into Moltmann's thought. Despite his emphasis on the active nature of God's waiting,[77] his notion of God acting to save by patiently suffering creation's opposition has moved him very close to the position he opposed in *Theology of Hope*, where salvation depends on human action rather than God's faithfulness.

Moltmann published a third major volume on Christology in 1990 and another shorter book in 1994.[78] By this point, he had developed a dynamic vision of God active in history toward the coming of God's reign; the ecological crisis had become a major concern, and he was now keenly aware of the differences between his privilege as a tenured professor in Germany and the situation of the poor of the third world.[79]

Moltmann described his Christology here as postmodern in the sense of including nature in the consideration of Jesus' saving significance.

In keeping with his dynamic understanding of God, he now wrote of Jesus as "on the way" to his rule in five stages: as the earthly Jesus in history, as the crucified, as the risen, as the present, and as the coming One.[80] Jesus himself is the way to this future, the road that those who believe in him must follow.[81] In a world full of violence and injustice, this road, which seeks the fullness of life over against the powers of death, frequently leads to suffering and sometimes to martyrdom. Following it brings an existential understanding of Christ that complements what can be gained through study and worship. Faith in Christ alienates people from the injustice of the world and brings hope to its victims, displacing both and setting them on this road to a liberated future.

## Douglas John Hall

Douglas John Hall was born in 1928 and grew up in a village in southwestern Ontario, Canada,[82] where Protestant churches were a major influence on English-speaking society. Hall attended The United Church of Canada but found "little of depth" in the church life of his village.[83] He found more as a young man when he was introduced to the thought of Martin Luther, who has remained a formative influence on Hall.[84] In 1948, he went to study music at the Royal Conservatory in Toronto, then completed a B.A. at the University of Western Ontario in London, Ontario. In 1953, he went to Union Theological Seminary in New York to study theology. There he studied under Paul Tillich and Reinhold Niebuhr but was also influenced by reading Karl Barth and Dietrich Bonhoeffer.[85] In 1960, he married Rhoda Palfrey Hall, who became his lifelong theological dialogue partner. Together they had four children. He also became the ordained minister of The United Church of Canada congregation in the town of Blind River in northern Ontario. In 1962 he became the first principal of St. Paul's College, a liberal arts college established by the United Church in Waterloo, Ontario. In 1965, he became MacDougald Professor of Systematic Theology at St. Andrew's College, a seminary of the United Church in Saskatoon, Saskatchewan. In 1975, he moved to Montreal to become Professor of Christian Theology in the faculty of religious studies at McGill University until his retirement. He remains in Montreal and continues to be active as a public lecturer in Canada and the United States. In many respects, he is the best-known Canadian Protestant theologian of his time.

In Canada, the decade from 1965 to 1975 was a time of creative social chaos.[86] This ended the volunteer establishment[87] of the church there. According to Hall, it created an openness in theology and society to previously excluded voices and new readings of the gospel, but it also led to a loss of concern to wrestle with "the whole tradition" of Christian faith.[88] Hall's years at St. Andrew's were the culmination of his theological apprenticeship. There he developed his own theological voice in dialogue with Marxists, the natural sciences, and students. While on sabbatical in Westphalia, Germany, in 1972 and 1973, he wrote *Lighten Our Darkness*,[89] which lays out the social analysis, theological approach, and Christology that became characteristic of his mature work. This was followed by a steady stream of public lectures, articles, and books, culminating in a trilogy in which his Christology found mature expression.[90]

Hall's Christology grows out of his understanding that Christian theology must be contextual, addressing the predominant alienation of humanity from God in its time and place. Failing to do so, it may actually contribute to this alienation rather than help alleviate it.[91] According to Hall, characteristic of the dominant cultures in Canada and the United States is an official optimism. This is "a carefully cultivated and nurtured construct, deliberately drawing upon well-rehearsed positive data or past and present achievement, and judiciously omitting, suppressing, and repressing the data of despair."[92] This official optimism has become an ideology blinding middle-class Americans and Canadians to the havoc their lifestyles—and the economies and military dominance they are based on—wreak in other countries[93] and the natural environment. For Hall, certain kinds of suffering, such as the experience of limits, anxiety, loneliness, and temptation, are intrinsic to human life.[94] Humanity is always tempted to flee these through sloth or deny them through hubris.

According to Hall, the official optimism of the United States and Canada is a denial of the suffering intrinsic to being human, an expression of hubris that attempts to mask an inner despair. The Protestant Christian churches in Canada and the United States have for the most part functioned as the purveyors of "the 'positive religion' of empire,"[95] and supporting its ideology. However, Canada and the United States are in a process of cultural change. The modern worldview and its optimism are yielding to growing disillusionment.[96] Modern secularism is giving way to a new openness to spirituality. Western modernity is now "visibly in decline."[97] In this context, average members of the dominant culture of North America experience themselves as Sisyphus, toiling desperately but to no purpose. They hide this despair by masquerading as Prometheus, pretending to defy the limits imposed on them. The reason for their masquerade is partly that the role of Prometheus is the only one they know.[98] In this context, the task of Christian theology and Christian churches is to offer people a framework of meaning within which they can acknowledge the suffering intrinsic to being human and find spiritual resources that enable them to accept and rejoice in their creaturely condition. Without this framework or these resources, people will continue to repress their spiritual and physical suffering in ways leading to more suffering for others and worse destruction of the environment.

Hall believes that such a framework can be found in the theology of the cross, as classically articulated by Martin Luther. In Hall's view, Christianity became the civil religion of Western society under Constantine and since then has succumbed in the main to the temptation of triumphalism, celebrating Jesus' resurrection as a final and immediately effective victory over sin and death, leaving behind its Jewish roots, and banishing or persecuting all that would question this, including Judaism. The theology of the cross begins with a critique of this triumphalism and every claim on the part of humanity to mastery. Through this critique, it seeks to reduce people "to the status of a beggar,"[99] for only as such can one receive the grace of God. In doing so, it brings one to the knowledge of one's true status as a creature and delivers one from false hope.

In his mature trilogy, Hall identifies seven components of the North American context that Christian theology must address: the disestablishment of the church, religious pluralism, coming to terms with Auschwitz, the Marxist challenge, the rebellion of nature against the attempts of humanity to master it, the threat of nuclear annihilation, and the rise of religious fundamentalism.[100] Hall's theology addresses these issues by taking Jesus' suffering on the cross as the key to understanding the nature of God and humanity. Jesus Christ is the decisive revelation of God, though not the only one. He is the culmination of a trajectory in the Hebrew Scriptures, which Hall calls the "tradition of Jerusalem," that reveals God as having an orientation toward being in relationship with creation.[101] The primary ontological category for this tradition and the theology of the cross is relationship. The cross of Jesus reveals that God wills to be in relationship with humanity whatever the cost. The relationship God seeks is one of love, and therefore one of freedom for both God and humanity. For Hall, the fate of creation rests on the righting of the divine-human relationship.[102] The work of Jesus is directed primarily to this.

According to Hall, the early Christian witness to Jesus as the Messiah and the experience of his continuing presence in the Holy Spirit led to the development of the doctrine of the Trinity.[103] For Hall, this doctrine is important for its affirmation that, in Jesus, God has entered into the human condition, experiencing its negative aspects, taking them into God's self, and so transforming them that they serve life as God originally intended.[104] The revelation of God in Jesus reveals God to be active in history but requires that traditional attributes of God, particularly that of divine power, be redefined in light of Jesus' death on the cross.[105] God is truly great in being willing and able to suffer in Christ for the sake of entering into communion with humanity, which leads Hall to argue that the power of God's love is the ability of God to refrain from exercising coercive power. Unfortunately, here and elsewhere, Hall works with very abstract concepts. He speaks of "power" without discriminating between different kinds and dimensions of power, in a way that obscures the many forms and aspects of power and powerlessness attributed to Jesus and God throughout the New Testament.[106] This level of abstraction leads to his important insight degenerating into a simplistic dichotomy between love and power,[107] which overlooks how love can only attain what it seeks through the exercise of some form(s) of power and how the death of Jesus has been variously experienced by Christians as a source of empowerment.

But while Hall opposes love to power, he insists that God's love includes an element of judgment. The encounter with Jesus involves judgment on sin that hopefully leads to repentance necessary for communion between God and humanity. God judges because God is love, and only through judgment can healing of the human condition occur. However, God's judgment is not expressed through punishment but through Jesus' suffering on the cross. For Hall as for Luther, there is something in humanity that revolts against God and that must be overcome before communion with God can be established.[108] This happens through God in Jesus enduring humanity's rejection on the cross. While

Hall insists that Jesus must be understood contextually, in his own time and in the present, he tends to see Jesus' cross as a transcendent symbol of the human condition, the nature of God, and how the gulf between them has been overcome.[109] His emphasis is on Jesus' cross as a decisive event necessitated by God's desire to redeem humanity and not on Jesus' death as the murder of a prophet.

Hall acknowledges the importance of the quest for the historical Jesus for informing the church's understanding of Jesus,[110] which is drawn from the biblical witness and the experience of Jesus as risen in the Holy Spirit. Hall does not study the public ministry of Jesus at length, but he generally sees it to have been characterized by a preferential option for the poor. As part of this, Jesus heightened the demands of the Jewish Law so that those who proclaimed themselves righteous over against the poor and sinners would see the error of their claim,[111] which Hall sees to be the central theme of Jesus' prophetic ministry. This and Jesus' critique of Roman power led to his cross. Following Calvin, Hall organizes Jesus' saving significance under the threefold office of prophet, priest, and king. The prophetic ministry of Jesus, outlined above, leads to his death, in which he is the priest who offers himself as the sacrifice. In describing the saving significance of Jesus' death, Hall emphasizes the efficacy of Jesus' suffering, following Anselm, but sees its effectiveness to lie in what it demonstrates, following Abelard. This leads to a central theme of Hall's Christology.

For Hall, the saving significance of Jesus is primarily the change he effects in an individual's will and through this in the "collective spirit" of a culture.[112] Both the will of an individual and the collective spirit of a culture can be altered without destroying the people involved only if the change happens from "within."[113] This notion of "change from within" is central to Hall's Christology and has several interrelated meanings. First, the change that is needed is not in the being of people but in their will. It cannot be caused by external coercion but only by the appeal of a demonstration of love. The change happens through the free response of the person to the love of God revealed in Christ. In this respect Hall's understanding of the atonement resembles Abelard's moral influence theory. But according to Hall, for change to occur in this way, God must enter into history and the human condition.[114] Thus, the key to Hall's understanding of atonement is God's becoming incarnate in Jesus. Entering the human condition means experiencing the suffering intrinsic to it, most profoundly on the cross. Like Anselm,

Hall emphasizes what God has suffered in Jesus and how this makes reconciliation between God and humanity possible.

Jesus' office as king is his present reign. For Hall, this is noetically prior to Jesus' other offices. Jesus reigns when he is recognized as the Christ. People only appreciate Jesus' prophetic and priestly work after they recognize him as king. Hall leaves factual questions about Jesus' resurrection "in abeyance."[115] For Hall, Jesus' resurrection flows into Pentecost and the pouring out of the Holy Spirit.[116] Its importance lies in the way it floods his ministry, death, and person with meaning and calls the church into being. The crucial point of Jesus' office as king is the transvaluation of values it effects on contemporary notions of glory and rule. As king, Jesus reveals that true rule is service that seeks the preservation of life.[117]

In seeking to understand how Jesus effects atonement, Hall critically appropriates the Chalcedonian Definition, of Jesus as fully human and fully divine, the two natures united without confusion in his one person. Hall argues that, for this to be meaningful today, its categories must be reinterpreted. Jesus is the Christ not because divine and human natures are united in his person but because he represents God to humanity and humanity before God, in a uniquely decisive way. Borrowing the concept of representation from Dorothee Soelle, Hall argues that in North America it is implicit in almost every area of life.[118] According to Hall,

> The metaphor of representation permits us to sustain the fundamental profession of belief that the newer Testament as well as Chalcedon, in its way, wished to affirm, without indulging in the substantialistic-ontological language of the latter. Instead of translating the biblical profession of Christ's unique relation with the Father into his divinity, we may profess Jesus Christ as God's representative; and instead of translating the biblical witness to Jesus' real humanity as his human nature . . . we may affirm that he is our human representative.[119]

For Hall, "there is no rational explanation" for how Jesus is uniquely able to represent humanity to God and God to humanity; it "is a matter of experience and of faith; it can only be professed and confessed."[120] But while Hall does not explain how it came to be, he does see a distinct dynamic in Jesus' person and work that intertwines the two. Through his personal development, Jesus comes to know of God's presence and himself as called by God in a unique way, so that he comes to identify with God. His identification with God leads him to also identify with humanity. The divine quest for humanity and the human quest for God come together in his one person, as Jesus, distinct from both, freely identifies with both.[121] The decisive moment of this occurs in the Garden of Gethesmane, where Jesus chooses to go all the way in his identification with God and humanity.

Hall argues that Jesus can only represent contemporary North Americans if he experiences their anxiety of meaninglessness and despair, their fundamental alienation of feeling themselves to be alone in the universe. He sees Jesus to experience this in Gethsemane. Hall is particularly impressed with the portrayal of this in the rock opera *Jesus Christ Superstar*.[122] The confluence of the divine quest for humanity and the human quest for God in Jesus' person involves a moment of rejection of God by humanity, a justified outcry at the suffering intrinsic to the human condition, just as it involves divine judgment on humanity. Having vented in Gethsemane, Jesus freely chooses to continue representing God to humanity and humanity to God. His decision made here is actualized on his cross. Crucial here is Jesus' genuine humanity manifest in his protest and suffering. He experiences the spiritual and physical suffering of the human condition yet affirms the meaningfulness of his mission and human life by going through with it. In this, Jesus withstands the temptations afflicting the human condition. His resurrection simply confirms this victory.[123] On the cross, he represents God to humanity, making God present to all in the midst of their suffering. Through the mediation in his broken person of God's presence with people in their brokenness, they can find the spiritual resources to acknowledge their suffering and fears and go on to rejoice in their creaturely condition nonetheless. The work of Christ on the cross, confirmed in his resurrection and made present through the Holy Spirit, calls the church into being, which continues his work by celebrating his presence and message and following his example of service.

In this way, the crucified Christ gives the disestablished church resources and a mission that call it away from being the established religion of dominant Western societies. As people accept their creaturely condition, they are enabled to rejoice in religious pluralism and benefit from it. Jesus as representative of God and humanity calls the church back to the tradition of Jerusalem and to dialogue with and respect for Judaism. As this theology of the cross enables people to accept their humanity and live in a more human and less aggressive fashion, it meets the Marxist challenge to transform the world. According to Hall, this more effective presentation of the gospel can provide an alternative to religious fundamentalism. Through accepting their creaturely condition, people learn to live in peace with the natural environment and as stewards that care for it. According to Hall, the nuclear arms race is an extension of a sinful desire for mastery over nature, and of a deep underlying death wish on the part of humanity.[124] People learning to rejoice in their creaturely condition helps deflate this drive and subdue this wish.

For Hall, the cross of Jesus affirms three things: a high estimation of humanity as loved by God and able to represent God in the world, a grave realism about human sin, and the determination of God to redeem humanity so it can fulfill its creaturely potential.[125] The church is called to take up the cross by continuing to represent Christ in the world by word and deed. The cross means that the church must exercise a preferential option for the poor and continually engage issues of suffering and oppression in the world around it.[126] Hall does not articulate any concrete hope or ethical goals arising from his Christology. Rather, the church moves from age to age, doing what it can where it is.[127] Jesus in his compassion for others and faithfulness to God models the fullness of humanity that the church should seek and live out. But this is not so much a task as a possibility created by the presence of God that Jesus' humanity mediates.[128]

## Marilyn McCord Adams

Marilyn McCord Adams was born in 1943 in a small town in western Illinois. She was a happy and intellectually precocious child. She enjoyed the Disciples of Christ congregation that her grandfather pastored but found the public school system restrictive. In adolescence, she entered into a series of intellectual and spiritual crises.[129] A love of learning took her to the University of Illinois at age seventeen, where she began as a physics major but switched to philosophy, coming first in her graduating class. Here she encountered the theologies of Reinhold Niebuhr and Paul Tillich and became confirmed in the Episcopal Church. In 1964, she enrolled as a graduate student at Cornell University. Her consciousness was raised by the anti–Vietnam War movement. She met and married Robert Adams. She completed her doctorate in three years, with a dissertation on divine foreknowledge in medieval thought. Though her experience of the philosophy department at Cornell was traumatic,[130] the analytical approach to philosophy of religion and the background in medieval thought that she gained there became major influences on her Christology.

When her husband was hired at Perkins Theological Seminary, Adams became a visiting lecturer at the University of Michigan and began to publish articles and books on medieval philosophy and theology. They both received offers from University of California, Los Angeles, where she enjoyed its cosmopolitan ethos and came under the influence of Allan Wolter, an expert on Duns Scotus. While on sabbatical in 1979–80, at Princeton Theological Seminary, she became involved in a charismatic prayer group and sensed a call to ministry. The rejection of her application for ordination in the Episcopal Church provoked a spiritual crisis, during which she found Jesus' death on the cross to be a definitive revelation of God's love.[131] She enrolled in a master of theology program at Princeton Theological Seminary and, returning to UCLA in 1981, began to also work in an Episcopal parish in Hollywood. Ministering to homosexual members of the parish dying of AIDS convinced her that the church's condemnation of gay and lesbian sexual orientation was wrong. She also began to work on "how Jesus solved the problem of evil."[132] Her Christology developed from this. She applied for ordination again and was ordained deacon on June 20, 1987. In the mid-1990s, she became Horace Tray Pitkin Professor of Historical Theology at Yale University. On January 1, 2004, she became Regius Professor of Divinity at Oxford University and Canon of Christ Church Cathedral, where she remains.

Adams's Christology has three main roots. Her training as an analytical philosopher of religion orients her thought toward logical clarity but away from concern for contextuality in theology. Her constructive christological reflections began as she attempted to address a central problem of philosophy of religion, how to rationally reconcile the existence of a loving and omnipotent God with evil. A second root is her study of medieval philosophy, which (1) insists on the radical transcendence of God to creation, which she refers to as the "metaphysical size gap between God and creatures,"[133] and (2) seeks logical clarity in understanding the incarnation of God in Jesus Christ. A third root is the existential comfort she found in understanding Jesus' suffering and death as the decisive expression of God's love.

Adams describes her theoretical approach as skeptical realism. She is a realist in believing that "there is some fact of the matter," independent of what people think.[134] But she is a skeptic in believing that any philosophical position "will eventually involve premises that are fundamentally controversial and so unable to command the assent of all reasonable persons."[135] Given this, she embraces coherence as a criterion for the pursuit of truth through integrating data and intuitions gained from diverse fields of experience and inquiry. Other criteria for a theological position include internal clarity, consistency, explanatory power, and fruitfulness.[136] As a skeptical realist she accepts that there will be other positions than hers from which she can learn, but the existence of which do not disprove hers. According to Adams, Christian theology "is tradition-based creativity," formed out of a conversation with texts and traditions from the past, present experiences, and deeply entrenched data,[137] such as the scandal of Jesus' death on the cross. Church traditions, historical creeds, and the biblical witness are authoritative but not infallible. She takes the Gospels to be primarily interpretive documents attempting to understand Jesus in relation to issues current when they were formed. She questions the reliability of the quest for the historical Jesus as a source of data for Christology, preferring to read the New Testament as "among other things—a variety of loosely integrated systematic proposals which—insofar as Scripture is authoritative—demand the Christologian's serious consideration."[138] From this theoretical standpoint she argues apologetically that it is not unreasonable for Christians to hold a "robust Christology,"[139] which understands Jesus to have been fully human and fully divine. On a more evangelical note, she attempts to show how one can find in the crucified Christ a revelation of God that gives meaning to life even amid great suffering.

Adams's Christology began with her attempt to address the problem of how to reconcile the existence of horrendous evils with Christian claims about the goodness of God. She defines horrendous evils as acts that threaten to rob the life of those subject to them, or those who perpetrate them, of any positive meaning.[140] Adams has a stock list of such evils, which includes "betrayal of one's deepest loyalties" and "participation in the Nazi death camps."[141] Horrendous evils reach beyond moral categories into aesthetic ones. What is most horrible about them is their degrading nature, the way they destroy the possibility of a meaningful life. If God's goodness can be defended in relation to these, then it can be defended in relation to lesser evils as well. She insists that in thinking about the problem of evil, the understanding of God specific to a given religion must be considered, rather than a generic concept of deity.[142]

Adams defines people as potential or actual meaning-makers.[143] Meaning comes from being positively related to something valued as good. Horrendous evils, whether people suffer or perpetrate them, are by definition so degrading that nothing people can do can positively outweigh the negative meaning accruing to them. However, people and their actions are finite in relation to the infinite goodness of God. Because God's goodness is infinite, a positive relation to it more than counterbalances any horrendous evil, which can never be more than finite. The incommensurable relation between God's infinite goodness and the finite nature of horrendous evils means that God's goodness can impart a positive meaning to a person's life regardless of what they have experienced.[144]

The problem of evil is only solved if one can understand how God can overcome or "defeat" its destructive power, both to creation and to the meaning that created life might have.[145] In an analysis reminiscent of Reinhold Niebuhr's account of the roots of sin,[146] Adams argues that the source of horrendous evils lies in the way human nature straddles the metaphysical divide between the spiritual and the material worlds.[147] The perishable material nature of humanity makes people vulnerable to horrendous evils. It distracts and distorts the human mind with anxieties over its own survival. Conversely, the mind struggles to discipline the body to attain spiritual goals. In the course of pursuing them, one may commit horrendous evil. According to Adams, death itself is a horror that God must ultimately defeat.[148] By being part of a nation and society, virtually every human being shares in the collective responsibility for some horrendous evil.[149] Human life is set in a web of causal effects that can never be fully comprehended, such that people are liable to perpetrate horrendous evils without intending to. In short, everyone needs a positive relation to God in order to have a meaningful life.

On the basis of this analysis, Adams argues that God's defeat of horrors must include three stages.[150] Stage one is the overcoming of the degrading power of horrendous evils. The key to this is the incarnation of God in Jesus Christ and his death on the cross, which offers people a positive relation to God's infinite goodness in and through their vulnerable human condition. In Jesus, the Second Person of the Trinity assumed a fully human nature, vulnerable to horrors and participation in them. Jesus' birth and ministry occasioned horrors, like the slaughter of the innocents[151] and his own death, although Jesus did not intend these. Jesus also suffered horrors, primarily on the cross.[152] The cross signifies that God identifies with victims of horrendous evils, thus bestowing meaning on their lives that outweighs the degradation of horrendous evils. By becoming cursed or guilty of sin through dying on the cross, Jesus also identifies with the perpetrators of horrors, bestowing infinite meaning on their lives as well. In this way, God nullifies "the power of horrendous evils to degrade."[153] Adams is bold enough to argue that, through faith in Christ, crucified people can see their suffering of horrendous evils as "moments of intimacy with God," and "not wish them away from their life histories."[154] In this way, she sees Jesus' suffering on the cross as able to defeat the evil aspects of horrors from the perspective of the individual who suffered them. At this point, her argument overreaches itself. It is hard to imagine a mother, having watched her child killed, who would not wish that away.[155] Here Adams's concern for a logically consistent explanation ultimately undermines some of the values she seeks to affirm; in this case, the value of life.

Adams posits that God created the world because God "wants to be the Lover of this sort of material creation."[156] God becomes this through becoming incarnate in Jesus Christ. Adams seeks to understand what is involved here in some detail by asking, what sort of human nature did the divine Word assume, and how did it assume it? According to Adams, the Synoptic accounts demand that Jesus' human nature be understood as such that he could have clarity about his calling and relationship to God. They do not portray Jesus' humanity as godlike in perfection or as the ideal in human development. Jesus did not commit radically evil deeds and was probably not mentally ill, but he could have had a learning disability.[157] As a fully human person, Jesus would have experienced fears, frustrations, and doubts and would have been subject to some of the biases of his day. It is the sinlessness of Christ's divine nature that enables him to overcome sin. His human nature enables him to participate in and so overcome horrors. It does not need to have been utterly sinless for this.[158] Given these requirements for Jesus' human nature, how was his divine nature united with it? According to Adams, conciliar pronouncements claim that Jesus was fully human, but they do not require that this be understood according to any one theory of human nature. Adams argues that, following Duns Scotus and William of Ockham, one can argue that the divine Word assumed a fully human body and soul as an alien supposit.[159] This notion, developed by Scotus and Ockham to understand the incarnation, does not translate easily into contemporary forms of thought. Adams uses it to say that the divine Word is the ultimate subject of Jesus' person, which ensures the clarity of his sense of mission and relationship to God. But the divine Word is not the subject of Jesus' typically human actions, such as bodily functions or fear in the face of death. According to Adams, how Jesus' divine and human natures interacted in his one person can be derived from church pronouncements and Scripture. For the purposes of theoretical explanation, it is enough to know that such an alien supposit is logically possible. It occurs through the transcendent power of God. This understanding of the incarnation is central to Adams's Christology[160] and her understanding of Christ's presence in the Eucharist. But it trades on an understanding of divine power and human nature that, in relation to contemporary understandings of life as an organic whole in which matter and mind are intricately related, seems to devalue human life to the level of an inanimate object, by making it something the divine Word can assume simply by fiat.

By becoming incarnate, Christ makes a meaningful life possible for both victims and perpetrators of horrors,[161] thus accomplishing stage one horror-defeat. However, due to the composite aspects of human nature, people remain vulnerable to temptation. Stage two horror-defeat involves the overcoming of sin and evil from within, through sanctification. This happens through people developing personal relationships to Christ and participating in the life of the church, so that Christ becomes their inner teacher, present in their hearts and minds. As such, Christ guides people in participating in his work of loving material creation and all that dwell therein. Christ on the cross offers emergency assistance, overcoming the degrading effects of horrendous evils. Christ present in the Holy Spirit offers ongoing guidance as people seek to cope with a world and challenges that are ultimately beyond their ken.[162] This inner work of Christ's divine nature draws on the ministry carried out in his human nature. Jesus' death on the cross is the culmination of actions on God's part directed toward overcoming evils. It expresses judgment, revealing the horror of evil acts. It also reveals how vulnerable people are to abuse, and how vulnerable people are to becoming abusers.[163] Jesus' ministry, focused on creating an inclusive community through his practice of inclusion and forgiveness and through teaching that "pressured the self-righteous to recognise their own inner bias towards hatred and death,"[164] led to his death. It serves to instruct the church in its ministry of solidarity with the victims and testimony to Christ.

For Adams though, the focal point of Jesus' work toward stage two horror-defeat lies in his presence as priest, on the cross and in the Eucharist. Here God in Christ is sacrificer, priest, and victim. Adams's writing frequently suggests that she has an intensely personal relationship to God and Jesus Christ. She is also a master of wringing multiple, imaginative meanings out of symbols like the cross. Both characteristics come to the fore in her discussion of the Eucharist. Adams considers the human condition to be nonoptimal to the extent that God can be said to have sacrificed "humankind by setting us up for horrors." In turn, God overcomes horrors by "sacrificing God's own self."[165] The Eucharist liturgically condenses all this so that it is "many sacrifices at once."[166] Here Christ represents God to humanity and humanity to God, so as to guide and sustain the church in its ministry. Drawing on the medieval theory of impanation,[167] Adams argues that in the Eucharist, the divine Word assumes the eucharistic bread as a "body" just as it previously assumed a human nature in the incarnation. Christ's risen body is thus present in the eucharistic bread and can be handled and chewed "according to its bread nature."[168] Christ's presence in this way is a gift sacrifice honoring those who receive it. It is also a sin offering, atoning for God's responsibility for the sufferings people endure as a result of their nonoptimal condition. By being present in the bread, Christ invites people to vent their rage at God for horrendous evils by biting and tearing him with their teeth. In this way, Christ is sacrificed to propitiate human anger.[169] Finally, the passing of the bread–body of Christ through the human digestive system represents "a continuation of Divine solidarity that descends to the depths of human degradation to be God-with-us!"[170]

Adams argues that for God to be true to Godself as omnipotent, omniscient, and perfectly good, God must save all people.[171] For many, stage two horror-defeat requires an ongoing existence after death, and for all, stage three horror-defeat requires a cosmic renewal of material creation and embodied life in which death will be no more.[172] This will bring an end to horrors, including death, through the coming of a new creation in which people will be as Godlike as possible and all will enter into a personal relationship with God.[173] Jesus' healings of the sick and his resurrection express God's intention and ability to achieve this.

# Summary

Moltmann, Hall, and Adams all see Jesus' cross as an event and symbol with many levels. It is an act of violence, injustice, cruelty, and oppression and as such symbolizes much of what is most evil in the world. At the same time, because it is this and in light of Jesus' resurrection, they also see Jesus' cross on another level as in some ways the defining act and symbol of God's love. Here, through his suffering and death, Jesus enters into the situation of victims and the guilty, bridging the distance between God and them, effecting reconciliation between perpetrator and victim, God and suffering and fallen humanity, reestablishing the relationship that sin, violence, and inexplicable evil seemed to have permanently ruptured.

Moltmann, Hall, and Adams view Jesus' death from an existential perspective, as the reaching out of God to the suffering and the guilty. They focus on what this achieves, not on an objective evaluation of Jesus' death as a means to an end. For them, Jesus' cross is the culmination of God's saving actions in Jesus Christ directed toward the salvation and well-being of humanity and creation. This helps guard against their understanding of Jesus' death becoming a warrant for abusive cruelty. Yet in the New Testament Jesus' death always remains something that his resurrection overcomes and thus opposes. Moltmann, Hall, and Adams do not always stress this sufficiently.

According to Charles Taylor, the "great spiritual visions of human history have also been poisoned chalices, the causes of untold misery and even savagery."[174] This is particularly true of this way of understanding of Jesus' death as an act and sign of God's love, as past and recent critiques of it have shown. Identifying Jesus' suffering and death as a definitive expression of God's love can encourage passivity in the face of abuse and the acceptance of suffering as God's will. Yet it can also speak to a particular kind of alienation, a spoiled identity that no act on a person's part can fix, in a powerful and sustaining way. It can enable a person whose identity is irredeemably spoiled to be reconciled to themselves despite this and to continue to live in hope, and to love.

# Suggestions for Further Reading

Adams, Marilyn McCord. *Christ and Horrors: The Coherence of Christology*. New York: Cambridge University Press, 2006.

Bauckham, Richard. *The Theology of Jürgen Moltmann*. Edinburgh: T&T Clark, 1995. A good overview of Moltmann's theology, with attention to his later Christology. It includes a valuable bibliography of secondary sources.

Bell, Daniel, Jr. "Only Jesus Saves: Towards a Theopolitical Ontology of Judgment." In *Theology and the Political: The New Debate*, ed. Creston Davis et al., 200–27. Durham: Duke University Press, 2005. An appropriation of Anselm's atonement theory in the vein of Radical Orthodoxy.

Cahill, Lisa Sowle. "Salvation and the Cross." In *Jesus as Christ*, ed. Andrés Torres Queiruga, et al., 55–63. London: SCM, 2008. A brief feminist reappropriation of Anselm's interpretation of the cross.

Hall, Douglas John. *The Cross in Our Context: Jesus and the Suffering World*. Minneapolis: Fortress Press, 2003. A succinct summary of Hall's theology of the cross.

Meeks, M. Douglas. *Origins of the Theology of Hope*. Philadelphia: Fortress Press, 1974. A good study of the early sources of Moltmann's eschatology.

Moltmann, Jürgen. *The Crucified God: The Cross as the Foundation and Criticism of Christian Theology*. Minneapolis: Fortress Press, 1993 [1974].

———. *The Way of Jesus Christ*. Minneapolis: Fortress Press, 1993 [1990].

———. *Jesus Christ for Today's World*. Minneapolis: Fortress Press, 1994.

## Discussion Questions

1. What are some tensions in Anselm's theory of atonement?

2. What innovations does Douglas John Hall make to Anselm's theory in his appropriation of it?

3. What are the strengths and weaknesses of Marilyn McCord Adams's appropriation of Anselm's theory?

4. Do Moltmann, Hall, and Adams answer and/or reinterpret Anselm's theory so as to avoid the criticisms of it outlined at the start of this chapter?

5. What makes this model of the atonement meaningful to some people?

♦

# CHAPTER 5

# Jesus as Source
# of "Bounded Openness"

## Raimon Panikkar,
## John B. Cobb Jr.,
## Jacques Dupuis

The novel *Life of Pi*[1] tells the story of a teenage boy named Piscine who abbreviates his name to Pi. He lives in southern India, becomes interested in Hinduism, Christianity, and Islam and begins to practice all three. The pandit of the temple, the Imam of the mosque, and the priest of the church he goes to hear that he is frequenting these other places of worship. One day, all three meet Pi and his parents at the beach. An angry conversation ensues in which each denounces the other's religion. Finally, the pandit states that Pi's piety is admirable. All agree on that. But they also declare, "He can't be a Hindu, a Christian and a Muslim. It's impossible. He must choose."[2] When asked his opinion, Pi replies, "Bapu Gandhi said, 'All religions are true.' I just want to love God."[3] Pi is already a Hindu by birth. He is subsequently baptized a Christian, and he continues to pray as a Muslim. The unfolding of the story soon takes him away from this controversy. In the novel as in real life, the issue remains unresolved.

Pi recognizes that there is truth in all three religions and finds each meaningful to practice. There are similarities among all three and they can be complementary. But the pandit, the imam, and the priest recognize that while Pi speaks of God generically, these three religions do not conceive of God or ultimate reality in the same way. They differ in their respective understandings of the goal of human life. While religions inevitably absorb elements from their surroundings, including other religions, to some degree, fundamental differences can still be recognized between their teachings.[4] This makes it difficult to be a Hindu, a Christian, and a Muslim all at the same time.

This is a central dilemma of the twenty-first century. How do the truth claims of different religions relate to one another? In Christian theology, a typology of exclusivism, inclusivism, and pluralism has emerged, denoting three different approaches to this question.[5] Exclusivism, often associated with theologians Karl Barth and Hendrik Kraemer, asserts the importance of religious differences and that Jesus Christ is the only source of salvation.[6] Inclusivism, often associated with Karl Rahner and his theory of anonymous Christians, tends to argue that while truth and salvation can be found outside Christianity, wherever this occurs it is in some way derivative from and secondary to the truth and saving significance of Jesus Christ. Pluralism, often associated with theologian John Hick, tends to assert that different religions are to be seen as many ways—each having a partial vision of the truth—that lead to the same God who transcends them all.

Raimon Panikkar,[7] John B. Cobb Jr., and Jacques Dupuis all develop their Christologies in relation to this dilemma. They reject the claim that salvation can be found only through faith in Jesus Christ, but they affirm that Jesus is the Christ. They affirm that truth and salvation can be found in other religions, but they reject that this is simply a derivative or secondary version of Christian truth. They also reject the idea that a universal theology or theory of religion can be developed as a neutral basis for adjudicating the truth claims of different religions, or that all religions are equally true in their own way. They find in Jesus a source of truth for resisting evil yet also for discerning truth elsewhere. In this way, Jesus is a source of "bounded openness,"[8] a sense of identity and defined values, but one that is open to critique, reformation, recognizing truth in other religions and receiving from them.

## Raimon Panikkar

Raimon Panikkar was born in Barcelona, Spain, on November 3, 1918. His mother was Spanish and Roman Catholic. His father was an Indian Hindu. He was raised Roman Catholic, becoming a priest in 1946. He earned a doctorate in philosophy from the University of Madrid the same year and a doctorate in chemistry from there in 1958. He taught at the University of Madrid from 1946 to 1953 then went to India, where he studied Indian philosophy and participated in Hindu-Christian dialogue. From this emerged his dissertation for a doctorate in theology from the Lateran University in Rome in 1961, published as *The Unknown Christ of Hinduism*.[9] He taught in Rome from 1962 to 1963 then was visiting professor of comparative religion at Harvard University from 1967 to 1971. From 1971 to 1978, he taught comparative religions at the University of California, Santa Barbara.[10] He has lived for parts of many years in India. At age seventy, he married. He currently resides in Tavertet, Spain. He has been an immensely prolific lecturer and writer, authoring over forty books and hundreds of articles, primarily in the areas of interreligious dialogue, hermeneutics, spirituality, and theology. His vision of reality has remained remarkably consistent over the course of his career.[11]

According to Panikkar, "we are on the brink of a mutation in human civilization [such] that . . . no religious tradition is any longer capable of sustaining the burden of the present-day human predicament and guiding Man[12] in the 'sea of life.'"[13] Partly as a result of globalization, encounters between different world religions, and the civilizations they help shape, have greatly increased. Because religions encounter each other as different ways of being human, their encounters can be mutually enriching or destructive. In the present context, religions need to develop so as to be able to recognize the truth claims of other religions while holding to their own. This new context of religious pluralism is complicated by the challenge of Western technology and secularism, which threatens to turn all reality into objects to be manipulated and life into a competition for ever greater productivity and amassing of wealth.[14] Panikkar is convinced that life can only be sustained by a religious vision. A new understanding of religions and reality, what Panikkar calls a new "cosmovision,"[15] is needed to enable different religions to live in peace and to sustain religious beliefs so that they can guide human life in a technological age. In his view, allowing "this new vision to spring forth constitutes the great challenge of our times."[16]

Panikkar attempts to articulate this cosmovision in his many writings. He sees in the present global context and in his own person a remarkable correspondence between phylogenesis, the development of the human race, and ontogenesis, his development as an individual.[17]

His frequently repeated self-description states that he left Europe as a Christian, found himself a Hindu, and returned a Buddhist, "without having ceased to be a Christian."[18] He sees the understanding of religious truth he gained through this pilgrimage to be a model for the development that the race as a whole must undergo.

For Panikkar, a historical religion like Christianity is a symbol system and way of life oriented to the transcendent reality of God. This reality is mediated through the symbols and practices of a religion but transcends them. Religions express their understanding of this transcendent reality in their doctrines. Religions are historical entities in that their doctrines and practices always reflect their historical context and are limited by it. The real, which is beyond doctrine[19] and expressed in symbols, is transhistorical. As such, it is beyond conceptual grasp. But faith experiences and perceives it through symbols and religious experience. If a doctrine becomes confused with the transcendent reality it seeks to conceptualize, it becomes idolatrous.

Panikkar argues that as people can only known God, or the "real," through symbols[20] and religious practices, religions are indispensable and insurmountable, which makes the idea of developing a universal theory of religion that rises above different world religions impractical. He also argues against a universal theory of religion on the grounds that any such theory "is loaded with political overtones."[21] Because the concepts and values of any such theory are inevitably based on the ideas and experiences of a particular people or culture, its claim to be universally valid in relation to other religions and cultures is in effect a form of cultural imperialism. What is needed instead is a "'theology' for a postcolonial era."[22] No one can surmount their historical particularity. The key is to recognize that religions are oriented to a reality beyond rational conceptualization. This is experienced through religions, which are inherently diverse and cannot be conceptually unified. Yet members of different religions can enter into dialogue with one another about the reality they worship. Instead of ostensibly offering a theoretical solution to religious pluralism, Panikkar advocates a practice of intrareligious dialogue and mystical quest on the grounds that our "deepest human fellowship . . . arises because we all live by faith in spite of the diversity of our beliefs."[23]

While Panikkar opposes the idea of a universal theory of religion, his argument implicitly presents one.[24] He argues that religious truth is relational but not relativistic.[25] Religions are relational to what he calls the cosmotheandric[26] process. All of reality, composed as it is of the divine and the material, is involved in a continuous process of exit from and return to the eternal, which is beyond being. This process is ongoing on the level of individuals' lives and history as a whole. Intrareligious dialogue facilitates the mutation needed in religions to carry this process forward, on the level of history as a whole, in the present context.

Panikkar sees this cosmotheandric process symbolized in the Trinity. His interpretation provides the framework for his understanding of intrareligious dialogue and human history as a whole. According to Panikkar, the Father, or First Person of the Trinity, symbolizes the transcendently real, which is beyond being, the infinite Source from which everything comes. The Father begets the Son by a process of total self-emptying.[27] Through this kenotic process God comes into being in the person of the Son. The Son is the knowledge and being of God, at once identical with and yet totally other than the Father.[28] The Son creates the universe. He is its point of emergence and way of return to its origin. The Spirit is the unity of the Father and the Son and as such, the goal of creation. The Spirit is beyond being[29] but present in creation, though hidden, as creation exists in the Spirit without being aware of it. Salvation is coming to conscious awareness of and participation in the Spirit. This occurs through experiencing what Panikkar calls christophany, the christic process by which a person's true identity is actualized.[30] All of reality exists within this eternal process of divine self-emptying and return that the Trinity symbolizes.[31]

Christophany occurs through self-emptying, or kenosis, as symbolized for Christians in Jesus' death on the cross. For Panikkar, kenosis is the means of creative transition to another level of existence. It is through the self-emptying of the Father that the Son is begotten, who then creates the world. In turn, as Jesus' example shows, the way of return to unity with the Father in the Spirit is by self-emptying through the death of the ego. According to Panikkar, intrareligious dialogue, to be an authentic encounter with another religious tradition, involves a self-emptying on the part of Christians, a relinquishing of the egocentricity of doctrinal knowledge in imitation of Christ on the cross.[32] Through the sharing and receiving in intrareligious dialogue that this self-emptying facilitates, Christ becomes incarnate in the participants. They move closer to the fulfillment of their divine destiny and, in doing so, participate in the cosmotheandric process. The paschal mystery, the death and resurrection of Christ, is thus the model for and the vision motivating intrareligious dialogue.

This involvement in intrareligious dialogue contributes to and reflects a similar process that has occurred repeatedly in the historical development of religions over the centuries. According to Panikkar, religions develop a greater understanding of the truths their symbols mediate through encounter with other cultures and religions. This encounter can bring a violent clash, or it can result in a fecundation of the religions involved, in which they mutually enrich each other. This fecundation occurs as each religion dies to its previous understanding of its symbols, only to rise again in a new understanding[33] better able to sustain life by offering greater insight into the cosmotheandric process. Panikkar's vision of this process is inspired by a "cosmic confidence"[34] in the goodness of reality, which empowers one to empty oneself and so open oneself to the other. It is this openness and the new understanding of each other that it leads to that will enable members of different religions to live together in peace.

For Christians, Jesus Christ is the primary source of this cosmic confidence and the model for this process. Panikkar's intervention in it has been to develop his cosmovision and, as part of this, to develop a Christology from "an Indic perspective,"[35] aimed at converting Western or "tribal" Christologies "into a christophany less bound to a single cultural current."[36] Against Christologies from above and below, he presents a Christology from within,[37] aimed not at grasping the empirical truth of Jesus as a figure in history but at understanding and sharing in Jesus' self-consciousness and experience of God. For Panikkar, Jesus saves not by doing as much as by enlightening. Accordingly, his interest lies in the inner life of Jesus, which reveals "a universal experience"[38] available to everyone regardless of their religious tradition.

Panikkar describes Jesus as follows:

> He was one with the Origin of the universe, although in fact he was not the Origin; he had come from the Source and he had to return to the Source. He spent the time granted him doing good deeds without any programmatic calculation. . . . He was simply a man who went about without joining any extremist groups, a man wholly disposed to forgive everything but hypocrisy. . . . Though he did not discriminate against any

group, he always seemed to take the side of the oppressed and the disinherited, and thus he ended his life.[39]

He also describes Jesus as never experiencing "any frustration whatsoever," as despising power and as never employing violence.[40] Panikkar sees here a person whose lack of attachment to worldly things freed him from mental and spiritual anxieties and allowed him to care for others.

According to Panikkar, the human condition is theandric, a union of the divine and the material. Because the divine has been emptied into the material and lies hidden within it, there is a kenotic dimension of "nakedness" or abasement intrinsic to human life.[41] Jesus shared this spiritual nakedness, with the difference that he accepted it in the awareness that the divine, while hidden, is still present. The hiddenness of people's divinity leads them to seek a sense of self-value in attachment to material possessions, historical identities, and religious doctrines. This attachment leads to intolerance of and violence toward others. Jesus taught and revealed that salvation is experienced through a kenoticism that reverses the initial kenotic dimension intrinsic to creation. The first form of kenoticism gave rise to historical life with its egos and anxieties. The second form is a self-emptying of the ego through the recognition that human life, precisely because "it is limited in form and manifestation," is infinite in value.[42] Through accepting our finitude, we discover the divinity hidden within us. As the Christ, Jesus reveals the infinite value of finite human life through sharing it, living as a human person, and accepting his finitude. His example shows that people find salvation by doing the same. As people do so, emptying themselves of their ego, they participate in the cosmotheandric process. Christ is revealed in them, and they enter consciously into the life of the Spirit while still on earth.

What Jesus reveals as the Christ is not so much himself but the presence of the divine in human life and the potential everyone has to experience it more fully.[43] Adherents of other religions can have the same experience and so encounter Christ through the religious practices and symbols of their own traditions.[44] The Christian "encounters Christ in and through Jesus,"[45] but Christ cannot be limited to or identified solely with Jesus. The issue of the uniqueness of Christ is a "pseudo-problem" that arises when one mistakenly tries to objectify Christ scientifically rather than approaching him in love.[46] Panikkar does not contest the historicity of Jesus' cross and resurrection,[47] but his interest lies in the "actual reality" of these events, which transcends their historical occurrence.

The ethical vision Panikkar draws from his thought has some ambiguities. Coming to consciousness of the Spirit's presence and one's own participation in it comes with a detachment from worldly possessions and material needs. This detachment creates openness to and love for others. The recognition that people may experience Christ through other religions creates openness to them and fosters desire for dialogue. Faith in Jesus Christ is thus a source of bounded openness. But Panikkar's pluralism makes him ambivalent as to when, where, and how love for others might give rise to opposition to those who commit evil in the name of their beliefs or religion.[48] According to him, pluralism "is not blind to error or evil, but [it] does not absolutize any position."[49] He endorses the option for the poor, but for him "purity of heart" in the sense of detachment from earthly concerns is more efficacious than commitment to a project of historical liberation.[50] He presents this as a cross-cultural comment on a Western ideal from an Eastern perspective. This leads to the heart of Panikkar's challenge, and that of other Indian Christian theologians, to contemporary Christologies.

Jesus and much of the early church thought in terms of a vision of God acting in history to move it to a final fulfillment. Panikkar's interpretation of Jesus replaces this vision of history with a cosmology more of Hindu origin.[51] In the former, God effects salvation through history. In Panikkar's vision, salvation is experienced through detachment from history. This replacement of the deep thought structure underlying most of the New Testament with a more mystical vision drawn from advaitic Hinduism has a decisive influence on Panikkar's Christology and ethical vision. Many have questioned how substantially the New Testament proclamation of Jesus informs his Christology. However, this proclamation has an impulse toward its enculturation in the worldview of believers[52] that legitimates Panikkar's concern to develop an understanding of Jesus that is "meaningful to the Indian tradition."[53] But his argument is not simply for the legitimacy of enculturating Christology into the culture of India. It is also that interpreting Jesus as he does is the "mutation" Christianity needs to be adequate to the global challenge of religious pluralism.[54] On this level, Panikkar does see history moving toward a goal, but the goal is embracing a vision of reality inspired by advaitic Hinduism, in which history is not oriented to any goal.

Panikkar's objection, noted earlier, that any universal theory of religion is inevitably culturally imperialistic can be turned against his second argument here. But his claim that Christology should not be developed only in terms of the underlying assumptions of Western cultures is more challenging. Must Christology remain Western, in Panikkar's terms, in its underlying vision of history?[55] How essential to the gospel is the view of history that Jesus and much of the early church inherited from first-century Judaism? Many Christian theologians in India are critical of Panikkar's devaluation of the historical details of Jesus' life, arguing that these are intrinsic to Jesus' identity as the Christ.[56] There is the danger that Panikkar is repeating here the error of patristic theology of understanding Jesus abstractly, in a way that forsakes his historical concreteness as a first-century Palestinian Jew. This concreteness is particularly important for Dalit Christologies, which have developed in the struggle against caste oppression in India. Yet other Indian Christian theologians affirm the need to understand Jesus in terms of their own culture, which is deeply informed by Hindu traditions. The issues raised here regarding the enculturation of the gospel in cultures shaped by other religions remain open and continue to be discussed by Christian theologians around the world.

## John B. Cobb Jr.

John B. Cobb Jr. was born in Japan on February 9, 1925, the youngest of three children. His parents were Methodist missionaries from the United States. He lived mostly in Hiroshima and Kobe until 1940, when World War II led to his moving to the United States.[57] He lived in Georgia with his grandmother while completing high school and junior college. At this time, he was noted for his remarkable Christian piety, demonstrated in personal devotions, worship, acts of charity, and seeking social justice. When he joined the United States Army in 1944, he encountered a broader intellectual world, which he explored through reading. On advice from army friends, he went to the University of Chicago to continue his exploration. There he and Jean Lofitin were married. Together they had three sons.

Cobb enrolled in an interdepartmental program at the University of Chicago to subject his Christian faith to the intellectual challenges of modern worldviews. Within six months, his faith was shattered.[58] Sensing that the faculty at the University of Chicago Divinity School were engaged with the ideas and issues he had encountered, he went there, where Charles Hartshorne introduced him to process philosophy. This eventually gave him a conceptuality from which he could speak of God with conviction.[59] Cobb received a Ph.D. from the University of Chicago in 1952, with a dissertation on the relationship of Christian faith to speculative belief, a topic that remains central to his thought. While completing his dissertation, he worked for a year as a minister in a seven-congregation circuit in rural Georgia and taught part-time at Young Harris Junior College. He then taught at Young full-time for two years before moving to Emory for five and then, in 1958, to Clare-mont School of Theology in California. On February 15, 2008, a dinner in his honor and a three-day conference on his theology celebrated his fifty years at Claremont.

Cobb's initial writings were mostly concerned with demonstrating the intellectual credibility of Christian faith, primarily in relation to the challenges of secularism and other world religions.[60] He spent the academic year of 1965–66 as a Fulbright professor in Mainz, Germany, where he was influenced by Wolfhart Pannenberg's emphasis that Christian faith is oriented to the future. Thomas Altizer led him to see that human action is guided by images as well as rational understanding. In 1969, his thought underwent a major "turn,"[61] as he gained a new appreciation of the unsustainability of modern Western societies and their devastating impact on other nations, the poor, and the environment. This led him to develop his theology more as a critical theory in relation to crises of the present.

In the first part of his career, Cobb sought to legitimate Christian faith by showing that the human autonomy cherished in modern Western societies stemmed from Jesus Christ. Cobb argued that human consciousness is structured by a symbolic view of the world, present in the unconscious but dialectically related to conscious experience.[62] He accepted Karl Jaspers's theory of an "axial period" in which the "basic modes of thought and existence"[63] characteristic of modern civilizations arose, and then argued that these developed further in the ministry of Jesus and the experience of the early church. Jesus' proclamation of the reign of God issued out of a new sense of God as a "presently active reality . . . incomparably greater . . . than the world of creaturely things."[64] Following Jesus' death and resurrection, early Christians experienced God as an empowering presence in the Holy Spirit. Jesus' proclamation and the subsequent experience of the Holy Spirit created a specifically

Christian structure of experience, characterized by a sense of peace with God, empowerment to love others, and freedom to take responsibility for one's own actions.[65] This structure of existence is oriented toward continually seeking a deeper relationship with God and others. Any given actualization of this structure can be surpassed, but not the orientation itself, or the structure of existence deriving from it.[66] Jesus is the Christ as the one to whom this structure of existence is owed, and as the one who actualized it superlatively. This understanding of Jesus as the source of authentic contemporary existence, as the full actualization of creative possibility, and as such, continuing to transcend the present, remained central to Cobb's Christology through its further developments.

Cobb's shift from an apologetic to a more socially critical theology reflected the transition from the modern to a postmodern era that he observed in the late 1960s.[67] This transition resulted partly from the emergence of a new awareness of injustices "with respect to race, religion, sex, consumption, the natural environment, and their profound conjoint interconnection with all our values and attitudes."[68] The emergence of this awareness shattered previous restrictions on intellectual credibility "established by the secular consciousness,"[69] and created a new openness to images of hope.

With this change in his theological concerns and social ethos, Cobb began to emphasize more the transcendence of Jesus to contemporary society. He had already begun to describe the meaning of Jesus for the present as "the call to go forward beyond the achievements of the past and the security of what is established and customary,"[70] and to argue that inherited notions of God must be reinterpreted in light of Jesus.[71] He continued to describe Jesus as the source of the modern structure of existence, but he began to focus more on Jesus as giving comfort and hope and as judging and disturbing.[72] Here Cobb introduced a new note into his Christology. Jesus is always an expression of God's love. He disturbs in order to creatively transform and empowers people to respond to his call.[73] Cobb thus came to see Jesus' expression of God's judgment and grace as a source of creative transformation. A call for faithfulness to Jesus who calls people out of the present to a future as yet unrealized became an important theme in his theology.

For Cobb, apologetics play an important role in contemporary Christology. In his view, Karl Barth's repudiation of any attempt to build a conceptual bridge between the message of the Bible and the forms of knowledge and experience characteristic of modernity paved the way for the eruption of "death of God" theologies in the 1960s.[74] Cobb argues that speculative thought supports faith by building this kind of bridge. The power of Jesus' words and life to move people to love and faith in Jesus Christ can only be sustained by a rational conceptuality demonstrating the intelligibility of this belief in relation to contemporary knowledge and experience.[75]

Cobb uses the process philosophy of Alfred North Whitehead to build such a bridge in his major work on Christology, *Christ in a Pluralistic Age*. According to Whitehead, God has a primordial and a consequent nature.[76] The flow of history, which is made up of occasions and which is itself an occasion, occurs between the two. The primordial nature of God accompanies every occasion as it becomes actual, conceiving the possibilities for beauty, truth, and goodness that it may realize and presenting these to it as an initial aim or "lure" in its becoming. In this way, God introduces order, value, and novelty into the world.[77] The occasion in its becoming responds to the initial aim provided by God with its own subjective aim, which it seeks to actualize. The consequent nature of God experiences this becoming of the occasion, remembering and treasuring what is good in it, while dismissing what is evil.[78]

Cobb identifies the patristic idea of the Logos as a transcendent principle of order and rationality, drawn from the prologue to John's Gospel, with Whitehead's idea of God's initial aim for every occasion.[79] The Logos aims at a creative transformation in the actualization of every occasion. The Logos, however, is not identical with the Christ. The possibilities for creative transformation that the Logos presents are not always realized, and when they are, it is generally imperfectly. The Christ is the actualization of the creative transformation that the Logos presents as a possibility for a particular occasion—the Logos become incarnate and effective in history. Christ for Cobb is thus the occurrence of creative transformation. Jesus is named the Christ because he is experienced as the occasion in which the possibility for creative transformation was fully actualized.

For Cobb, there is a reciprocal relationship between Jesus as the Christ and the Logos. The concept of the Logos makes the belief that Jesus is the Christ intelligible. Conversely, naming Jesus as the Christ designates the Logos as having a certain character. Jesus experienced as the Christ reveals the Logos, the creative source of order in the universe to be "dynamic, trustworthy, loving."[80] This recognizes creative transformation as love in action, and makes love the hallmark of it. It also makes the love discernible in the person and work of Jesus the guiding image by which the presence of Christ can be recognized, even where Christ is not named: in "creative transformation in art, in persons of other faiths, and in the planetary biosphere."[81] For Cobb, creation and redemption coalesce as two aspects of creative transformation.[82] Jesus as the Christ is the unique paradigmatic instance of this. But what happens in him is continuous in terms of how it happened and what happened with creative transformations occurring elsewhere.

For Cobb, it is the transformative effect of Jesus' message expressed primarily in his words and the experience of the Holy Spirit following his death that make Jesus the Christ. The death of Jesus is important as an example of love, though it requires careful interpretation.[83] But like Jesus' resurrection, it does not play a major role in Cobb's Christology. However, Jesus' saving significance cannot be reduced to his moral influence. Cobb uses the term *force field* from Whitehead's understanding of how past events become part of a new occasion to interpret Paul's notion of life in the Spirit.[84] Jesus is the source of the force field of the Holy Spirit because he overcame in his person the temptations that afflict people. Thus he is a decisive image of hope for the continued creative transformation of self and society in the future.[85] Here Cobb understands Jesus' saving significance along the lines of the Christus Victor theory of atonement, though in muted form.

Jesus' decisive overcoming of sin raises the question of what enabled him to do this. This question, combined with Cobb's emphasis on the need for a conceptual understanding to undergird belief, leads him to take up the questions that led to the formulation of the Chalcedonian Definition,[86] except on the basis of Whitehead's thought. For Cobb, Jesus is fully human in having a self structured like everyone else, but he is distinct as a source of creative transformation. Cobb explains how this could be by postulating that while the initial aim provided by the Logos challenges most people from outside the center of their selves, it is possible that the Logos could "share in constituting" the selfhood of a person by being identical with that center.[87] In that case, "the usual tension between the human aim and the ideal possibility of self-actualization that is the Logos would not occur."[88] Cobb suggests that this coinherence of the Logos with the center of Jesus' self need not have been constant in Jesus' life. The stories of his temptations and his struggle in Gethsemane suggest that his disciples did not believe it had been.[89] But Jesus' implicit identification of his words and actions "as directly expressive of God's purposes"[90] indicates that in his public ministry he did experience the Logos as identical with the center of his self. In light of this and the continued emanation of transforming power from his person, Cobb argues that it is possible to affirm that in Jesus' life the possibility for creative transformation was fully actualized so that he literally was the Christ.[91] The Logos becoming fully incarnate in Jesus in no way denied or displaced his humanity. In Cobb's conception, the more fully the Logos becomes incarnate in a person, the more their humanity is fulfilled. As the Christ, Jesus is the paradigm of a fulfilled human life.

Using Whitehead's conceptuality thus, Cobb is able to affirm what he sees to be the central statements of the Chalcedonian Definition about Jesus' person, that he was fully human and also that the divine was fully present in him. He also argues that this conceptualization enables Jesus' humanity to be fully acknowledged, which corrects distortions introduced into Christology by the use of substantialist categories in patristic theologies. These categories led to the implicit denial of aspects of Jesus' humanity (Alexandrian Christology), or to difficulty conceptualizing the unity of God and humanity in Jesus' person (Antiochean Christology).[92] This conceptualization also relativizes certain aspects of the Chalcedonian Definition so as to enable the recognition of Christ's presence in other religions.

Cobb's 1960s work *The Structure of Christian Existence* presents other religions as alternatives to Christianity that it surpassed.[93] By the mid-1970s, his central concern had become developing a Christology that could provide ethical guidance, hope, and engender commitment while recognizing the validity of other religions and ways of life.[94] His answer was that Jesus Christ, understood as the paradigm of creative transformation, "is the Way that excludes no Ways."[95] For Cobb, the church extends the incarnation as it makes Jesus present through its worship, community life, and public witness.[96] Christ is most effectively present in the church, despite the many ways it betrays and distorts its message, because "the church names the Logos as Christ and understands that Christ is the Logos."[97] But Christ is also present in other realms, and sometimes more effectively. The church, because of its faith in Christ, is impelled by him as the paradigm of creative transformation and the call to a greater future to seek out other religions and domains where he is present, in order to be itself creatively transformed through encounter with them.[98] Having understood Christ as creative transformation, Cobb later supplemented this by describing Christ as the center of Christians' lives that calls for openness to others:

> We must show that we are open to the other because we are truly faithful to our heritage. For Christians this means that because Christ is the center there can be no boundaries. Because we are faithful to Christ, we seek truth wherever it can be found.[99]

In this way, "Christocentrism provides the deepest and fullest reason for openness to others."[100] Jesus Christ thus demands recognition of other religions and constructive encounter with them. Through these encounters, the church's understanding of Christ will be transformed. In the encounter with Judaism, Christ as the center of a Christian's history calls and empowers Christians to acknowledge and repent for the history of Christian anti-Semitism. Cobb's understanding of Christ as the center also has critical implications for society. Christ as the center should encourage Christians to work to overcome the fragmentation brought on by the differentiation of social systems and forms of knowledge in modern Western societies, as this impedes effective response to the environmental crisis.

Cobb developed this notion of Christ as the center that has no boundaries through the 1980s and 1990s. Other ethical dimensions of his notion of Christ as creative transformation grew stronger at the same time. In the 1970s, Cobb defined creative transformation as the arrangement of the given elements of the world into a novel constellation, providing a broader perspective, a more intense experience, and a greater harmony among contrasting elements.[101] He argued that this dynamic is "discoverable in nature, in history, and in personal experience."[102] Understood as such, Jesus Christ offers insights "into how every aspect of life is to be lived and every aspect of nature and history is to be understood."[103] There is an element of dying to the old to be born to the new in this, but for Cobb, the focus is on the new to be attained rather than the sacrifice it cost.[104] In general, the dynamic of creative transformation that Jesus exemplified, his revelation as the Christ that the Logos is love, his assurance that creative transformation is possible, and his call to continually seek to realize it on the way to a more just, inclusive, and beautiful future, have remained more important to Cobb than the particulars of Jesus' teachings and actions.[105]

However, Cobb always saw that creative transformation involves progression toward a greater justice, in theory and practice. As Christ is the center that has no boundaries, Christ must be good news for all,[106] the bearer of a universal principle of justice. When the church's understanding of Jesus does not function as such, it must be rethought, creatively transformed, until it does.[107] This pushed him to a new understanding of Christ beyond creative transformation.

As the social crises of the 1980s deepened and Cobb engaged in dialogue with liberation and feminist theologies, he began to argue that while "Christ is not limited to the historical figure of Jesus," the figure of Jesus does provides criteria for its use, as do the notions of salvation and God.[108] The openness of Christ is a bounded openness. As the notion of Christ is bounded by that of salvation, creative transformation must be life giving. But as the threat of nuclear war increased, injustices between rich and poor worsened, and the destruction of the environment continued during the Reagan administration, Cobb came to see that the tie of Christ to salvation meant that Christ "must be the life that struggles against the death-dealing powers that threaten us."[109] In this struggle, Christ is often present more in the victims and in martyrdom[110] than as creative transformation. Liberation theology's emphasis on the preferential option for the poor led Cobb to see that Christ not only acts for the poor but identifies with them and is present in their suffering and joy. This led Cobb to realize that Christ is not just creative transformation but also the truth of the world found in the faces of the poor. As the truth of the world, Christ is not only the incarnation of the Logos, God's primordial nature; Christ is also the incarnation of God's consequent nature.[111] This led Cobb to affirm that "it is God who is incarnate in Jesus and . . . this God is the Trinity in its totality. . . . Christ names God in God's relation to the World without limitation."[112]

This affirmation stresses Cobb's reliance on Whitehead's philosophy, as Whitehead does not usually speak of God's consequent nature becoming incarnate. It is partly in the consequent nature of God that God transcends the tumult of history so as to give it meaning, as the beauty and goodness remembered there are objectively immortal.[113] If Christ present in the faces of the poor is the truth about the world, then Jesus Christ can only be the transcendent principle of hope that Cobb insists he is in light of Jesus' resurrection, and a more differentiated understanding of God, such as that found in the Trinity. After the shattering of his faith in his undergraduate years, Cobb concluded that the "traditional transcendent prophetic God"[114] could no longer be affirmed. This meant that he could no longer affirm God's power to do something radically new in history, as in the resurrection of Jesus Christ. For Cobb, such an affirmation was untenable in relation to other forms of knowledge and raised insolvable questions concerning theodicy. Yet he does affirm the need for the kind of hope that this faith provides. There remains an ambivalence in Cobb's Christology here between what he can speculatively affirm through Whitehead's philosophy and what he sees to be the truth of Jesus Christ.[115]

Cobb's Christology was also transformed through his encounter with feminist theology. Feminist critiques of the ideological uses made of Jesus' maleness led him to supplement his notion of Christ as the incarnation of the Logos by identifying Christ as Wisdom. Christ then names Sophia, or Wisdom, "as she embodies herself in the world and receives the world into herself."[116] Cobb experienced feminist concerns to be a greater challenge to his Christology than other religious traditions and liberation theology.[117] Yet his Christology seemed to accommodate these without substantial change.

## Jacques Dupuis

Jacques Dupuis was born in Huppaye, Belgium, on December 5, 1923, the second of four children in a pious Roman Catholic family.[118] He entered a Jesuit elementary school when he was five years old, attended a Jesuit secondary school, and joined the Jesuit order when he was seventeen. When it was time for him to begin teaching, he volunteered to go to India. He was ordained there in 1954 and completed his doctorate, working in India and Rome, with a dissertation on Origen. He then taught theology at St. Mary's, a Jesuit theological college at Kurseong in northern India. In 1971, this college moved to New Delhi. He taught there until 1984, when he was transferred to the Pontifical Gregorian University in Rome to teach Christology. In India, he edited *Vidyajyoti Journal of Theological Reflection* for many years and participated in the theological work of the Indian church. In Rome, he edited the journal *Gregorianum*. During his career, he produced many articles, book reviews, five books in the area of Christology and the theology of religious pluralism,[119] and coedited a collection of doctrinal documents of the Catholic Church. His fourth book, *Toward a Christian Theology of Religious Pluralism*, garnered wide attention. The Congregation for the

Doctrine of the Faith began to investigate it in 1998. In November 2000, a Notification was issued, stating that Dupuis's book "contained notable ambiguities and difficulties on important doctrinal points, which could lead a reader to erroneous or harmful opinions."[120] No further action was taken. Dupuis resumed writing and lecturing. He died December 28, 2004. In all, he spent thirty-six years in India. He is reported to have said: "I consider my exposure to Hindu reality as the greatest grace I have received from God in my vocation as a theologian."[121]

This exposure led Dupuis to believe that Hindus had encountered God through their faith.[122] For Dupuis, Jesus Christ is the decisive revelation of God and the saving event of God's grace, on which the salvation of all depends.[123] This raised the question of how the gospel should be seen in relation to other religions and vice versa. Dupuis viewed this question as a contextual challenge to Christology in Asia equal to the challenge of secularism in North Atlantic countries, that of poverty and oppression in Latin America, and that of enculturating Christology in Africa.[124] However, in presenting things this way, Dupuis excluded the possibility that enculturating Christology might also be a challenge in his Indian context.

As religion tends to form the substance of culture,[125] enculturating the gospel in India has generally meant interpreting it in terms derived from Hinduism. In the opening section of his book *Jesus Christ at the Encounter of World Religions*, Dupuis examines Hindu responses to Jesus Christ, attempts to enculturate the gospel in Hindu terms, and the attempt of Swami Abhishiktananda to combine Hindu and Christian spiritualities in his own person.[126] Dupuis notes the similarity of some Hindu concepts to Christian ones.[127] He recognizes the challenge to enculturate the gospel in Hindu terms posed by Brahmabandhab Upadhyaya on the grounds that he was a Hindu by culture, a Christian by baptism.[128] But Dupuis believed there is a fundamental incompatibility between Hinduism and Christianity. In his view, "it is the mystery of Jesus Christ himself," the occurrence of his incarnation and resurrection, "and not just his message, that is at the very center of faith."[129] This attributes a "theological density"[130] to the event of Jesus Christ and a value to history irreconcilable with Hinduism's relativization of the value of history and perception of the absolute as categorically beyond it.[131] The gospel cannot be enculturated in a Hindu culture because this means trying to combine these two incompatible views of reality. Therefore, the challenge to Christology in India is instead to relate the gospel to other religions like Hinduism, which are distinct from Christianity and yet have been channels of grace.

With this decision, Dupuis refused to follow an extensive tradition in India of seeking to enculturate Christology in Hindu terms.[132] His reason for this seems open to question when one examines his description of the interpretation of the gospel in Hellenistic terms affirmed at the Councils of Nicaea and Chalcedon. Here Dupuis speaks of "a grace of inculturation" occurring as the gospel was "transposed" into the linguistic register of Hellenistic thought.[133] This was necessary because the church had to proclaim the gospel in this context and to do so had to use and adapt terms available there. Here one might ask: why would the church not have to do the same in order to proclaim the gospel in India? Dupuis suggests that the process of enculturation leading to Nicaea and Chalcedon may have to be repeated in other contexts. He sees that, in the transposition leading to Nicaea and Chalcedon, crucial aspects of the gospel were lost that must be recovered.[134] But in relation to enculturating the gospel in India, Dupuis asks whether there might be cultures in which enculturation is not possible because they have essential elements "that are hermetically sealed and impenetrable to the Christian message."[135] He never answered this directly. His implied answer was yes, and that Hindu culture is one of them.

Given Dupuis's emphasis on the event of Jesus Christ, one could ask why the Hellenistic notion that the absolute is unchangeable was not a similar barrier to Christology's enculturation in the patristic era.[136] Dupuis's turn away from seeking to enculturate the gospel in India also conflicts to some extent with his anthropological principle that people are formed as persons partly by the religious communities and cultures in which they live.[137] This was precisely Upadhyaya's point. He had been formed by Hindu culture. It was part of him. The gospel would remain foreign to him if not enculturated into it. Dupuis noted Upadhyaya's challenge but argued that religion cannot be separated from culture[138] and that one cannot effect a symbiosis of these two religions.[139] But while culture and religion are closely related, they are not identical. There are aspects of the relationship of religion and culture and possibilities of a hybridity between them in the enculturation of the gospel that Dupuis did not acknowledge.

Enculturating the gospel is most often a dialectical process. As Dupuis argues, the enculturation of Christology leading to the Councils of Nicaea and Chalcedon involved a gain in conceptual clarity but a loss of some distinctive characteristics of the Christ event. Dupuis chose not to pursue the enculturation of Christology in India. Instead he developed his Christology in light of interreligious dialogue with Hinduism. However, Dupuis's attempt to do this can be seen as having been facilitated by another long-term process of enculturation: that of the Roman Catholic Church into the modern world during the twentieth century. This occurred through a dialectical process of doctrinal development[140] that led to the affirmation at Vatican II of a new, more positive relationship between the Roman Catholic Church and the modern world, other religions included.[141]

This enculturation is reflected in Dupuis's theological method. He notes that, in the past, Western theologians reasoned about other religions deductively: they began with statements from the New Testament and understood other religions on that basis.[142] He argues instead that one must begin inductively with one's own experience of "a praxis of interreligious dialogue."[143] This move from an exclusive reliance on church authority and tradition to beginning instead with experience reflects an acceptance of modern values and approaches to knowledge in Roman Catholic theology that was part of the enculturation of the Roman Catholic Church in Western modernity. But Dupuis also notes that Christians have to understand their experience in light of their faith, which means that the reality apprehended inductively must then be understood deductively in light of church teaching. Dupuis follows this approach in *Jesus Christ at the Encounter of World Religions*. This combination of inductive and deductive approaches is replicated in his approach to Christology. Here he argues that one must begin inductively, with a Christology from below—which begins with what can be known historically about Jesus. This Christology from below must then be supplemented by a Christology from above, which seeks to show how what is known about Jesus inductively can be understood deductively in light of the church's faith.[144] The inductive approach shows the continuity and the discontinuity between the historical Jesus and the church's understanding of him as the Christ. The continuity demonstrates the truth of the church's faith. The discontinuity reveals the difference between Jesus during his public ministry and his glorified state as the risen Christ. By attending to this difference in the deductive trajectory of his christological thinking, Dupuis created space for a positive understanding of other religions in relation to Jesus Christ.

Dupuis developed the outline of his Christology and his basic approach to other religions in *Jesus Christ at the Encounter of World Religions*. He then fleshed his Christology out in *Who Do You Say I Am?* His magnum opus *Toward a Christian Theology of Religious Pluralism* develops the position of the first book in more detail and introduces a distinction between the Word of God apart from the incarnation (Logos *asarkos*) and the Word of God incarnate (Logos *ensarkos*). His final book, *Christianity and the Religions*, restates his position with the modification of characterizing the complementarity between Christianity and other religions as asymmetrical.[145]

Dupuis begins his Christology by noting that the ministry of Jesus focused on proclaiming and inaugurating the reign of God, the expression of Jesus' sense of mission, which in turn reflected his sense of having a unique filial relationship to God.[146] Jesus inaugurated the reign of God by his words and actions and by his death and resurrection. The reign of God is already present in Jesus' ministry yet is still to come in fullness. There is a relationship of continuity and discontinuity between these two states. There is also a parallel relationship of continuity and discontinuity between Jesus and the First Person of the Trinity. Jesus is conscious of being one with the Father, yet he also knows himself to be distinct as the Son. The continuity in both cases gives the church a firm sense of identity. The discontinuity reveals a space between the church and the whole of what it believes in, in which there is room for complementarity between Christianity and other religions.

According to Dupuis, Christianity complements Hinduism in that the Hindu notion of advaita, being one with Brahman, finds its truest instance and new meaning in Jesus' consciousness of oneness with the Father. In turn, the concept of advaita can deepen Christians' understanding of Jesus' and their own relationship to the Father.[147] In this relationship, God the Father is a "Thou" to Jesus' and Christians' "I." This differentiates it from the advaita experience of Brahman's impersonal transcendence to creation. But the advaita awareness of Brahman's radical transcendence can render the Christian relationship to God more profound by increasing Christians' awareness that the Father is the radically transcendent ground of being. Dupuis argues that, in this way, Christianity and Hinduism are mutually complementary. Christianity adds a sense of personal relationship to the Hindu experience of advaita. Advaita gives Christians a heightened sense of divine transcendence and mystery. Thus, the continuity and discontinuity between Jesus and the

First Person of the Trinity makes room for a complementarity between Christianity and Hinduism that can enrich both. Through this enrichment, the reign of God inaugurated in Jesus' ministry, death, and resurrection moves closer to its fulfillment.

Dupuis sees another relationship of continuity and discontinuity between Jesus as a person in history and as the Christ proclaimed in faith. Between the two lies Jesus' death and resurrection. Once the inductive approach of ascending Christology has determined the continuity and discontinuity between the two, a descending Christology, or deductive approach, must be employed to interpret the historical person, ministry, death, and resurrection of Jesus in light of his being the Second Person of the Trinity. In this combination of ascending and descending Christologies, Dupuis sees the contemporary interpreter following the trajectories of interpretation of the first followers of Jesus, who knew him in his public ministry, but who then had to reinterpret him in light of his resurrection.[148] The turning point between an ascending and a descending Christology, then and now, and the warrant for moving from an inductive to a deductive approach lies in Jesus' resurrection and the experience of this in faith.[149] Here a revelation of truth is given that transcends what can be known inductively and that puts the results of inductive inquiry in a new light. This twofold way of knowing reflects the nature of Jesus' being as the Christ.[150]

In his resurrection, Jesus was "constituted" by God as the Christ.[151] This notion is at the heart of Dupuis's Christology and his understanding of how Christianity can be bounded by a sense of Jesus' uniqueness yet open to other religions. God's resurrection of Jesus' person transforms it into the "eschatological condition"[152] awaiting all humanity. This constituting of Jesus as the Christ affects all of reality. Following Rahner, Dupuis argues that it effectively ensures the salvation of all humanity in a quasi-sacramental way.[153] What happens to Jesus' humanity in his resurrection decisively (though mysteriously) affects the humanity of everyone, thus ensuring the final salvation of all. Here God's salvific will comes to final expression and has decisive effect. God's resurrection of Jesus makes Jesus' person "transhistoric,"[154] universally and effectively present throughout history. Jesus' person becomes the "'concrete universal' in which universal meaning and historical particularity coincide."[155] The resurrection reveals that Jesus was the incarnation of the Logos, the Second Person of the Trinity. In the event of Jesus Christ, there occurs both the "personal insertion of God into history" and the integration of history "into the mystery of God itself."[156] This is the theological density that the event of Jesus Christ has as "an actual, decisive, divine intervention in history."[157] It establishes a reality that cannot be revoked or stopped from coming to full fruition in the future. As Jesus is constituted the Christ through his resurrection, the event of his person becomes "constitutive" for the salvation of all. It is the "'punctual' moment in which God 'becomes' God-of-all-peoples-in-a-fully-human-way."[158]

The "event" character of this constitutive moment is important to Dupuis's emphasis on the continuity and discontinuity between the present and the eschatological future and between Jesus as the incarnate Logos and other religions. Though Jesus is the incarnate Logos, he remains a finite human being during his lifetime. His filial relationship to God is real, but so is the finitude of his humanity. He is only able to express God's love in finite ways. As the constitutive event of salvation, the fullness of the revelation he effects is qualitatively unsurpassable but also relative, in that it occurs through the limitations of his humanity.[159] The risen Christ universally present and effective wherever salvation occurs is always continuous with what is revealed in Jesus but is not limited to the church.

In *Toward a Christian Theology of Religious Pluralism*, Dupuis introduces a distinction between Jesus as the incarnate Word, the Logos *ensarkos* (within the flesh), and the Word apart from becoming incarnate, the Logos *asarkos* (without the flesh).[160] For Dupuis, salvation history and Jesus Christ must be understood in a trinitarian perspective. The Logos, or Word of God, is continually going forth to address humanity. This address reaches its constitutive and ultimate expression in Jesus Christ, but it was occurring before Jesus and continues afterward in other modes.[161] The address of the Word takes effect in people's lives through the Holy Spirit inspiring and empowering them to respond to it. As God is one, all salvation is effected by God through the Word and Spirit. Any authentic religious experience results from their presence. Dupuis argues that all human life takes place within communities, and all authentic religious experience is formed through religious traditions. These can be different modalities of the christic mystery,[162] even if not to the same degree as the church. While the tradition in which religious life occurs is important, so is the existential attitude with which it is lived out.[163] From the praxis of interreligious dialogue, it is apparent that there is existentially authentic experience of God in other religions.

This authentic experience of God in other religions reflects the work of the Logos *asarkos* and the Holy Spirit. The Logos *asarkos* can never contradict the Logos *ensarkos* in Jesus Christ, but the manifestation of the Logos *asarkos* in other religions can complement the revelation of the Logos *ensarkos*, just as the Hindu notion of advaita could enrich a Christian's experience of the Father, as outlined earlier. Thus, the uniqueness and universality of Jesus Christ is constitutive of salvation but is relational in terms of other religious traditions.[164] A Christian's perception of it can be deepened by dialogue with other religions,[165] through which all partners may come to a more profound conversion to God.[166] Interreligious dialogue is thus an end in itself. Recognizing this leads to the conclusion that the multiplicity of religions has its source in the overflowing goodness of God.[167]

By developing his notion that Jesus is constituted the Christ through his resurrection—and by his insightful emphasis on the continuity and discontinuity between the fullness of the reign of God in the future and its presence now, the revelation of God in Jesus Christ, and the fullness of the Logos in eternity—Dupuis shows that Christology can be a source of bounded openness in relation to other religions. Resistance to the openness to the world and other religions affirmed at Vatican II that Dupuis received from the Congregation for the Doctrine of the Faith caused him to qualify his notion of complementarity between Christian and other religions as "asymmetrical." But though asymmetrical, it remains real.

One can only wonder how much Dupuis's insight into the continuity and discontinuity between the fullness of God in eternity and the revelation of God in history may have resulted from his prolonged exposure to Hinduism's emphasis on the transcendence of Brahman to the maya (unreality) of history. Dupuis rejected the notion of the unreality of history, but he integrated into his Christology a deepened sense of the transcendence of God in eternity to God's revealed presence in history without severing the connection between the two. In this way, he saw himself as correcting limitations and shortcomings that entered Christology through its encounter with Hellenistic thought centuries earlier while preserving the gains that this encounter brought. Seen thus, his Christology represents an example of how Christology can be enriched through dialogue with Hinduism.

Perhaps this rethinking of Christology in light of interreligious dialogue represents a different approach to enculturating the gospel in

India from that proposed by Upadhyaya. Dupuis retained traditional Christian terms and eschatology but reinterpreted them in light of dialogue with Hinduism. In doing so, he maintained the view of history forming the deep structure of Jesus' identity as the Christ through most of the New Testament even while changing the way this is understood so as to create within it an openness to other religions. The result is not a Christology in Hindu terms but a Christology open to dialogue with Hinduism. This might represent an enculturation of Christology in a Hindu culture by someone whose person was not formed in it. However, in his dialogue with Hinduism, Dupuis seems not to have appreciated how the view of history he sees to be intrinsic to the gospel is experienced by some Indian Christian theologians as Western and entangled in a history of Western imperialism.

## Summary

Panikkar, Cobb, and Dupuis interpret Jesus as the Christ in different ways. Yet all understand Christ as a source of bounded openness in relation to other religions. This openness is bounded by the record and interpretation of Jesus' ministry, death, and resurrection, which gives Christians a sense of identity and ethical direction. Yet while bounded, this identity is open to learning from others and being transformed through encounter with them. Jesus Christ as the center that has no boundaries impels and enables one to enter into dialogue with others.[168]

All three authors see that this bounded openness is not a static state but a shifting, dynamic identity, moved by the Word and Spirit as recognized on the basis of the Word incarnate and as encountered in other religions, social movements, forms of knowledge, and historical events. The shifts that happen in one's identity often occur by a process, "which incarnates the paschal mystery revealed by Christ."[169] Through the give and take of encounter with others, there is a dying to the old understanding of Jesus and self in order to be born again into a new one. Yet all three note that at times this dynamic of openness must give way to resistance and determined opposition. Christ is the source of an identity that combines openness to others with resistance to evil.[170]

All three reject the idea of constructing a universal theology that would achieve harmony among different religions by transcending their differences. Instead, they opt for entering the dialogue with other religions as Christians, seeking to understand Jesus Christ anew in this context and through dialogue with others. This dialogue is not aimed at overcoming differences, but at mutual understanding and enrichment. All three see this dialogue as transformative. Faith in Jesus Christ is not a barrier to it but a basis for it. In the context of religious pluralism, Christ is transformed from the only way to salvation to a source of truth transcending the church. By being transformed in this way, Christ remains the giver, the source of guidance, hope, and strength that the church and others need.

Finally, Panikkar and Dupuis represent two different ways of enculturating the gospel. Panikkar interprets and merges Christology with a Hindu cosmology. Dupuis keeps the two separate, but reinterprets Christology in light of insights gained from a prolonged encounter with Hinduism.

# Suggestions for Further Reading

Aleaz, K. P. *An Indian Jesus from Śaṅkara's Thought*. Calcutta: Punthi Pustak, 1997. An interpretation of Jesus from a cultural perspective shaped by Vedanta Hinduism, which enters into dialogue with Panikkar's Christology.

Cobb, John B., Jr. *Christ in a Pluralistic Age*. Philadelphia: Westminster, 1975. This is Cobb's major effort in Christology. It is a very original and stimulating work.

———. *Transforming Christianity and the World: A Way beyond Absolutism and Relativism*. Edited and Introduced by Paul F. Knitter. Maryknoll, N.Y.: Orbis, 1999. This collection of essays helps document the development of Cobb's Christology through the 1970s, 1980s, and 1990s.

D'Costa, Gavin. *Theology and Religious Pluralism: The Challenge of Other Religions*. New York: Basil Blackwell, 1986. Gives a concise account of the exclusivist, inclusivist, and pluralist approaches to relating Jesus Christ to other religions.

Dupuis, Jacques. *Jesus Christ at the Encounter of World Religions*. Maryknoll, N.Y.: Orbis, 1991. This book focuses primarily on the encounter of Christianity and Hinduism in India, and develops the basis of Dupuis' mature position.

———. *Who Do You Say That I Am?: Introduction to Christology*. Maryknoll, N.Y.: Orbis, 1994. This book focuses directly on Christology and provides the Christological underpinnings for Dupuis's theology of interreligious dialogue.

—. *Toward a Christian Theology of Religious Pluralism.* Maryknoll, N.Y.: Orbis, 1997. This is Dupuis's mature statement of his understanding of the relationship of Christian faith to other religions.

Hick, John, and Brian Hebblethwaite, eds. *Christianity and Other Religions: Selected Readings*, rev. ed. Oxford: Oneworld, 2001. Gives a representative selection of different approaches to the question of how Jesus Christ relates to other religions.

Knitter, Paul. *No Other Name? A Critical Survey of Christian Attitudes toward the World Religions.* Maryknoll, N.Y.: Orbis, 1985. An important critical survey of various understandings of Jesus' relationship to other religions from a pluralist perspective.

Panikkar, Raimon. *Christophany: The Fullness of Man.* Maryknoll, N.Y.: Orbis, 2004. Panikkar's most recent contribution. A beautifully written presentation of his mature vision.

—. *The Unknown Christ of Hinduism,* revised and enlarged edition. Maryknoll, N.Y.: Orbis, 1981. This was Panikkar's first major work in Christology.

Young, Pamela Dickey. *Christ in a Post-Christian World: How Can We Believe in Jesus Christ When Those Around Us Believe Differently—Or Not at All?* Minneapolis: Fortress Press, 1995. An attempt to formulate an understanding of Jesus as enabling a stance of bounded openness to other religions from a feminist perspective.

## Discussion Questions

1. Can one be a Muslim, a Hindu, and a Christian all at the same time? If so, how? If not, why not?
2. How does Cobb see Jesus as enabling a critique of injustice and openness to other religions at the same time?
3. Panikkar and Dupuis are both Roman Catholics, born in Europe, who spent considerable time in India. How do you account for their different approaches to the question of how Jesus relates to other religions?
4. Is Dupuis correct that certain fundamental differences between Christianity and Hinduism prevent the gospel from being expressed in Hindu terms and thus from being enculturated in a culture shaped by Hinduism?

# CONCLUSION

## Fifteen Christologies Later . . .

Coming to the conclusion of this pilgrimage through fifteen contemporary Christologies from four continents, it is time to reflect on what can be gleaned from them. This can be divided into traditional issues in Christology of continuing relevance and new issues arising from contemporary contexts and developments.

## Traditional Issues of Continuing Relevance

Almost all the Christologies studied here developed in theological contexts that became significantly more ecumenical after World War II, but most of them continue to reflect denominational traits. John B. Cobb Jr. does not present his Christology as Methodist in outlook; but, in his emphasis on the experience of Christ, Christ as creative transformation, and the importance of communal worship for sustaining faith, one can hear echoes of a Methodist emphasis on the experience of salvation, ongoing sanctification, and the importance of gathering for worship and study. Mark Lewis Taylor does not advertise himself as a Reformed theologian, yet his continually evolving Christology reflects a Reformed emphasis on the need to continually rethink doctrine in light of the witness of the Word and Spirit, and a Reformed concern for the reformation of society. Denominational background continues to be an influence on contemporary Christologies.

The issues debated at the Councils of Nicaea and Chalcedon continue to be discussed in most contemporary Christologies. Theologians who claim that Jesus has a saving significance beyond that of his moral influence generally have to explain how this is so. This means that questions debated at these councils of how Jesus is related to God, what enables him to save, and how the divine is related to his human nature in his one person continue to be wrestled with. Most of the Christologies studied here affirm that in Jesus Christ God acted in a new and decisive way in history. All emphasize the genuine humanity of Jesus. None portray him, for instance, as enjoying omniscience all his life, as Anselm did. Those who affirm an understanding of Jesus as fully human and fully divine, the two natures united in his one person, emphasize that the Gospels portray him as experiencing spiritual struggle and needing to learn. The genuine humanity of Jesus is a basic assumption of contemporary Christologies.

Anselm taught that Christ became incarnate to save humanity from the penalty of sin. But the Christologies studied here that understand Jesus in a trinitarian perspective and that take up speculative questions tend to follow Duns Scotus, who argued that Christ would have become incarnate even if there had been no sin. According to Scotus, the world was created and Christ became incarnate to express God's goodness, so that there might be others to share in God's joy.[1] Contemporary Christologies following this line of thought see creation as existing for the further expression, communication, and celebration of God's love. This Franciscan innovation in the understanding of the incarnation and its use in contemporary Christology can provide a moral framework that understands creation as having intrinsic value apart from its use by humanity, without falling into antihumanism.[2] Christologies developed on a trinitarian basis can thus make an important contribution to thinking about creation in the context of the environmental crisis.

Contemporary Christologies continue to draw on the three models of atonement that Gustaf Aulén identified to articulate how Jesus provides hope for an end to suffering and death, a beauty and example that move people to love, or comfort that comes from a sense of God's nearness, acceptance, and forgiveness. Some use only one or two of Aulén's models. This study has shown that each of Aulén's models addresses a different form of sin, evil, or suffering, and each sees Christ exercising a different kind of power to overcome it. Abelard's moral influence understanding of the atonement recognizes the basic truth that Christ came to make a difference in the way people live. Christ makes this difference through the power of the beauty of his example, which evokes love and a passion for justice. But how can these be sustained in the face of structural evils like racism, economic oppression, or genocidal violence? The moral influence of Jesus cannot sustain moral concern alone. It strengthens and directs the individual and perhaps the group, but it does not address the root causes of these evils, the cosmic powers of sin and death. Without the hope that in the end God's love is greater than human sin, of the oppressors and of the victims, a passion for social justice is difficult to sustain. It may even degenerate into contempt and aggression toward those one claims to care for.[3]

The Christus Victor model addresses the powers and principalities of sin and death at a mythic or ontological level and can provide a principle of transcendent expectation to undergird the passion for justice that the moral influence of Jesus evokes. It also focuses on how the divine power of being, which eternally overcomes nonbeing, is decisively revealed and actualized in Jesus' resurrection.[4] But the Christus Victor theory can lead to dualistic thinking that becomes an excuse for violence.[5] Neither it nor the moral influence theory addresses the problem of a spoiled identity or the cry for God's presence in suffering and despair, as versions of Anselm's theory do. Where the moral influence theory is at work, sooner or later there will be a sense of failure, guilt, or unworthiness. That is why moral communities ultimately rest on a transmoral basis, and only this can sustain them.

Anselm's theory articulates how Jesus provides this transmoral basis for communion with God and other people in combination with his moral demand. With its impulse toward universal salvation, this theory can also correct the tendency of the Christus Victor model to divide the world into friend and foe. In versions of Anselm's theory, Christ exercises the power of God's unconditional love to accept the unacceptable, to endure the unendurable, to create communion and reconciliation with creation. But Anselm's stress on the salvific nature of Jesus' suffering and death has potentially destructive implications. If employed, it needs the impulse of the other two models toward the coming of God's reign and life lived in all its fullness to guard against its intrinsic danger of valorizing suffering per se. Aulén's three models need and complement each other.[6] They have continuing validity in the way they identify different forms of evil or alienation and the dynamics by which Christ works to overcome them.

An analysis of sin and evil in postmodern societies will need to be complex because of the many different forms of oppression and sin running through them.[7] People's identities in these societies are equally complex. Most are victims of one form of evil and perpetrators of another. While the diverse facets of different people's identities are not all the same or equal, they are real. Contemporary Christologies need to use all of Aulén's atonement models to develop an adequate understanding of Jesus' saving significance in relation to them.

This survey has shown that Aulén's three types have continuing relevance. But it also shows contemporary Christologies to be using them somewhat differently from the way patristic or medieval theologians did. When patristic theologians like Gregory of Nyssa employed the Christus Victor theory, their emphasis was on how Christ is able to save from death those who believe in him. In contemporary Christologies, Aulén's models of atonement tend to function more as "moral sources"[8] that move people to do what is good and resist evil. The emphasis is more on how Jesus empowers those who believe in him to love others, accept themselves, and remain faithful than on the difference he will make for them after death. In contemporary Christologies, Christ's saving significance is articulated chiefly in terms of what it means for life in this world. The same atonement models are used, but it is often their ethical implications that are stressed. This altered focus partly reflects a modern social imaginary that sees society as a project to be constructed through common action[9] and a new emphasis on the meaningfulness of daily life,[10] both of which blossomed in Western modernity. But contemporary Christologies are not completely swept up in a Western concern for productivity. The hope of eternal life, forgiveness of sin, and the meaningfulness of moral action remain bound together. Most contemporary Christologies continue to see Jesus as a source of hope for eternal salvation. Most also endorse a vision of universal salvation. Many also see Christ as a source of meaning that lies in communion with God as much as action. But their focus tends to be more on Christ's meaning for the present than for eternity.

In conjunction with their use of atonement theory as moral sources, these Christologies also differ from their patristic and medieval predecessors in that they have absorbed elements of modern Western liberalism. They see Christ as the bearer of a universal principle of justice that is not limited by creed or race, and they emphasize how he enhances life in this world. They see Christ as supporting notions of democracy,[11] human rights, freedom of speech, and equality before the law. Yet all these Christologies reject liberal notions that religion is a private matter and does not belong in public discourse. Most have played a part in the return of religion to the public sphere.[12] These Christologies also reject liberal notions of human autonomy and the sufficiency of reason, education, and diligence to solve humanity's troubles. They reject the notion that humanity can find fulfillment on its own. Instead, they see people as needing and benefiting from what Christ has to give. Contemporary

Christologies understand Christ as a gift of God that enables one to be more fully human and who reveals what the fullness of humanity is like. They set liberal notions of human autonomy within a broader and deeper view of a humanity in need of God's judgment and grace and finding fulfillment through Christ.

This survey has also shown that there are more atonement models than Aulén described. Jesus as revealer of God's loving presence and Jesus as a source of bounded openness are not new atonement models. Rudolf Bultmann found the first in the Gospel of John.[13] Serene Jones finds the second in the theologies of John Calvin and Martin Luther.[14] The first addresses the experience of the absence of God. This is not a sense of transgression, a lack of moral commitment, or fear of death. Aulén's three models all suppose or supply a moral code in relation to which Jesus has saving significance. But the experience of the absence of God is partly about the lack of a moral code or a sense of value. With this lack comes a loss of meaning in life that can create openings to terrifying idolatries. It may be a kind of alienation unique to secularized societies. In this model, Christ exercises the power to disclose the presence of God that others cannot see. Whether this understanding of Jesus as the revealer of God's loving presence can express all the meanings of Aulén's three models in addition to its own remains an open question. The gospel contains contrasting meanings that relate to people's circumstances in different ways. Attempting to express these in one all-encompassing formulation or according to one dynamic risks losing various facets of the gospel's meanings and glossing over the different circumstances and aspects of people's lives.

None of Aulén's three types directly addresses the challenge of living with religious commitment amid religious pluralism. This has become a crucial issue for contemporary Christologies. Jesus becomes a source of bounded openness when his transcendence to the church and universality as the risen Christ are recognized together with the particular nature of his presence in the worshiping community. Recognizing the diverse ways the risen Christ is present in and to history plus a wide-ranging appreciation of the work of the Holy Spirit can help the church maintain commitment to him while remaining open to other sources of truth. Here Christ enables a power of discernment and exercises the power to transcend the church while being present within it. A sense of Christ's radical transcendence continues to be relevant in religiously pluralistic societies.

Another traditional issue in Christology that continues to be relevant in these Christologies is the distinction between law and gospel. The law stands for the moral demand, the imperative to seek justice and resist evil. Gospel stands for the unconditional acceptance of sinners by God, the transmoral love of God that justifies the ungodly and accepts all regardless of their righteousness. The contemporary Christologies studied here all see Christ as a source of both a moral demand and the transmoral love of God that forgives and accepts those who fail to live up to it. For instance, it is present in Mark Lewis Taylor's insistence that the "communal praxis that is of the Christ"[15] include both a dynamic oriented toward liberation of the oppressed and another oriented toward effecting reconciliation "within a differentiated humanity."[16] Christ expresses a moral demand through his teaching and example, but he also offers forgiveness to sinners and calls for reconciliation between enemies. Contemporary Christologies need to express both and hold them together in a productive tension.

A final traditional and continually relevant concern of Christology is the question of how Christ relates to culture. H. Richard Niebuhr developed a much-discussed typology of five different models, in which he showed how this relationship has assumed different forms, each of which appear in patristic, medieval, and modern Christologies.[17] But the Christologies studied here have all been developed during the cultural transition of modernity to postmodernity. In this transition, the cultures they relate to have become conflicted, fragmented, and diversified. Niebuhr's typology presupposed a unity to culture that no longer exists. Because culture has become fragmented in postmodernity, contemporary Christologies typically relate to it in more than one way, so few can be categorized as fitting any one of Niebuhr's types. For instance, Carter Heyward's Christology resembles Niebuhr's Christ of culture type, in which Christ is accommodated to surrounding culture by "selecting from his teaching and action as well as from the Christian doctrine about him such points as seem to agree with what is best in civilization."[18] In many respects, this is what Heyward's Christology does. She makes no claim about Christ that conflicts with culturally respected forms of knowledge like the natural sciences or the study of history. Her Christ expresses contemporary social ideals of compassion, justice, freedom, equality, self-fulfillment, and community. But if one focuses on her opposition to the religious right and her understanding of Christ's radical opposition to Western capitalism, her Christology seems to fit Niebuhr's Christ against culture type, with its vehement rejection of prevailing culture.[19] This last aspect of Heyward's Christology is representative of most Christologies studied here. Virtually all see a fundamental conflict between the person, teaching, and work of Jesus Christ and the capitalist and imperial ethos that has dominated Western cultures and societies in the last twenty years. Jesus Christ has become a countercultural and politically radical figure even in the Christologies of established theologians.

Niebuhr's typology has continuing relevance in the way it notes the strengths and weaknesses of each type and in its conclusion that there is an insurmountable ambivalence to whatever choice one makes among them.[20] One must make a decision about how Christ relates to culture, and yet there are shortcomings to whatever types are chosen and strengths in the types that are not. The fragmentary nature of postmodern cultures exacerbates this ambiguity so that any approach to Christology will be deficient in some respect. This fundamental ambiguity is evident in John B. Cobb Jr.'s comments on his own earlier Christology. It was very much of the Christ of culture type. Deeply impressed by the cultural achievements of modernity early in his career, Cobb believed that the only credible understanding of Christ was one that was accommodated to modern views of history and nature. Since the time of Schleiermacher (1768–1834) Christologies of this kind have played an important role in supporting the faith of many in the church.[21] But by Cobb's own admission, the factors that led him to interpret Christ in this way also caused him to neglect the aspects of Christ that stand in radical judgment on contemporary American society.[22] Similarly, Moltmann's interpretation of Christ's resurrection in *Theology of Hope* helped unleash the prophetic power of the gospel and directed the church to engage in struggles for social justice. But, as he later noted, the focus on history bound up with this interpretation of Jesus' resurrection was in some ways a withdrawal from concern with nature that needed to be corrected in light of the environmental crisis.[23] Every Christology studied in this book reflects a choice about how Jesus should be related to surrounding culture and in so choosing affirms some values and denies others.

The fragmented nature of postmodern cultures means that there will be various ways of relating Christ to culture such that each have a relative validity and integrity, even though they differ significantly in their theological method and understanding of Jesus Christ. Roger

Haight demonstrates this in an insightful study of the Christologies of Karl Rahner and Edward Schillebeeckx in relation to religious pluralism. Their respective Christologies differ significantly in their understanding of Jesus Christ and their approach to religious plural- ism. Rahner's understanding of Christ's relationship to other religions is controlled "'from above,' specifically by his reliance on the doctrine of the immanent trinity. By contrast, Schillebeeckx argues consis- tently from below and within a framework of history and historical consciousness."[24] On this issue, the Christology of each is vulnerable to critique from the other, and yet each arises from a theological posi- tion possessing "a coherent, comprehensive, and integral character."[25] The fragmentation of postmodern cultures results partly from the con- tradictions between globalized capitalism and the ideals of democracy and the needs of peoples. It results partly from the way globalization brings diverse cultures into constant contact with each other and causes them to become internally related. It also results partly from the explo- sion and fragmentation of knowledge in Western modernity.[26] The last two factors figure prominently in the differences between Rahner and Schillebeeckx's Christologies. Rahner responded to the explosion of knowledge by abstracting from history to the transcendental horizons of historical existence. Schillebeeckx responded by burying himself in New Testament studies for years in order to produce the two great volumes of his mature Christology. Haight concludes from his study of their Christologies in relation to religious pluralism that "a real pluralism of such theologies of religion is possible and even desirable within a single Christian church."[27] From the survey of contemporary Christologies in this book, one can similarly conclude that a pluralism of Christologies in the present is desirable and inevitable. An example of this can be found in John Cobb Jr.'s response to Stanley Hauerwas. Hauerwas's Christology is resolutely of the Christ against culture type, while Cobb's tends to combine more the Christ of culture and Christ the transformer of culture positions. But Cobb notes that while his under- standing of Christ is very different from Hauerwas's, still he admires Hauerwas's work and prizes the way he is able to engage people about Christ.[28] The continuing relevance of the different strengths and weak- nesses of each of Niebuhr's types means that in fragmented postmod- ern cultures there will be a pluralism of Christologies, each limited in some ways, each more adequate in others.

The Christologies studied here that developed in relation to religious pluralism recognize, in some sense, this limitation, inherent in every understanding of Jesus, and have responded to it. Built into each of these Christologies is a sense of the inadequacy of their own grasp of the truth they have received in Christ and of their need to be open to dialogue and correction from others. Out of faithfulness to Christ, all contemporary Christologies need to be developed with this kind of recognition. Christ must be a source of bounded openness. The dialectic of gospel and law also comes into play here. People must seek to understand Christ as adequately as possible, even though every Christology will inevitably be deficient in some respect. Recognition of the inescapable inadequacy of every Christology means that, in order to be authentic, each needs to express Christ's forgiveness as well as Christ's moral demand.

Finally, this survey of fifteen contemporary Christologies shows that, as Ernst Bloch insisted, there is future in the past; in this case, in past understandings of Jesus' person and saving significance. Jesus Christ continues to have a productive noncontemporaneity,[29] elements that do not fit with the present, that remain relevant to new social crises and people's personal lives. Many christological insights and formulations of the past, having been rethought and reframed for the present, continue to be efficaciously present in contemporary Christologies. Surveying the way Jesus Christ has been creatively interpreted so as to address racism, sexism, violent and economic oppression, the experience of the absence of God, horrendous evils, and the challenge of living with religious commitment in the company of other religious communities, one is struck by how these Christologies have been "able to bring forth, from their essential symbolism, new and unexpected meaning empowering people to respond, out of their religious heritage, to changed historical conditions."[30] This creativity in response to major historical events and social developments in the twentieth century can be seen as a sign of hope for the church and the world. Christian faith is not trapped in past understandings of Jesus Christ. Rather, Christians are able to draw on their past and, in fidelity to it, develop new Christologies that enable Christ to address the changing face of evil in a new day. The enabling inspiration for this can be traced to the Holy Spirit[31] and points to another aspect of traditional Christology that is of continuing relevance. In the end, Jesus Christ has to be understood in a trinitarian perspective.

## New Issues Arising from Contemporary Contexts

New issues in contemporary Christologies have arisen as a result of internal developments in Christian theology and external factors in contemporary contexts. A new issue that represents a development internal to Christian theology is the quest for the historical Jesus. Since the 1950s, this has become a field of its own in New Testament studies. While Jesus Christ is not limited to what can be known about the historical Jesus, any academically credible Christology needs to show the continuity between what it affirms about Jesus Christ and what can be known about Jesus historically. This quest, which has gone through several stages, is both a boon and a challenge to contemporary Christologies. The wealth of historical knowledge about Jesus, his milieu, and the early church is a great gift to contemporary Christology. This has enabled Christologies to become much more concrete in their understanding of Jesus in relation to the social structures of his time and consequently in relation to social structures in the present. It has also helped overcome some of the anti-Jewish tendencies prevalent in Christology prior to World War II. However, the quest, as an academic subdiscipline, has its own internal debates. The constant proliferation of competing and conflicting studies on the historical Jesus that these produce can make it difficult for a theologian who is not a specialist in the field to say anything with confidence about Jesus as a historical figure. Martin Kähler's (1835–1912) fear that that the quest for the historical Jesus might lead to faith in Christ becoming dependent on academic results has proven to have some substance.[32] Yet who would wish for less knowledge about Jesus instead of more, and this kind of knowledge is only generated through academic debate. The quest has been a source of new knowledge about Jesus that has benefited Christology. But right behind the proliferation of interpretations of the historical Jesus produced by the quest stands the endless proliferation of materials produced in biblical studies as a whole, and behind that, in Christology itself. The challenge that the proliferation of sometimes conflicting studies on the historical Jesus pose to contemporary Christology[33] is a particularly pressing aspect of the challenge posed to contemporary Christology by the explosion and fragmentation of knowledge in postmodern cultures.

A second new issue arising from developments internal to Christian theology is the question of how much one can say about God on the basis of Christology. Through the influence of Karl Barth, Karl Rahner, and Hans Urs von Balthasar, Christology has become central to the understanding of God in contemporary Christian theology. This helped spark a renewal of trinitarian theology in the twentieth century. Particularly in theologians like Jürgen Moltmann, this has led to dramatic portrayals of the triune life of God, describing the activities and interrelationships of the three persons of the Trinity in the cosmic drama of creation and redemption. A different approach is found in the Christology of Roger Haight. Here Jesus Christ is understood in a trinitarian perspective, but compared to Moltmann, it is a muted trinitarianism. Haight notes that the doctrine of the Trinity arose out of the experience of salvation in Jesus Christ.[34] Christian faith and the Christian understanding of God have an inherent trinitarian structure. This doctrine of the Trinity affirms that God really is as God is revealed and experienced to be through Jesus Christ and the Holy Spirit. On the basis of this, theologians like Moltmann and Elizabeth Johnson then develop descending Christologies that interpret Jesus' history, and particularly his death and resurrection, in light of the doctrine of the Trinity. These descending Christologies open up into detailed descriptions of the divine life. Here Haight parts company from Moltmann and Johnson. For Haight, though God is revealed in Jesus Christ, respect for the transcendence of God demands a theological humility that restricts the kind of description of the divine life that a person can make, even on the basis of Christology.

Moltmann, on the other hand, argues that a consistently Christian doctrine of God must be developed on the basis of Christology.[35] It was this concern that led to the development of the doctrine on the Trinity at the Council of Nicaea. In the twentieth century though, Karl Barth argued that a consistent doctrine of God meant going much further than patristic theologians had in rethinking all of the divine attributes in light of the revelation of God in Jesus Christ. While affirming the doctrine of the Trinity in light of their faith in Jesus Christ, patristic theologians had still clung to a notion of God as immutable that in the twentieth century has come to be known as classical theism. Barth critiqued this understanding of God, affirming the notion of God's transcendence that it expressed but criticizing its failure to affirm the living nature of God.[36] Elizabeth Johnson has made a similar affirmation and critique of classical theism, motivated in addition by concern to free the concept of God from the patriarchal ideology that classical theism seems to express.[37] In order to bring out the living nature of God that Christology demands, these theologians turn to dramatic descriptions of the triune life of God.

The survey of fifteen contemporary Christologies in this book shows no consensus as to what kind of description of God Christology demands. In general, those claiming a unique saving significance to Jesus or one that goes beyond moral inspiration are drawn to undergird this through the doctrine of the Trinity. But the question still remains: how much can one claim to know about the inner life of God? On the one hand, nature abhors a vacuum. Where the doctrine of God is not filled out in light of revelation in Jesus Christ, other sources of inspiration are sure to enter, as Barth suggested happened in patristic conceptions of God as immutable, which he saw to be drawn uncritically from Neoplatonism.[38] Also, as Barth and Moltmann argue, revelation should be taken seriously. If God really is as God is experienced in Jesus Christ, then Jesus Christ should become the basis for understanding God in a thoroughgoing way. A descending Christology must be undertaken in order to develop appropriate concepts that enable one to understand and appreciate what has been revealed of God in Jesus' cross.[39] On the other hand, there is the difference between God and humanity that Haight emphasizes. John Cobb Jr. argues that, in postmodernity, Christianity is often rejected because of the barrenness of its images. "Christians can share in shaping this postmodern mind only if we live more deeply into our images and dare to offer them seriously in the public marketplace."[40] But how much can one claim to know about the trinitarian life of God on the basis of God's revelation in Jesus Christ? There is widespread agreement that Jesus can only be adequately understood in a trinitarian perspective. But how much one can claim to know and how much one should seek to know about the inner dynamics of the divine life remain open questions in contemporary Christology.

A final internal development in Christian theology that can be observed in the Christologies studied in this book is the need to understand Jesus as the Christ in relationship to other people, the church, other religions, and movements for social justice. The new presence of religious pluralism as a topic in Christian theology requires that Christology articulate the relationship of Jesus Christ to other religions. This coincides with an emphasis on relationality in feminist theology and an emphasis in contemporary Christology that there is an internal relationship between Jesus being the Christ and the church. A new category is emerging in Christology here. Traditionally, Jesus has been understood in terms of his person and work. But in the contemporary context, this is no longer sufficient. Jesus must now be understood as the Christ in terms of a third category, relationships, that includes his relationship to the church, to social movements, and to other religions. In the diverse world of postmodernity, Jesus needs to be understood as the Christ in terms of his person, his saving work, and his relationships.

A new issue arising from external developments in contemporary contexts is the challenge of the environmental crisis to contemporary Christology. In the past forty years, there has been a growing emphasis on the presence of Christ in and in relation to nature and on the need for a materialization of Christian faith "in the sense of a thoroughgoing valuation of material creation and of that which preserves it,"[41] to overcome an all-too-frequent spiritualization of the gospel. The environmental crisis requires that this be taken further, that there be a rereading of the Gospels that reflects on the incarnation as an expression of God's love for the world and presence in it and that gives hope in the face of the overwhelming scope of the environmental crisis that empowers constructive action in relation to it.[42] The environmental crisis has emerged as an external factor that leads to the biblical witness being read in a new light. The bodily resurrection of Jesus, rather than being an embarrassing thought, now becomes a promise of hope for an imperiled creation. The incarnation similarly takes on radical new meaning in terms of God's presence in and to material creation.

A second new issue arising from external developments in contemporary contexts is that of enculturating Christology in cultures shaped largely by other religious traditions. The issues here run very deep. Some theologians working in India repudiate the Chalcedonian Definition as Western, abstract, and narrow in its soteriological concern. As the discussions of the Christologies of Raimon Panikkar and Jacques Dupuis show, the dialogue with Hinduism raises the question of how intrinsic the vision of God acting in history to bring it to fulfillment is to Christology. As the church in Asia and Africa grows and continues to produce its own theologians, and as indigenous peoples around the world reclaim their cultures and Christians within these communities begin to articulate Christologies in terms derived from them, a new diversity is likely to enter contemporary Christology. It is unclear how this will affect the unity of denominations that have a global presence.[43] In cultures shaped by other religions, Christologies are likely to develop a hybridity that may in turn affect Christologies in North Atlantic cultures. The challenge of enculturating the gospel is not simply to understand Jesus as the Christ in terms derived from non-Christian cultures and other religious traditions. The challenge is also that, as this happens, it raises questions about the enculturation of Christology in Western cultures as to what is authentic to Jesus in traditional and contemporary Christologies produced in North Atlantic contexts and what are cultural accretions that may not be essential to the gospel or even antithetical to it.

There are other internal and external developments of note. Issues of how Christ relates to the differently abled[44] have not been mentioned here and probably should have been. Questions of how Christ relates to the experience of communities with hybrid identities, Asian American,[45] Japanese-Canadian, could also have been mentioned. The use of theories of cultural memory to understand Jesus as the Christ may become important in the future.[46] But it is time to bring this conclusion to a close. After surveying fifteen contemporary Christologies, there is still more that could be said, and there are issues that have been left untouched. This reflects a dynamic in Christology, expressed in the patristic axiom, "that which is unassumed is unhealed," that continually leads to reflection on the person, work, and relationships of Jesus Christ to new issues, contexts, and horizons. This dynamic means that Christology is always on the way, never finished but continually developing; encountering new questions, returning again to its sources, rediscovering riches in its past, being enriched by encounter and dialogue with new forms of thought, other religions, cultural developments. As this survey shows, the tradition of reflection on Jesus Christ continues, deepened by these contemporary Christologies and yet still moving on.

## Suggestions for Further Reading

Bohache, Thomas. *Christology from the Margins*. London: SCM, 2008. Develops a queer Christology.

Delio, Ilia. *Christ in Evolution*. Maryknoll, N.Y.: Orbis, 2008. Writing from a Franciscan perspective, Delio develops a Christology in relation to the findings of the natural sciences and the pluralism of religions and cultures.

Pannenberg, Wolfhart. *Jesus—God and Man*. 2nd ed. Philadelphia: Westminster, 1977. Pannenberg's unique apologetic approach, while politically conservative, did much to establish the theological significance of the quest for the historical Jesus for contemporary Christology.

Placher, William C. *Jesus the Savior: The Meaning of Jesus Christ for Christian Faith*. Louisville: Westminster John Knox, 2001. An accessibly written and insightful Christology from an American postliberal approach.

Schillebeeckx, Edward. *Jesus: An Experiment in Christology*. New York: Seabury, 1979.

———. *Christ: The Experience of Jesus as Lord*. New York: Crossroad, 1980. These huge books by Schillebeeckx were an important and influential attempt to develop Christology in sustained dialogue with contemporary biblical scholarship.

Trelstad, Marit, ed. *Cross Examinations: Readings on the Meaning of the Cross Today*. Minneapolis: Fortress Press, 2006. An important collection of contemporary interpretations of Jesus' cross.

Wells, Harold. *The Christic Center: Life-Giving and Liberating*. Maryknoll, N.Y.: Orbis, 2004. Argues that Christology is at the center of Christian thought and life.

## Discussion Questions

1. If you have a denominational affiliation, does it influence your understanding of Jesus Christ?
2. Which models of the atonement do you find most adequate?
3. Would you agree that Christology needs to have the third category of "relationships" in addition to that of the "person" and "work" of Christ?
4. Is the quest for the historical Jesus important for contemporary Christologies?

# GLOSSARY

**Abelard, Peter** (1079–1142): Born in Pallet, Brittany, Abelard was an intellectual sensation in medieval Europe and contributed to the development of medieval logic and theology. He is famous for his moral influence theory of the atonement, in which Christ "saves" through the beauty of his moral example, which moves one to imitate his love for others.

**Advaita:** This is a school of thought within Hinduism emphasizing the identity of the self (Atman) with the divine ground of being (Brahman).

**Alexandrian Christology:** This was one of two approaches to understanding Jesus' person as both human and divine involved in the christological crises leading to the Council of Chalcedon. Its most influential proponent was Cyril of Alexandria (378–444). Cyril followed Athanasius in stressing that the Word of God assumed a human nature and functioned as the subjective center of the person of Jesus Christ.

**Anselm** (c. 1033–1109): Born in Aosta, Italy, Anselm became a monk in 1060 and, in 1093, archbishop of Canterbury. Anselm is famous for his theoretical proof of God and his understanding of the atonement, in which Christ became incarnate and died on the cross to pay the penalty for human sin, thus winning the forgiveness of and reconciliation to God for people.

**Anti-Judaism:** A slightly more benign form of anti-Semitism, anti-Judaism is a denigrating portrayal of Judaism frequently found in New Testament texts and Christologies from the New Testament to the present, which presents Judaism and Jewish leaders and movements like the Pharisees as the antithesis to the moral righteousness of Jesus.

**Antiochene Christology:** This was one of two approaches to understanding how Jesus was both human and divine involved in the christological crises leading to the Council of Chalcedon. The most influential theologian of this school was Theodore of Mopsuestia (d. 428). Theodore stressed the individual person of Jesus, his development as a person, and his struggle to follow the will of God, inspired by the indwelling of the Word.

**Apologetics:** Apologetics is a defense of the legitimacy of Christian faith. This may be developed in relation to challenges coming from contemporary forms of knowledge and experience, or regarding the historical effects of Christianity.

**Arius:** A presbyter of Bishop Alexander, in 320, Arius's questioning of his bishop's christological views, and his promotion of his own, began the Arian controversy over the divinity of Jesus, which led to the Council of Nicaea (325), which affirmed Jesus' divinity and the trinitarian nature of God. Arius believed that, as God was absolute and immutable, Jesus could not be fully divine but was rather the highest part of creation.

**Ascending Christology:** The term *ascending Christology* was coined by Karl Rahner. It refers to a study of Jesus Christ that traces the continuity of the confession of Jesus as the Second Person of the Trinity with Jesus of Nazareth and the experience of him as the Christ. This is sometimes called a "Christology from below," with the difference that an ascending Christology is usually supplemented and completed by a descending Christology, whereas a Christology from below is usually seen as an alternative to a Christology from above.

**Atonement:** This term refers to the saving significance of Jesus Christ, what Christ does to effect a change in people's lives that "saves" them from sin and brings them closer to God. While it is often understood to refer to forgiveness of sin, its meaning is actually much broader, encompassing a variety of the changes Christ effects, such as empowerment, reorientation, and providing comfort and hope, that affect a person's whole life.

**Atonement models:** These refer to ways in which Jesus' atoning work or significance is understood. For instance, the moral influence theory or model of atonement sees Jesus saving people by reorienting people's will and strengthening their love, moving them to act in efficacious ways. The three classical atonement models are the Christus Victor (chapter 3), moral influence (chapter 2), and substitutionary or vicarious satisfaction theory (chapter 4).

**Aulén, Gustaf** (1879–1977): A Swedish theologian, composer, and bishop, Aulén belonged to a Swedish movement known as the Lundsenian school of theology. His chief contribution to contemporary Christology has been his formulation of a typology of three types of atonement theory in his book *Christus Victor*. Aulén's much discussed typology continues to be referred to and remains insightful regarding the characteristics of the atonement models he analyzed.

**Barth, Karl** (1886–1968): One of the most influential twentieth-century Protestant theologians, Barth was born in Switzerland and studied liberal theology in Germany. His shock at his liberal professors' support for Germany's involvement in World War I was one of several factors leading him to renounce the approach of liberal theology in favor of an emphasis on the otherness of God and the defining significance of Jesus Christ for all knowledge of God.

**Bloch, Ernst** (1885–1977): Born in Germany of Jewish descent, Bloch developed a humanistic interpretation of Marxism that stressed hope for the future as expressed in religion, visual arts, literature, and music. His philosophy deeply influenced the theologies of Wolfhart Pannenberg and Jürgen Moltmann in their initial stages.

**Bonhoeffer, Dietrich** (1906–1945): Dietrich Bonhoeffer was raised in a nominally Protestant German family with academic leanings. He studied theology and was briefly a pastor. He was influenced by Karl Barth but remained an independent thinker and became a leading figure in the German Protestant resistance to Hitler. He was hung by the Nazis. His theology, including his idea of Christ as representative and as the person for others, has become widely influential in the post–World War II era.

**Bultmann, Rudolf** (1884–1976): Bultmann was foremost a New Testament scholar, but his wide-ranging work on the New Testament and hermeneutics made him an influential figure in twentieth-century Protestant thought. Bultmann argued that the New Testament message could only be meaningful in the present if it was demythologized and reinterpreted in terms corresponding to experience in the modern West. For Bultmann, Jesus is risen in the faith of his followers, and it is primarily the Christ of faith, not the historical Jesus, that is significant for Christian faith.

**Chalcedonian Definition:** This is the statement of faith issued at the Council of Chalcedon, which has become a much-discussed landmark regarding how the person of Jesus Christ should be understood. The relevant text of the Definition is as follows:

Therefore, following the holy Fathers, we all with one accord teach men to acknowledge one and the same Son, our Lord Jesus Christ, at once complete in Godhead and complete in manhood, truly God and truly man, consisting also of a reasonable soul and body; of one substance . . . with the Father as regards his Godhead, and at the same time of one substance with us as regards his manhood; like us in all respects, apart from sin; as regards his Godhead, begotten of the Father before the ages, but yet as regards his manhood begotten, for us men and for our salvation, of Mary the Virgin, the God-bearer . . . ; one and the same Christ, Son, Lord, Only-begotten, recognized in two natures, without confusion, without change, without division, without separation; the distinction of natures being in no way annulled by the union, but rather the characteristics of each nature being preserved and coming together to form one person and subsistence . . . , not as parted or separated into two persons, but one and the same Son and Only-begotten God the Word, Lord Jesus Christ; even as the prophets from earliest times spoke of him, and our Lord Jesus Christ himself taught us, and the creed of the Fathers has handed down to us (from *Documents of the Christian Church*, ed. Henry Bettenson, 2nd ed. [New York: Oxford University Press, 1963], 51–52).

**Christology from above:** *See* descending Christology.

**Christology from below:** *See* ascending Christology.

**Classical Christology:** This is generally another term for the Christologies of Nicaea and Chalcedon.

**Congregation for the Doctrine of the Faith:** This is the oldest of nine Vatican congregations. It originated in 1542 under Pope Paul III and was called the Sacred Congregation of the Universal Inquisition, as it was to defend the church from heresy. Its current role is to safeguard the orthodoxy of Roman Catholic teaching and morals.

**Consubstantiality:** Consubstantiality is defined as sharing a common substance or nature with others of the same species or genus.

**Council of Nicaea:** The Council of Nicaea was an ecumenical church council, held in the year 325. It was called and presided over by the Roman emperor Constantine, who called it to establish unity in the church, which had been disrupted by the Arian crisis. One of the council's landmark decisions was that Jesus was fully divine, and that God was eternally triune.

**Council of Chalcedon:** The Council of Chalcedon was held in 451, at the instigation of the emperor Marcian, to restore the unity of the church that had been fragmented by the Christological crises arising from the dispute between the Antiochene and Alexandrian schools of Christology. The council is famous for its affirmation of the Chalcedonian Definition, stating that Jesus was fully human and fully divine, the two natures united without confusion in his one person.

**Descending Christology:** A term coined by Karl Rahner, *descending Christology* denotes an approach to understanding Jesus as the Christ from a trinitarian perspective, seeking to understand his incarnation, life, death, and resurrection in terms of the trinitarian life of God. A descending Christology usually follows, supplements, and completes an ascending Christology, sometimes called a "Christology from above," with the difference that a descending Christology depends on a prior ascending Christology, whereas "Christologies from above," such as Karl Barth's, usually do not.

**Demythologization:** *See* Bultmann, Rudolf.

**Dualism:** This is a view that sees differences in gender, race, religion, or ethnicity as signaling essential differences between people and that values one as morally superior to the other.

**Enculturation:** Enculturation refers to the reinterpretation of Christian faith in the terms and concepts of a culture different from that in which the basis for its present terms and concepts arose.

**Enlightenment:** The Enlightenment was a epochal western European cultural, philosophical, and political movement straddling the eighteenth century, partially provoked by the carnage of the wars of religion. It was marked by a turn away from external authorities and traditions and toward autonomous and critical thinking. Many Enlightenment thinkers opposed traditional Christian beliefs as superstition and repudiated or sought to rationalize them in relation to developing fields of knowledge like the natural sciences and modern historiography.

**Heidegger, Martin** (1889–1976): Possibly the most influential philosopher of the twentieth century, Martin Heidegger was born in Germany and raised as a Roman Catholic. His early philosophy followed existentialism in exploring the nature of human existence. His later philosophy was profoundly critical of the history of much of Western philosophy in its analysis of the nature of language, technology, and the philosophical task. Heidegger's early philosophy provided Bultmann and others with categories in terms of which the gospel could be interpreted in a pastorally powerful but nonmythological way.

**Historical Jesus:** This refers not to Jesus as portrayed in the New Testament but to what can be known about Jesus through historical inquiry into the New Testament and other documents. The quest for the historical Jesus began in the eighteenth century, with Hermann Samuel Reimarus. The quest has gone through several stages, each marking some change in criteria and interest. Though it remains controversial, it became an important aspect of many Western Christologies in the 1960s.

**Hypostatic union:** *Hypostasis* is a Greek term of variable meaning referring to substance. Over the course of the christological debates, it came to mean "concrete reality." The hypostatic union was the teaching affirmed at the Council of Chalcedon that in Jesus the divine and human natures were united in his one person, or *hypostasis*.

**Incarnation:** In Christian thought, the teaching that the Second Person of the Trinity assumed flesh and became uniquely present in the person of Jesus of Nazareth is referred to as the incarnation.

**Kenosis:** Kenosis is a Greek term meaning "emptying." Philippians 2:6-7, where Paul describes the incarnation as occurring through Christ emptying himself, is the source for kenotic Christologies, which see the incarnation as involving a humble emptying of Christ's self. In Christian thought, this has come to be paradigmatic for Christian understanding of kenosis.

**Liberation theology:** This is a theological movement originating in Latin America in the late 1960s, flowering in the 1970s and 1980s, which reconceived salvation as including liberation from economic and military oppression. Liberation theology analyzes societies in terms of the social conflicts within them between rich and poor. It argues that Jesus reveals God to have a preferential option for the poor and that the church must express this in its social presence.

**Logos:** "Word" is the literal translation for this term, but in Hellenistic thought, particularly Stoic philosophy, it referred to the rational structure or law of the universe. This term was adopted as a christological title in the early church because of its use in the Gospel of John and its resonances in Hellenistic culture. Logos Christologies tend to be descending Christologies, seeing Jesus as the Word of God incarnate, following the lead of John's Gospel.

**Logos *asarkos*:** The Word of God or Second Person of the Trinity, prior to becoming incarnate in Jesus of Nazareth.

**Logos *ensarkos*:** The Word of God or Second Person of the Trinity, having become incarnate in Jesus of Nazareth.

**Patristic theology:** The patristics, or "fathers," are the theologians of the first centuries of the church, as it became enculturated in the Roman Empire. The patristic period is variously described as stretching from roughly 150 to 500 or 800. Patristic theology and Christology was produced in this era.

**Pluralism:** Pluralism is a situation characterized by a number of different and not easily reconciled views of reality.

**Political theology:** This is a term for the concern by German theologians like Dorothee Soelle, Johann Baptist Metz, and Jürgen Moltmann to emphasis the public dimensions and meanings of Christian faith and theology. It developed in the 1960s through Christian-Marxist dialogues and was an influence on the rise of Latin American liberation theology. The term was also used by Carl Schmitt in pre–World War II Germany for his theology, which supported an authoritarian state.

**Postmodern:** A term that first became popular in North Atlantic discourse in the late 1970s, *postmodern* refers to a cultural context marked by a pluralism of forms of knowledge, experience, religions, and cultures, frequently difficult to reconcile with one another, though each often has a local validity. The postmodern cultural context has emerged out of the modern and is characterized by an ethos that values highly the recognition of and respect for difference.

**Preferential option for the poor:** The preferential option for the poor is a guiding principle for Christian thought and life, formulated first in black theology (James Cone) and Latin American liberation theology, deriving its name from the latter. The preferential option for the poor acts to effect salvation in social terms by siding with the poor and marginalized in their conflicts with the powerful. The preferential option demands that one interpret society from the perspective and experience of the poor, and that one express public solidarity with them in their struggles against oppression.

**Process theology:** This was a major theological movement of the twentieth century, using the process philosophy of Alfred North Whitehead (1861–1947) as a conceptual basis for expounding a contemporary understanding of the Christian faith.

**Proleptic:** A proleptic event is one occurring ahead of its time and in anticipation of its coming in fullness. Thus, the ministry of Jesus is said to be a proleptic revelation of the coming reign of God.

**Schleiermacher, Friedrich** (1768–1834): Schleiermacher is often described as the initiator of modern Protestant theology. He repudiated belief in miracles, arguing that religions was based on a feeling of absolute dependence shared by all, and that Christ saved by the influence of his God-consciousness on the consciousness of others. Once described as an atheist, Schleiermacher is one of the most influential of modern theologians.

**Scholasticism:** Scholasticism was an approach to philosophy and theology that flowered in the Middle Ages, particularly in the thought of Thomas Aquinas. Scholasticism assumes the teaching authority of the church and hence the contents of Christian faith as a given. Medieval scholastics then sought to understand this teaching and to answer questions arising in relation to it with the aid of the philosophy of Aristotle primarily, but also Plato, and by drawing on the teachings of preceding theologians who had become accepted as authoritative within the church.

**Secularism:** This is an ethos in which large portions of life and society are independent of direct religious influence or control, and in which religion is typically seen as a private matter and not afforded public recognition or support.

**Secularization:** Secularization refers to the removal of aspects of life and society from direct religious influence or control.

**Soteriology:** Soteriology is the understanding of the saving significance of Jesus Christ.

**Spirit Christology:** Spirit Christologies tend to see Jesus as a person inspired by the Holy Spirit, to the point that he becomes paradigmatic for all those who are so inspired. Spirit Christologies tend to stress the inspired humanity of Jesus and are often characterized as ascending Christologies or Christologies from below.

**Substance:** Substance is a category in Aristotelian philosophy pertaining to the essential nature of any entity. According to Aristotle, horses, carrots, and human beings each have their particular kind of substance (nature or being), distinct from that of others. Aristotle's notion of substances influenced the debates about the divinity and humanity of Jesus Christ that led to the Councils of Nicaea and Chalcedon and up until the Enlightenment. The influence of this category in Christian thought has waned as the result of developments in modern Western philosophy and the natural sciences.

**"The unassumed is the unhealed":** This phrase was the articulation by Gregory of Nazianzus (Letter 101) of a principle underlying what was affirmed at the Councils of Nicaea and Chalcedon as orthodox Christology. It is present in the Christologies of Athanasius, Origen, Cyril of Alexandria, as well as the Cappadocians. It states that any part of humanity that God has not taken on in the incarnation is not saved.

**Theodicy:** Literally "theos"—God, "dicy"—justice; theodicy refers to the question of the justice of God in relation to the experience of evil. Classically expressed, the question of theodicy is, If God is good and God is powerful, why is there evil?

**Tillich, Paul** (1886–1965): Tillich, a German Lutheran, broke with liberal theology in response to his experiences as a German army chaplain in World War I. He subsequently became involved in religious socialism and had to flee Germany as a result of his 1930s book *The Socialist Decision*. He went to the United States, where he developed his systematic theology, in which the gospel message is correlated as the answer to questions arising out of human cultural activity. Christ represents the new being for Tillich, in whom the alienation and contradictions of historical being are overcome.

**Trinity:** The Christian concept of God, affirmed at the Council of Nicaea, that developed under the impact of faith in Jesus Christ and the enculturation of the gospel as Christianity became a Gentile religion in a culture profoundly influenced by Hellenistic thought. The doctrine of the Trinity affirms that God is one yet exists in three persons: God the Creator and Redeemer, Jesus Christ, and the Holy Spirit, who share one divine nature.

**Vatican II:** The Second Ecumenical Council of the Vatican (Vatican II), the twenty-first Ecumenical Council of the Roman Catholic Church, opened under Pope John XXIII on October 11, 1962. It closed under Pope Paul VI on December 8, 1965. The council, an epochal event in the history of the Roman Catholic Church, marked a major turn in direction, inaugurating a new openness to the modern world, other churches, and religions.

**Western modernity:** Western modernity denotes a cultural epoch originating in Europe, centered in Europe and North America, stretching from the 1700s to roughly the 1960s, characterized by the rapid advance of the natural sciences, both in their findings and social influence, the functional differentiation of society, the application of advances in technology to many aspects of life, globalization, an unsustainable consumption of natural resources, and an emphasis on freedom and autonomy coupled with colonial conquests.

**Wiesel, Elie** (1928–): Wiesel is a Jewish author and essayist, a Holocaust survivor whose writings reflect his experience of Nazi death camps. His memoir *Night* is frequently quoted and referred to in Christian theology reflecting on the Holocaust.

# NOTES

## Introduction

1. John Meier, *A Marginal Jew: Rethinking The Historical Jesus*, vol. 1, *The Roots of the Problem and the Person* (New York: Doubleday, 1991), 407.

2. For instance, Romans 1:3-4.

3. For an analysis of the theological significance of many of the events and developments mentioned here, see *The Twentieth Century: A Theological Overview*, ed. Gregory Baum (Maryknoll, N.Y.: Orbis, 1999).

4. David Tracy, *Blessed Rage for Order* (Minneapolis: Winston/Seabury, 1975), 5.

5. Edith Wyschogrod, "Man-Made Mass Death: Shifting Concepts of Community," *Journal of the American Academy of Religion* LVII, no. 2 (1990): 165.

6. Gustaf Aulén, *Christus Victor* (London: SPCK, 1950).

7. For an introduction to contemporary African Christologies, see Diane Stinton, *Jesus of Africa: Voices of Contemporary African Christology* (Maryknoll, N.Y.: Orbis, 2004).

## Chapter 1. Jesus as Revealer

1. Martin Buber, *Eclipse of God* (New York: Harper & Row, 1952), 3–9.

2. Charles Taylor, *A Secular Age* (Cambridge, Mass.: Belknap Press of Harvard University, 2007), 542–43.

3. *The Music Man*: http://www.stlyrics.com/t/themusicman.htm (accessed June 8, 2007).

4. Herbert Vorgrimler, *Karl Rahner: His Life, Thought and Work* (London: Burns and Oates, 1965), 16–17.

5. For an estimation of Heidegger's influence on Rahner, see Gaspar Marquez, *Confronting the Mystery of God* (New York: Continuum, 2001), 3–4.

6. Marquez describes this as follows: "*Geist in Welt* can be defined as a Maréchalean interpretation of Aquinas's metaphysics of knowledge in a Heideggerian key that takes up the questions raised by Kant's critique of knowledge, bearing in mind Hegel's critique of Kant's position," Marquez, *Confronting the Mystery of God*, 2.

7. Karl Rahner, *Spirit in the World*, revised by J. B. Metz (London: Sheed and Ward, 1968).

8. Karl Rahner, *Hearers of the Word*, revised by J. B. Metz (London: Sheed and Ward, 1969).

9. J. A. Di Noia, "Karl Rahner," in *The Modern Theologians*, ed. David Ford, 2nd ed. (Malden, Mass.: Blackwell, 1997), 119.

10. Anne Carr, "Starting with the Human," in *A World of Grace*, ed. Leo O'Donovan (New York: Seabury, 1980), 18.

11. Karl Rahner, *Theological Investigations* (Baltimore: Helicon, 1966), 4:106.

12. Karl-Heinz Weger, *Karl Rahner* (New York: Seabury, 1980), 5.

13. Otto Muck, *The Transcendental Method* (New York: Herder and Herder, 1968).

14. Weger, *Karl Rahner*, 21–22.

15. Karl Rahner, *Foundations of Christian Faith* (New York: Crossroad, 1989), 32.

16. Ibid., 33.

17. Patrick Burke, *Reinterpreting Rahner* (New York: Fordham University Press, 2002), 37.

18. Rahner, *Foundations of Christian Faith*, 39.

19. Karl Rahner, in *Sacramentum Mundi*, ed. Karl Rahner, et al. (New York: Herder and Herder, 1969), s.v. "Jesus Christ: 4. History of Dogma and Theology."

20. Rahner, *Theological Investigations*, 4:128.

21. John McDermott, "The Christologies of Karl Rahner—2," *Gregorianum* 67, no. 2 (1986): 312.

22. Karl Rahner, *The Love of Jesus and the Love of Neighbor* (New York: Crossroad, 1983), 56–57. See also the translator's note in Karl Rahner, *Theological Investigations* (London: Darton, Longman & Todd, 1961), 1:175n1.

23. Rahner, *The Love of Jesus and the Love of Neighbor*, 60.

24. Rahner, *Foundations of Christian Faith*, 220.

25. John McDermott, "The Christologies of Karl Rahner," *Gregorianum* 67, no. 1 (1986): 114; McDermott, "The Christologies of Karl Rahner—2," 317.

26. Rahner, *Theological Investigations*, 4:237.

27. Rahner, *The Love of Jesus and the Love of Neighbor*, 56; Joseph Wong, *Logos-Symbol in the Christology of Karl Rahner* (Rome: Libreria Aléno Salesiano, 1984), 203–5.

28. Gregory of Nazianzus, *On God and Christ* (Crestwood, N.Y.: St. Vladimir's Seminary Press, 2002), 158.

29. Jaroslav Pelikan, *The Christian Tradition*, vol. 1, *The Emergence of the Catholic Tradition (100–600)* (Chicago: University of Chicago Press, 1971), 268.

30. Burke, *Reinterpreting Rahner*, 154–58.

31. Rahner, *Foundations of Christian Faith*, 224.

32. Karl Rahner, *Theological Investigations* (New York: Crossroad, 1983), 19:30.

33. This enables Rahner to develop his theory of anonymous Christians, in which other religions perceive something of the truth of God, who is always present, but not the fullness of that truth that is revealed in Jesus Christ. In discussions of religious pluralism, Rahner's position is often referred to as "inclusivism." Other religions are included within Christianity as "anonymous Christians." But Christianity is seen to have a fuller apprehension of the truth; Jeannine Hill Fletcher, "Rahner and Religious Diversity," in *The Cambridge Companion to Karl Rahner*, ed. Declan Marmion and Mary Hines (New York: Cambridge University Press, 2005), 242.

34. Rahner, *The Love of Jesus and the Love of Neighbor*, 71.

35. Rahner, *Theological Investigations*, 4:129.

36. See Burke, *Reinterpreting Rahner*, 139n41, for a list of the many places where Rahner invokes this argument.

37. Wong, *Logos-Symbol in the Christology of Karl Rahner*, 235.

38. Gustavo Gutiérrez, *The Truth Shall Make You Free* (Maryknoll, N.Y.: Orbis, 1990), 22–25.

39. Dorothee Soelle, *Against the Wind* (Minneapolis: Fortress Press, 1999), 18–20.

40. Ibid., 24.

41. Ibid., 37–41, 86–89.

42. Dorothee Soelle, *Stations of the Cross* (Minneapolis: Fortress Press, 1993), 93.

43. Dorothee Soelle, *The Truth Is Concrete* (New York: Herder and Herder, 1969), 21–26.

44. Ibid., 14.

45. Dorothee Soelle, *Thinking about God* (Philadelphia: Trinity Press International, 1990), 187–88. For a somewhat different analysis of shifts in Soelle's Christology, see Dianne Oliver, "Christ in the World," in *The Theology of Dorothee Soelle*, ed. Sarah Pinnock (Harrisburg, Penn.: Trinity Press International, 2003), 117–18.

46. Dorothee Soelle, *Christ the Representative* (London: SCM, 1967), 39–42.

47. Dorothee Soelle, *Death by Bread Alone* (Philadelphia: Fortress Press, 1978), 4.

48. Dorothee Soelle, *The Window of Vulnerability* (Minneapolis: Fortress Press, 1990), 13.

49. Ibid., 12–13.

50. Ibid., 13.

51. Soelle, *Christ the Representative*, 15.

52. Soelle, *Death by Bread Alone*, 130.

53. Michael Welker, *God the Spirit* (Minneapolis: Fortress Press, 1994), 44.

54. Soelle, *Death by Bread Alone*, 3–10.

55. Soelle discusses her relationship to the institutional church in *Against the Wind*, 90–95.

56. Soelle, *Christ the Representative*, 10–12. For Soelle, the phrase "theology after the death of God" refers to theology done in the context of secular Western societies, which has adopted the immanent perspective on reality characteristic of those societies, in which interventions by God in history are no longer expected and religion is viewed ambivalently.

57. Dorothee Soelle, *Suffering* (Philadelphia: Fortress Press, 1975), 7–8.

58. Dorothee Soelle, *Beyond Mere Obedience* (New York: Pilgrim, 1982), 4.

59. Dorothee Soelle, *Political Theology* (Philadelphia: Fortress Press, 1974), 64.

60. Dorothee Soelle and Luise Schottroff, *Jesus of Nazareth* (Louisville: Westminster John Knox, 2002), 140–41.

61. Ibid.; Soelle, *Political Theology*, 27–28.

62. Soelle, *Christ the Representative*, 104–5, 134–35.

63. Ibid., 46.

64. Ibid., 31, 46–47.

65. Ibid., 148–49.

66. Ibid., 105.

67. Ibid., 69–71. At this point, and occasionally throughout her later writings, Soelle described God as personal and as an active agent. But in her later writings

she generally described God as the power of relationship; Soelle, *Thinking About God*, 192–95. This ambiguity may reflect in part her never having worked out an understanding of Jesus' person to account for her understanding of his saving significance.

68. Soelle and Schottroff, *Jesus of Nazareth*, 122.

69. Soelle, *Christ the Representative*, 121.

70. Ibid., 143.

71. Soelle, *Stations of the Cross*, 92.

72. Jürgen Moltmann, *The Crucified God* (London: SCM, 1974), 262–64.

73. Dorothee Soelle, *The Mystery of Death* (Minneapolis: Fortress Press, 2007), 124–28.

74. Helmut Peukert, *Science, Action, and Fundamental Theology* (Cambridge, Mass.: MIT Press, 1984), 205–10, 231–45.

75. Soelle, *Thinking about God*, 171–82.

76. David Tracy, *Blessed Rage for Order* (Minneapolis: Winston/Seabury, 1975), 4–7.

77. Ibid., 13.

78. Information at: http://www.utsnyc.edu/Page.aspx?&pid=341 (accessed July 11, 2007).

79. Information at: http://divinity.uchicago.edu/alumni/awards/haight.shtml (accessed July 11, 2007).

80. Congregation for the Doctrine of the Faith, "Notification on the book 'Jesus Symbol of God' by Father Roger Haight S.J.; http://www.vatican.va/roman_curia/congregations/cfaith/documents/rc_con_cfaith_doc_20041213_notification-fr-haight_en.html (accessed July 11, 2007).

81. Roger Haight, *Jesus, Symbol of God* (Maryknoll, N.Y.: Orbis, 1999), xii; idem, *The Future of Christology* (New York: Continuum, 2005), 129.

82. Haight, *Jesus, Symbol of God*, 331.

83. Haight, *The Future of Christology*, 34, 129–30; *Jesus, Symbol of God*, 333.

84. For the four characteristics that follow, see Haight, *The Future of Christology*, 128–29.

85. Haight, *Jesus, Symbol of God*, 24.

86. Ibid., 430–31.

87. Ibid., 333.

88. In terms of relating Christian faith to other religions, Haight represents a position that has come to be known as religious pluralism. Here, Jesus is normative for Christians and the basis by which they evaluate other religions and discern God's presence therein. But the Christian perception of truth can be enriched by dialogue with other religions, and there is no sense that Christianity represents an objectively superior apprehension and relationship to God; Haight, *Jesus, Symbol of God*, 410.

89. Ibid., 333.

90. Ibid., 334.

91. Haight, *Jesus, Symbol of God*, 428–29.

92. Ibid., 183.

93. Haight, *The Future of Christology*, 95–96, 101.

94. Haight, *Jesus, Symbol of God*, 238, 239, 342.

95. Ibid., 359. This is very close to the summary Haight gives of Schleiermacher's understanding of Jesus' saving significance; ibid., 350.

96. Ibid., 392.

97. Ibid., 410.

98. Ibid., 415.

99. Ibid., 465.

100. Ibid., 464.

101. Ibid., 461.

102. Ibid., 296.

103. Ibid., 463–64.

104. Gerd Theissen, *The Religion of the Earliest Churches* (Minneapolis: Fortress Press, 1999), 273–74.

105. Wolfhart Pannenberg, *Jesus—God and Man*, 2nd ed. (Philadelphia: Westminster, 1977), 156.

106. Haight, *Jesus, Symbol of God*, 484–85.

107. Ibid., 488.

108. Gregory Baum, *Religion and Alienation* (New York: Paulist, 1975), 222.

109. Taylor, *A Secular Age*, 542.

## Chapter 2. Jesus as Moral Exemplar

1. Abelard, "A Solution," in *A Scholastic Miscellany: Anselm to Ockham*, trans. and ed. Eugene Fairweather (Philadelphia: Westminster, 1956), 283.

2. This is the third of Gustaf Aulén's three types, or models, of the atonement; Gustaf Aulén, *Christus Victor* (London: SPCK, 1950), 163, 112–13.

3. Charles Taylor, *A Secular Age* (Cambridge, Mass.: Belknap Press of Harvard University, 2007), 545.

4. Paul Tillich, *Systematic Theology* (Chicago: University of Chicago Press, 1957), 2:171.

5. Rosemary Radford Ruether, "Religion and Society: Sacred Canopy or Prophetic Critique?" in *The Future of Liberation Theology*, ed. Marc Ellis and Otto Maduro (Maryknoll, N.Y.: Orbis, 1989), 174–75; Carter Heyward, *Our Passion for Justice* (New York: Pilgrim, 1984), 113–14; Mark Lewis Taylor, *The Executed God: The Way of the Cross in Lockdown America* (Minneapolis: Fortress Press, 2001), 134–35.

6. Of the three authors studied in the previous chapter, Dorothee Soelle is closest to Ruether, Taylor, and particularly to Heyward in her understanding of Jesus' saving significance. But Soelle resisted restricting Jesus' meaning to the action he inspires. For Soelle's resistance to this kind of restriction, see Dorothee Soelle, *Death by Bread Alone* (Philadelphia: Fortress Press, 1978), 36.

7. "Rosemary Radford Ruether biography," http://www.bookrags.com/biography/rosemary-radford-ruether (accessed Dec. 21, 2007).

8. Rosemary Radford Ruether, "Beginnings: An Intellectual Autobiography," in *Journeys,* ed. Gregory Baum (New York: Paulist, 1975), 41.

9. Ibid., 54; Rosemary Radford Ruether, *Disputed Questions* (Nashville: Abingdon, 1982), 76–80.

10. Grant D. Miller Francisco, "Rosemary Radford Ruether (1936–)" http://people.bu.edu/wwildman/WeirdWildWeb/courses/mwt/dictionary/mwt_themes_908_ruether.htm (accessed Dec. 21, 2007).

11. Mary Hembrow Snyder, *The Christology of Rosemary Radford Ruether: A Critical Introduction* (Mystic, Conn.: Twenty-Third Publications, 1988), 29. For an account of the development of Ruether's theological methodology, see ibid., 3–26.

12. Rosemary Radford Ruether, "Religion for Women: Sources and Strategies," *Christianity and Crisis* 39 (1979): 308

13. Rosemary Radford Ruether, "Asking the Existential Questions," in *Theologians in Transition*, ed. James Wall (New York: Crossroad, 1981), 162–68.

14. Rita M. Gross and Rosemary Radford Ruether, *Religious Feminism and the Future of the Planet* (New York: Continuum, 2001), 148, 186.

15. Rosemary Radford Ruether, "The Development of My Theology," in *Religious Studies Review* 15, no. 1 (1989): 2. Ruether lists the social issues in relation to which she has pursued this approach as follows: "racism, religious bigotry, especially anti-Semitism, sexism, class hierarchy, colonialism, militarism, and ecological damage," ibid.

16. Ruether, *Disputed Questions*, 142.

17. Ibid.

18. Ibid., 46, 35–42. Ruether also notes the possible influence of her Jewish uncle; ibid., 43–44.

19. Ibid., 46.

20. Ibid., 47.

21. For Ruether's account of this work and its importance for her thought, see ibid., 51. For a discussion of some of its contents, see Snyder, *The Christology of Rosemary Radford Ruether*, 30–48.

22. Rosemary Radford Ruether, "An Invitation to Jewish-Christian Dialogue: In What Sense Can We Say That Jesus Was 'the Christ'?" *The Ecumenist* 10, no. 2 (1972): 19.

23. Ibid., 18, 20. Ruether seems to overlook that those who first proclaimed Jesus as the Christ were Jews, not least of all Paul of Tarsus.

24. Sarah Pinnock notes that in some respects, Jewish-Christian dialogue has moved beyond Ruether's rejection of classical Christology. In recent dialogue, there "is no demand on the Jewish side" for the reworking of classical Christology; Sarah Pinnock, "Atrocity and Ambiguity: Recent Developments in Christian Holocaust Responses," *Journal of the American Academy of Religion* 75, no. 3 (2007): 506.

25. Rosemary Radford Ruether, "The Adversus Jedaeos Tradition in the Church Fathers: The Exegesis of Christian Anti-Judaism," in *Essential Papers on Judaism and Christianity in Conflict*, ed. Jeremy Cohen (New York: New York University Press, 1991), 186–88.

26. Ruether, "An Invitation to Jewish-Christian Dialogue," 22.

27. Ibid.

28. Rosemary Radford Ruether, "Can Christology Be Liberated from Patriarchy?" in *Reconstructing the Christ Symbol*, ed. Maryanne Stevens (Mahwah, N.J.: Paulist, 1993), 22.

29. Rosemary Radford Ruether, *Faith and Fratricide* (New York: Seabury, 1974).

30. Ibid., 66.

31. Rosemary Radford Ruether, *Sexism and God-Talk* (Boston: Beacon, 1983), 33.

32. Rosemary Radford Ruether, *Introducing Redemption in Christian Feminism* (Sheffield: Sheffield Academic Press, 1998), 87.

33. Rosemary Radford Ruether, *To Change the World: Christology and Cultural Criticism* (London: SCM, 1981), 20. For an analysis of this term, which Ruether takes from Latin American liberation theology, see Gregory Baum, "Afterword," in *Faith That Transforms*, ed. Mary Jo Leddy and Mary Ann Hinsdale (Mahwah, N.J.: Paulist, 1987), 140–46. According to Baum, the preferential option for the poor means to analyze from perspective of the poor and to publicly stand in solidarity with them.

34. Ruether, *To Change the World,* 5.

35. Ruether, "Can Christology Be Liberated from Patriarchy?" 24.

36. Ruether, *To Change the World*, 5.

37. Ruether, *Introducing Redemption*, 102.

38. Ruether, *Faith and Fratricide*, 69.

39. Ruether, *Introducing Redemption*, 107.

40. A "critical theory" can be defined as an attempt at understanding reality that seeks to uncover the causes of suffering in the present and show how they can be overcome. For a discussion of Ruether's theology as a critical theory, see Marsha Hewitt, *Critical Theory of Religion* (Minneapolis: Fortress Press, 1995), 173–84, 198–206.

41. Ruether, "Can Christology Be Liberated from Patriarchy?" 22.

42. Ibid.

43. For this understanding of sin, see Sallie McFague, *The Body of God* (Minneapolis: Fortress Press, 1993), 112–15. Ruether presents a similar understanding in her book, *God and Gaia* (New York: HarperCollins, 1992), 141–42.

44. Rosemary Radford Ruether, *Women and Redemption* (Minneapolis: Fortress Press, 1998), 223.

45. Ruether, *Gaia and God*, 251–52. For a critique of Ruether's notion that hope of eternal life lessens ethical concern for the present and undermines concern for the environment, see Elizabeth Johnson, *Friends of God and Prophets* (New York: Continuum, 1999), 195–97.

46. Ruether, *Introducing Redemption*, 106, 119.

47. For Heyward's critical appreciation of Ruether's theology, see Carter Heyward, *Our Passion for Justice* (New York: Pilgrim, 1984), 55–68.

48. "Finding Aid for Carter Heyward Papers, 1967–1998," prepared by Leslie Reyman for The Archive of Women in Theological Scholarship, The Burke Library, Union Theological Seminary: www.columbia.edu/cu/lweb/img/assets/6396/Heyward_CFA51305PDF2.pdf (accessed Jan. 14, 2008).

49. Carter Heyward, *The Redemption of God* (New York: University Press of America, 1982), 196; idem, *Saving Jesus from Those Who Are Right* (Minneapolis: Fortress Press, 1999), 118.

50. Heyward, *Saving Jesus*, 117–18.

51. There is an account of this in Carter Heyward, *A Priest Forever* (Cleveland: Pilgrim, 1976).

52. Reyman, "Finding Aid for Carter Heyward Papers," 2.

53. Carter Heyward, *Flying Changes: Horses as Spiritual Teachers*, photographs by Beverly Hall (Cleveland: Pilgrim, 2005), 24–25.

54. Heyward, *The Redemption of God*, xv–xix. For Heyward's account of what led to this crisis, see Heyward, *Saving Jesus*, 28–29.

55. Carter Heyward, *God in the Balance* (Cleveland: Pilgrim, 2002), 28.

56. Heyward, *Saving Jesus*, 118.

57. Heyward, *Our Passion for Justice*, 212.

58. Carter Heyward, *Touching Our Strength* (San Francisco: Harper & Row, 1989), 117.

59. Heyward, *Saving Jesus,* 66.

60. The analysis is drawn from her 1980 sermon "Redefining Power" in Heyward, *Our Passion for Justice*, 116–22. See also Heyward, *The Redemption of God*, 47.

61. Heyward, *Touching Our Strength*, 22–23; idem, *Speaking of Christ*, ed. Ellen Davis (Cleveland: Pilgrim, 1989), 29.

62. Heyward, *Our Passion for Justice*, 121.

63. For Heyward, "bounded" relationships are ones in which people's desires and ability to enter into mutual, nonhierarchical relationships are restricted by rules, codes of conduct, or prejudices that keep them confined to certain roles and limits that they are forbidden to go beyond; Heyward, *Saving Jesus*, 137–41. This assessment grew in part out of her experience with a therapist, discussed in Carter Heyward, *When Boundaries Betray Us* (New York: HarperCollins, 1993).

64. Heyward, *Saving Jesus*, xi–xiv.

65. Carter Heyward, "Doing Theology in a Counterrevolutionary Situation," in *The Future of Liberation Theology*, ed. Ellis and Maduro, 404.

66. Heyward, *Touching Our Strength*, 66–67.

67. Heyward, *Saving Jesus*, 175.

68. Heyward, *The Redemption of God*, 6; Heyward, *Saving Jesus*, 61–62.

69. Heyward, *Saving Jesus*, 66.

70. Ibid., 140. Heyward's understanding of God is like that of process theology, but she denies that God has a primordial nature that transcends history; Heyward, *The Redemption of God,* 64–65.

71. Heyward, *The Redemption of God*, 160.

72. Heyward, *Saving Jesus*, 8, 57, 126.

73. Ibid., 111.

74. Heyward, *The Redemption of God,* 201.

75. Heyward, *Saving Jesus*, 9.

76. Ibid., 141.

77. Ibid., 167.

78. Ibid., 158.

79. Ibid., 3.

80. The Mud Flower Collective, Carter Heyward, ed., *God's Fierce Whimsy* (New York: Pilgrim, 1985), 46–54.

81. See Carter Heyward, "An Unfinished Symphony of Liberation: The Radicalization of Christian Feminism Among White U.S. Women: A Review Essay," *Journal of Feminist Studies in Religion* 1, no. 1 (1985): 113–14.

82. Heyward describes this relationship and reflects on it in Heyward, *When Boundaries Betray Us*. For a critique of Heyward's lack of moral discernment here, see K. Roberts Skerrett, "When No Means Yes: The Passion of Carter Heyward," *Journal of Feminist Studies in Religion* 12, no. 1 (1996): 71–92.

83. The biographical information in this paragraph comes from an e-mail from Mark Lewis Taylor, received on January 2, 2008. After Mark and Anita Kline were divorced in 1994, Mark changed his name from Mark Kline Taylor to his name from birth, Mark Lewis Taylor.

84. Mark Kline Taylor, *Beyond Explanation* (Macon, Ga.: Mercer University Press, 1986).

85. Mark Kline Taylor, *Remembering Esperanza: A Cultural-Political Theology for North American Praxis* (Maryknoll, N.Y.: Orbis, 1989), 1, 5–15.

86. Mark Kline Taylor, "Introduction," *Paul Tillich: Theologian of the Boundaries* (San Francisco: Collins Liturgical Publications, 1987), 26.

87. For the following four characteristics of symbols, see Mark Kline Taylor, "In Praise of Shaky Ground: The Liminal Christ and Cultural Pluralism," *Theology Today* 43 (April 1986): 38–40. See also Taylor, *Remembering Esperanza*, 18–22.

88. For this emphasis as characteristic of Reformed theology, see Jane Dempsey Douglass, "What Is 'Reformed Theology'?" *The Princeton Seminary Bulletin* 11, no. 1 (New Series 1990): 3–10.

89. Taylor, "In Praise of Shaky Ground," 47.

90. Ibid., 48–50. Some implications of this are explored in Mark Lewis Taylor, "Subalternity and Advocacy as Kairos for Theology," in *Opting for the Margins*, ed. Joerg Rieger (New York: Oxford University Press, 2003), 23–44.

91. Taylor, *Remembering Esperanza*, 220–21.

92. Ibid., 20. The first two challenges were explicitly acknowledged in his 1986 article.

93. Ibid., 157–62.

94. Ibid., 163–64.

95. Ibid., 159.

96. Ibid., 31–45.

97. Ibid., ix.

98. Ibid., 156.

99. Ibid., 159.

100. Ibid., 135.

101. Ibid., 82.

102. Ibid., 175.

103. Ibid., 172.

104. Ibid.

105. Ibid., 197.

106. Ibid., 212.

107. For these four arguments, see ibid., 219–42.

108. Taylor, *The Executed God*.

109. Ibid., 58–62.

110. Here Taylor develops a thicker description of Jesus' relationship to his context than was present in *Remembering Esperanza*; ibid., 70–78.

111. Ibid., 70.

112. Ibid., 101–5.

113. Ibid., 103.

114. Mark Lewis Taylor, "American Torture and the Body of Christ," in *Cross Examinations*, ed. Marit Trelstad (Minneapolis: Fortress Press, 2006), 264–77.

115. Ibid., 270.

116. Taylor, *The Executed God*, 102.

117. Ibid., 103.

118. For an account of how the concern to understand the nature of Jesus' person as that which enabled him to save interacted with the notion that the divine is immutable in the development of the doctrine of the Trinity, see Jaroslav Pelikan, *The Christian Tradition*, vol. 1, *The Emergence of the Catholic Tradition (100–600)* (Chicago: University of Chicago Press, 1971), 172–277.

119. Wolfhart Pannenberg, *Jesus—God and Man* (Philadelphia: Westminster, 1968), 45.

120. Jürgen Moltmann, *The Crucified God* (London: SCM, 1974), 223–24.

121. "Objective" theories of the atonement stress the new reality that God creates or that Christ brings, which changes in principle the reality in which people live. See Tillich, *Systematic Theology*, 2:171–72.

## Chapter 3. Jesus as Source of Ultimate Hope

1. *Voices United: The Hymn and Worship Book of the United Church of Canada*, (Etobicoke, Ont.: United Church Publishing House, 1996)

2. Natalie Sleeth, "In the Bulb There Is a Flower" (1986), in ibid., no. 703.

3. Ibid.

4. Gustaf Aulén, *Christus Victor* (London: SPCK, 1950), 20–23.

5. Ibid., 22. For the presence of this understanding in the thought of patristic theologians Irenaeus of Lyons (died 200) and Gregory of Nyssa (died after 394), see David Brondos, *Fortress Introduction to Salvation and the Cross* (Minneapolis: Fortress Press, 2007), 56–58, 70–71.

6. Aulén, *Christus Victor*, 163–64.

7. Paul Tillich, *Systematic Theology* (Chicago: University of Chicago Press, 1957), 2:171.

8. For this kind of focus as unique to the present era, see Charles Taylor, *A Secular Age* (Cambridge, Mass.: Belknap Press of Harvard University, 2007), 569.

9. Ibid., 590.

10. James Cone, *God of the Oppressed* (New York: Harper & Row, 1975), 1.

11. James Cone, *My Soul Looks Back* (Nashville: Abingdon, 1982), 22.

12. Ibid., 18.

13. Ibid., 31–33.

14. Union Theological Seminary website, James H. Cone, Charles A. Briggs Distinguished Professor of Systematic Theology: http://www.utsnyc.edu/Page. aspx?pid=353 (accessed Dec. 18, 2007).

15. These riots have also been described as "northern urban rebellions," Dwight Hopkins, *Introducing Black Theology of Liberation* (Maryknoll, N.Y.: Orbis, 1999), 53.

16. James Cone, *Black Theology and Black Power* (New York: Seabury, 1969).

17. Ibid., 37.

18. Ibid., 69.

19. James Cone, *A Black Theology of Liberation*, with a Foreword by Paulo Freire, 2nd ed. (Mayknoll, N.Y.: Orbis, 1986).

20. Cone, *My Soul Looks Back*, 93–113.

21. James Cone, *Risks of Faith* (Boston: Beacon, 1999), 130–31, 136. See also Cone's comments in "A Paradoxical Feeling," Interview with Hana R. Alberts, *Forbes*, March 24, 2008: http://www.forbes.com/2008/03/24/obama-black-liberation -theology-oped-cx_hra_0324cone.html (accessed Dec. 22, 2008).

22. For an overview of black theology and Cone's influential place in it, see Hopkins, *Introducing Black Theology of Liberation*.

23. Cone, *My Soul Looks Back*, 54–57.

24. Cone first noted the failure of white theologians to address racism as a theological issue during his graduate studies; ibid., 37.

25. James Cone, *For My People* (Maryknoll, N.Y.: Orbis, 1984), 102, 108, 119–20.

26. Ibid., 120.

27. Cone, *My Soul Looks Back*, 81. The influence of Barth's insistence that God be understood as trinitarian and God's being as dynamic on the basis of God's self-revelation in Jesus Christ is also present in the theologies of Jon Sobrino and Elizabeth Johnson. As Johnson notes, behind the attempts of Pannenberg, Moltmann, and other twentieth-century theologians to rethink the nature of God in light of God's incarnation in Jesus Christ lies the influence of Karl Barth, whose influence reached Sobrino and Johnson through the work of Pannenberg and Moltmann. See Elizabeth Johnson, "Christology's Impact on the Doctrine of God," *Heythrop Journal* 26 (1985): 161n9.

28. Cone, *God of the Oppressed*, 14.

29. Cone, *A Black Theology of Liberation*, 28; *God of the Oppressed*, 84–96.

30. Ibid., 116.

31. In addition to Barth, Cone drew theological concepts from Tillich, Bonhoeffer, and Bultmann. Martin Luther King Jr. and Malcolm X were both major influences, particularly on how these concepts were used, as was Stokely Carmichael. Albert Camus and Franz Fanon were important theoretical influences. By the mid-1970s, Pannenberg and Moltmann had become significant sources.

32. Cone, *Black Theology and Black Power*, 34, 120–21. Intially, Cone did not base his argument for the centrality of Jesus Christ as much on Christ's place in black experience as on Christ's importance in the New Testament and as affirmed

by Western theologians like Schleiermacher and Barth. He later corrected this in Cone, *God of the Oppressed*, 252–53n38.

33. Cone, *Black Theology and Black Power*, 36.

34. Ibid., 40–41.

35. Ibid., 42–43.

36. Ibid., 68–69.

37. Cone, *A Black Theology of Liberation*, 141.

38. Delores Williams notes that Cone's theology and black liberation theology in general up to 1993 had been dominated by the use of "a masculine indication of person and masculine models of victimization," and that its ethics had been developed in relation to these; Delores Williams, *Sisters in the Wilderness* (Maryknoll, N.Y.: Orbis, 1993), 158, 175.

39. Cone, *God of the Oppressed*, 130.

40. Cone, *A Black Theology of Liberation*, 116.

41. Kelly Brown Douglas, *The Black Christ* (Maryknoll, N.Y.: Orbis, 1994), 37–38, 83.

42. Cone, *A Black Theology of Liberation*, 30. For Cone, the question of the means by which liberation is sought is not irrelevant but is subordinate to the end to be achieved.

43. Cone, *God of the Oppressed*, 81, 120, 125.

44. Ibid., 80–81.

45. Ibid., 95–96.

46. Cone, *A Black Theology of Liberation*, 135.

47. Cone, *Speaking the Truth*, 34.

48. Cone, *God of the Oppressed*, 114.

49. Karl Barth, *Church Dogmatics* III/3 (Edinburgh: T&T Clark, 1960), 293–95.

50. Paul Ricoeur, *Figuring the Sacred*, ed. Mark Wallace (Minneapolis: Fortress Press, 1995), 257.

51. Cone, *God of the Oppressed*, 191–92.

52. Ibid., 147–48.

53. Cone, *Black Theology and Black Power*, 150.

54. Cone, *God of the Oppressed*, 232.

55. Examples of Cone's use of this can be found in Cone, *Black Theology and Black Power*, 40–41; *A Black Theology of Liberation*, 118–19; *God of the Oppressed*, 77, 232, 236–38; *For My People*, 188.

56. Cone, *God of the Oppressed*, 134.

57. Ibid., 135–36; Douglas, *The Black Christ*, 66–69.

58. For Cone, the literal color of Jesus' skin is irrelevant, though he is confident it was not white; Cone, *A Black Theology of Liberation*, 123.

59. Cone, *God of the Oppressed*, 136–37 .

60. For Christ as "truly present" in the Lord's Supper, see Michael Welker, *What Happens in Holy Communion?* (Grand Rapids: Eerdmans, 2000), 89–100.

61. Douglas, *The Black Christ*, 83, 88–92.

62. See Elisabeth Johnson, *She Who Is* (New York: Continuum, 1992), 262–64.

63. Cone, *Risks of Faith*, xxv.

64. Lisa Sowle Cahill, "Questio Disputata—The Atonement Paradigm: Does It Still Have Explanatory Value?" *Theological Studies* 68, no. 2 (2007): 423.

65. For an account of this, see Stan Granot Duncan, "Introduction: The Crime," in *Companions of Jesus: The Jesuit Martyrs of El Salvador*, by Jon Sobrino, et al. (Maryknoll, N.Y.: Orbis, 1990), xi–xxviii.

66. The text of the Notification and an Explanatory Note on it can be found as Appendixes 1 and 2 in *Hope and Solidarity: Jon Sobrino's Challenge to Christian Theology*, ed. Stephen Pope (Maryknoll, N.Y.: Orbis, 2008), 255–65, 267–70. For discussion of the Notification's criticisms of Sobrino's Christology, see William Loewe, "Interpreting the Notification: Christological Issues," in ibid., 143–52; James Bretzke, "The Faith of the Church, the Magisterium, and the Theologian: Proper and Improper Interpretations of the Notification," ibid., 171–84, and passim.

67. Jon Sobrino, *Christology at the Crossroads* (Maryknoll, N.Y.: Orbis, 1978), 35 (Spanish original 1976).

68. Jon Sobrino, *No Salvation outside the Poor* (Maryknoll, N.Y.: Orbis, 2008), 37–48.

69. For a discussion of Medellín, its impetus to Latin American liberation theology, and the historical influences that helped occasion it, see Arthur McGovern, *Liberation Theology and Its Critics* (Maryknoll, N.Y.: Orbis, 1989), 8–9.

70. Jon Sobrino, *Jesus in Latin America* (Maryknoll, N.Y.: Orbis, 1987), 4–6.

71. Rafael Luciani, "Hermeneutics and Theology in Sobrino's Christology," in *Hope and Solidarity*, 107–11.

72. Jon Sobrino, *Jesus the Liberator* (Maryknoll, N.Y.: Orbis, 1993); *Christ the Liberator* (Maryknoll, N.Y.: Orbis, 2001).

73. Sobrino defines "the poor" as "those whose greatest task is to try to survive . . . whose concrete lives are threatened by socio-economic structures;" Jon Sobrino, *Spirituality of Liberation* (Maryknoll, N.Y.: Orbis, 1988), 159.

74. Sobrino, *Christology at the Crossroads*, 34–36.

75. Sobrino, *Jesus the Liberator*, 15–17.

76. Ibid., 252.

77. Sobrino, *Christology at the Crossroads*, 37; *Jesus the Liberator*, 39; *Christ the Liberator*, 199.

78. Sobrino, *Jesus in Latin America*, 42.

79. Sobrino, *Christ the Liberator*, 118–21.

80. Sobrino, *Jesus the Liberator*, 15–17, 47.

81. Jon Sobrino, *The True Church and the Poor* (Maryknoll, N.Y.: Orbis, 1984), 129.

82. Sobrino, *Christology at the Crossroads*, 119–25.

83. Ibid., 50.

84. Ibid., 209.

85. Ibid., 265.

86. Jon Sobrino, "Spirituality and the Following of Jesus," in *Mysterium Liberationis*, ed. Ignacio Ellacuría and Jon Sobrino (Maryknoll, N.Y.: Orbis, 1993), 686.

87. Sobrino, *Christ the Liberator*, 324.

88. Jon Sobrino, *Archbishop Romero: Memories and Reflections* (Maryknoll, N.Y.: Orbis, 1990).

89. Ibid., 327.

90. Jon Sobrino, *The Principle of Mercy* (Maryknoll, N.Y.: Orbis, 1994), 49–57.

91. Sobrino, *Christ the Liberator*, 42.

92. Sobrino, *Jesus in Latin America*, 154.

93. Sobrino, *Christology at the Crossroads*, 112–13.

94. Ibid., 91–95. For a critique of Sobrino's position here, see Michael Cook, "Jesus from the Other Side of History: Christology in Latin America," *Theological Studies* 44, no. 2 (1983): 273–74.

95. Sobrino, *Jesus the Liberator*, 197–201.

96. Sobrino, *Christ the Liberator*, 309–10.

97. James Bretzke, "The Faith of the Church, the Magisterium, and the Theologian," 179, 181. For a defense of Sobrino's position here, see Loewe, "Interpreting the Notification," 149–50.

98. John Meier, "The Bible as a Source for Theology," *Catholic Theological Society of America Proceedings* 43 (1988): 3–7.

99. Clark Williamson, "Christ Against the Jews: A Review of Jon Sobrino's Christology," in *Christianity and Judaism: The Deepening Dialogue*, ed. Richard Rousseau (Scranton, Penn.: Ridge Row, 1983), 148–53.

100. Sturla Stalsett, *The Crucified and the Crucified* (New York: Peter Lang, 2003), 199–217.

101. Joseph Curran, "Mercy and Justice in the Face of Suffering," in *Hope and Solidarity*, 212.

102. As Stalsett notes, "although he is more directly influenced by the 'second quest,' the bulk of Sobrino's tenets does not seem to be seriously questioned by the third quest," ibid., 216.

103. Gary Dorrien, *The Making of American Liberal Theology: Crisis, Irony, and Postmodernity 1950–2005* (Louisville: Westminster John Knox, 2006), 437.

104. See Elizabeth A. Johnson, C.S.J., personal web page, http://www.fordham.edu/academics/programs_at_fordham_/theology/faculty/elizabeth_a_johnson_/sr_johnson_personal__26145.asp (accessed Jan. 28, 2009).

105. Elizabeth Johnson, "Worth a Life—A Vatican II Story," in *Vatican II: Forty Personal Stories*, ed. William Madges and Michael Daley (Mystic, Conn.: Twenty-Third Publications, 2003), 202.

106. For the final version that was promulgated on by Pope Paul VI on Dec. 7, 1965, see http://www.vatican.va/archive/hist_councils/ii_vatican_council/documents/vat-ii_cons_19651207_gaudium-et-spes_en.html (accessed Jan. 28, 2009).

107. Johnson, "Worth a Life—A Vatican II Story," 204.

108. Elizabeth Johnson, *Consider Jesus* (New York: Crossroad, 1990), 103. Johnson sees this principle to reflect statements and the general spirit of *Gaudium et Spes*.

109. Elizabeth Johnson, "Jesus, Wisdom of God," *Ephemerides Theologiae Louvaniensis* 61 (1985): 263.

110. Elizabeth Johnson, "Redeeming the Name of Christ," in *Freeing Theology*, ed. Catherine Mowry LaCugna (New York: HarperCollins, 1993), 116.

111. Ibid.

112. Johnson's theological method follows a dialectical pattern of doctrinal development discerned by Gregory Baum in the change in Roman Catholic

teaching that occurred at Vatican II. See Gregory Baum, *The Credibility of The Church Today* (New York: Herder and Herder, 1968), 156–75.

113. Johnson, *She Who Is*.

114. Ibid., 4–5. However, Johnson is not always attentive to how the way symbols function may vary with social location. For a critical discussion of her thought at this point, see Serene Jones, "Women's Experience between a Rock and a Hard Place," in *Horizons in Feminist Theology*, ed. Rebecca Chopp and Sheila Greeve Davaney (Minneapolis: Fortress Press, 1997), 37; Mary McClintock Fulkerson, review of *She Who Is* in *Religious Studies Review* 21, no. 1 (1995): 24.

115. Johnson, *She Who Is*, 5.

116. Johnson, "Christology's Impact on the Doctrine of God."

117. For Johnson's arguments for the importance of the quest for the historical Jesus in this regard and her summaries of its findings, see Elizabeth Johnson, "The Theological Relevance of the Historical Jesus: A Debate and a Thesis," *The Thomist* 48 (1984): 1–43; Elizabeth Johnson, "The Word Was Made Flesh and Dwelt among Us: Jesus Research and Christian Faith," in *Jesus: A Colloquium in the Holy Land*, ed. Doris Donnelly (New York: Continuum, 2001), 146–66.

118. Johnson, "Jesus, Wisdom of God," 261.

119. Ibid.

120. Johnson, *She Who Is*, 153.

121. Ibid., 156–58.

122. Ibid., 268.

123. Ibid., 124–87.

124. Ibid., 266.

125. Johnson, "Jesus and Salvation," 5–6, 14–15.

126. Elizabeth Johnson, "Passion for God, Passion for the Earth," in *Spiritual Questions for the Twenty-First Century*, ed. Mary Hembrow Snyder (Ottawa: Novalis, 2001), 121.

127. Taylor, *A Secular Age*, 543.

128. Gustavo Gutiérrez, *The Truth Shall Make You Free* (Maryknoll, N.Y.: Orbis, 1990), 23–24.

129. Johnson, "Jesus and Salvation," 9–10.

130. Douglas John Hall, *God and Human Suffering* (Minneapolis: Augsburg Publishing House, 1986), 100–1.

131. For the preferential option for the poor as a transcendent principle of justice, see Gregory Baum, "Afterword," in *Faith That Transforms*, ed. Mary Jo Leddy and Mary Ann Hinsdale (Mahwah, N.J.: Paulist, 1987), 143–44.

132. In James Cone's debate with J. Deotis Roberts about reconciliation, Cone's argument was that liberation of the oppressed must come first but then be followed by reconciliation with former oppressors; Cone, *God of the Oppressed*, 238–46.

## Chapter 4. Jesus as the Suffering Christ

1. Mark 6:5.

2. For an overview of Anselm's theory, see David Brondos, *Fortress Introduction to Salvation and the Cross* (Minneapolis: Fortress Press, 2007), 76–87.

3. Paul Tillich, *Systematic Theology* (Chicago: University of Chicago Press, 1957), 2:172.

4. Ibid., 176.

5. *Macbeth* 5.1.38–55.

6. Joanne Carlson Brown and Rebecca Parker, "For God So Loved the World?" in *Christianity, Patriarchy, and Abuse: A Feminist Critique*, ed. Joanne Carlson Brown and Carole Bohn (New York: Pilgrim, 1989), 1–30.

7. Ibid., 26.

8. Jürgen Moltmann, *A Broad Place: An Autobiography* (Minneapolis: Fortress Press, 2008), 3–10.

9. Ibid., 15.

10. Ibid., 17.

11. Moltmann states that this sense of shame still lingers; ibid., 29.

12. Ibid., 53.

13. *Prädestination and Perseveranz, Geschichte und Bedeutung der reformierten Lehre de perseverantia sanctorum'* (Neukirchen: Neukirchener Verlag, 1961).

14. Ernst Bloch, *The Principle of Hope*, vols. 1–3 (Cambridge, Mass.: MIT Press, 1986).

15. Moltmann, *A Broad Place*, 79.

16. Jürgen Moltmann, *Theology of Hope* (London: SCM, 1967).

17. Jürgen Moltmann, *The Crucified God* (London: SCM, 1974).

18. Jürgen Moltmann, *The Church in the Power of the Spirit* (New York: Harper & Row, 1977).

19. Jürgen Moltmann, *The Trinity and the Kingdom of God* (London: SCM, 1981), xi. Later, Moltmann noted that his approach was already changing in *The Church in the Power of the Spirit*; Moltmann, *A Broad Place*, 286.

20. Moltmann, *A Broad Place*, 227–32.

21. Ibid., 231.

22. Moltmann, *Trinity*, 52.

23. Jürgen Moltmann, *The Way of Jesus Christ* (New York: HarperCollins, 1990), 65. Moltmann drew this approach partly from Paul Tillich; see Jürgen Moltmann, *Theology Today* (London: SCM, 1988), 82–85.

24. For this approach in Moltmann's work, see Don Schweitzer, "The Consistency of Jürgen Moltmann's Theology," *Studies in Religion/Sciences Religieuses* 22, no. 2 (1993): 197–208.

25. Schweitzer, "The Consistency of Jürgen Moltmann's Theology," 205.

26. Moltmann lists a number of other influences on his thought at this point in Moltmann, *A Broad Place*, 97.

27. Ibid., 101; see also Moltmann, *Theology of Hope*, 33.

28. In doing this, Moltmann followed Karl Barth in seeking to understand God and reality on the basis of the particularity of God's revelation in Jesus Christ. See Moltmann, *Theology of Hope*, 140–43.

29. Ibid., 211.

30. Ibid., 199.

31. Ibid., 199–201.

32. Jürgen Moltmann, "Theology as Eschatology," in *The Future of Hope*, ed. Fredrick Herzog (New York: Herder and Herder, 1970), 24.

33. Moltmann, *Theology of Hope*, 181.

34. Jürgen Moltmann, "Antwort auf die Kritik der *Theologie der Hoffnung*," in *Discussion über die "Theologie der Hoffnung" von Jürgen Moltmann*, ed. Wolf-Dieter Marsch (München: Christian Kaiser Verlag, 1967), 209.

35. Moltmann, *A Broad Place*, 143. This was first raised by Douglas John Hall in "The Theology of Hope in an Officially Optimistic Society," *Religion in Life* 40 (1971): 376–90.

36. Langdon Gilkey, "The Universal and Immediate Presence of God," in Herzog, *The Future of Hope*, 101 and passim.

37. For Moltmann's response to this last criticism, see Moltmann, "Antwort auf die Kritik der *Theologie der Hoffnung*," 222–29.

38. Moltmann, *A Broad Place*, 124.

39. Moltmann, *Crucified God*, 2.

40. Ibid., 4; "blood" here refers to guilt for the Holocaust and World War II, and to the present suffering and death in third-world countries caused by the economies of North Atlantic countries and their struggles for global domination; ibid., 220.

41. Ibid., 105.

42. Ibid., 125.

43. Ibid., 130–33. Moltmann's argument here brought charges of anti-Judaism against him, most sweepingly by Roy Eckhardt, "Jürgen Moltmann, The Jewish People, and the Holocaust," *Journal of the American Academy of Religion* 44, no. 4 (1976): 675–91. According to Eckhardt, pp. 128–35 of *The Crucified God* and others, "reflect in many respects a closed-mindedness to the Jewish understanding of Judaism and of faith," ibid., 682. Moltmann later repudiated Eckhardt's critique; Moltmann, *A Broad Place*, 270–71, 276–82. On the whole, it is exaggerated. In the passage under discussion, Moltmann rejects Christian supersessionism, any notion of Jewish guilt for the death of Jesus, and argues that Judaism and Christianity remain dialogue partners; Moltmann, *Crucified God*, 134–35. Eckhardt too easily dismisses this; Eckhardt, "Jürgen Moltmann, The Jewish People, and the Holocaust," 682. However, Moltmann's interpretation of the Jewish law in this passage is problematic. Gregory Baum saw here a Christian theologian unwittingly repeating a pre-Holocaust negation of Jewish existence even when wanting "to adopt a new positive stance towards the Jewish people." Speaking of Hans Küng as well, Baum argues as follows:

> Instead of recognizing that the persecutors of Jesus stood for a legalism that threatens all religions and all societies, including the Church, and instead of clarifying the fact that Jesus' criticism of legalism was not foreign to the religion of Israel, but actually derived from ancient prophetic as well as rabbinic teaching, Moltmann and Küng, quite unthinkingly, accuse Torah of having crucified Jesus. They forget that there is an inward, liberated and surrendered manner of practicing Torah in keeping with the prophetic tradition, and hence not at odds with the teachings of Jesus.

Gregory Baum, "Catholic Dogma After Auschwitz," in *Antisemitism and the Foundations of Christianity*, ed. Alan Davies (New York: Paulist, 1979), 144–45.

44. Moltmann, *Crucified God*, 144.

45. Ibid., 149. Moltmann's emphasis on the historicity of Jesus' dying cry of abandonment in Mark's Gospel finds recent support in Joel Marcus, "Identity and Ambiguity in Markan Christology," in *Seeking the Identity of Jesus: A Pilgrimage*, ed. Beverly Roberts Gaventa and Richard Hays (Grand Rapids: Eerdmans, 2008), 141.

46. Moltmann, *Crucified God*, 151–52. Moltmann's use of masculine terms for the First and Second Persons of the Trinity is problematic for the many who share feminist concerns.

47. Moltmann, *Crucified God*, 153.

48. Ibid., 245.

49. Ibid., 205–6.

50. Ibid., 204.

51. Moltmann, *Trinity*, 184.

52. Ibid., 108.

53. Ibid., 116.

54. Jürgen Moltmann, *God in Creation* (London: SCM, 1985), 69.

55. Moltmann, *Way of Jesus Christ*, 102.

56. Ibid., 98.

57. Moltmann, *The Church in the Power of the Spirit*, 123.

58. Jürgen Moltmann, *History and the Triune God* (London: SCM, 1991), 36.

59. Ibid., 37. Moltmann also invokes the doctrine of Christ's two natures in relation to the environmental crisis. In this context, the risen body of Christ becomes a promise of the resurrection of nature, a sign that it is included in God's redemptive work and must be treated accordingly; Moltmann, *Way of Jesus Christ*, 258 and passim.

60. Jürgen Moltmann, *Jesus Christ for Today's World* (Minneapolis: Fortress Press, 1994).

61. "The unassumed is the unhealed, but what is united with God is also being saved"; St. Gregory of Nazianzus, *On God and Christ* (Crestwood, N.Y.: St. Vladimir's Seminary Press, 2002), 158.

62. Moltmann, *Way of Jesus Christ*, 164–70.

63. Moltmann, *Crucified God*, 248.

64. Gilkey, "The Universal and Immediate Presence of God," 91 and passim.

65. Moltmann, *Crucified God*, 248. Joy Ann McDougall notes this change but stresses the continuity of Moltmann's position in *The Crucified God* with *Theology of Hope*; Joy Ann McDougall, *Pilgrimage of Love* (New York: Oxford University Press, 2005), 42–43.

66. Moltmann's emphasis is not simply that sin requires punishment as Anselm taught, as some suggest; Celia Deane-Drummond, *Christ and Evolution: Wonder and Wisdom* (Minneapolis: Fortress Press, 2009), 177. It is rather that guilt, like other forms of spoiled identity, is experienced as alienation or separation from God. In Moltmann's view, it is overcome in principle by Christ's suffering, because through this, God in the person of Christ enters into the situation of the

sufferer or guilty person, thus reestablishing communion with them and so over-coming in principle their separation from God. It is the entry into the sufferer or guilty person's condition that is important, not the meting out of punishment. Moltmann does see Christ's suffering as a necessary atonement for guilt in a way that has some similarities to Anselm's view; Moltmann, *Jesus Christ for Today's World*, 40–42. But like Tillich, he argues that this is not simply a matter of what God decrees. It is a question of what is psychologically compelling to the guilty person by virtue of doing justice to the moral values involved in their experience of guilt; Tillich, *Systematic Theology*, 2:172–73. While Moltmann's emphasis is different, his argument continues to provoke criticism similar to that directed at Anselm.

67. Moltmann, *God in Creation*, 89.

68. Moltmann, *Theology of Hope*, 212.

69. Dorothee Soelle, *Suffering* (Philadelphia: Fortress Press, 1975), 26–27; John Macquarrie, "Today's Word for Today: I. Jürgen Moltmann," *Expository Times* 92 (1980): 6.

70. Moltmann, *Crucified God,* 243–44.

71. Moltmann, *A Broad Place*, 195.

72. Ibid., 199.

73. Moltmann, *Theology of Hope*, 123.

74. Moltmann, *Crucified God*, 248, 275–76.

75. Moltmann, *Trinity*, 209–10; *Way of Jesus Christ*, 290–91; *Jesus Christ for Today's World*, 146; "God's Kenosis in the Creation and Consummation of the World," in *The Work of Love: Creation as Kenosis*, ed. John Polkinghorne (Grand Rapids: Eerdmans, 2001), 149–50.

76. Moltmann, "God's Kenosis," 149. Here Moltmann writes, "We look in vain for God in the history of nature or in human history if what we are looking for are special divine interventions." This does not sit easily with his earlier emphasis on God's future becoming present and effective in history through the resurrection of Jesus Christ. Jürgen Moltmann, *Religion, Revolution, and the Future* (New York: Charles Scribner's Sons, 1969), 4.

77. Moltmann, "God's Kenosis," 149.

78. Moltmann, *Way of Jesus Christ*, and *Jesus Christ for Today's World*.

79. Moltmann, *Way of Jesus Christ*, 65.

80. Ibid., 33.

81. Ibid., 34; *Jesus Christ for Today's World*, 47–48.

82. Douglas John Hall, *Bound and Free: A Theologian's Journey* (Minneapolis: Fortress Press, 2005), 28.

83. Ibid., 33. For Hall's description of the church and village life of his upbringing, see Douglas John Hall, *The Future of the Church* (n.p.: The United Church Publishing House, 1989), 5–19; *Why Christian?* (Minneapolis: Fortress Press, 1998), 4–14.

84. Hall, *Bound and Free*, 33–34. For Hall's use of Luther, see Gordon Jenson, "Douglas John Hall's use of Luther's *theologia crucis*," *Toronto Journal of Theology* 7, no. 2 (1991): 196–210.

85. Hall, *Bound and Free*, 34–38.

86. Douglas John Hall, "Christianity and Canadian Contexts: Then and Now," in *Intersecting Voices: Critical Theologies in a Land of Diversity*, ed. Don Schweitzer and Derek Simon (Ottawa: Novalis, 2004), 19.

87. For a description of this volunteer establishment, which Hall often refers to as "Christendom," see Mark Noll, *What Happened to Christian Canada?* (Vancouver: Regent College Publishing, 2007), 16–18.

88. Hall, *Bound and Free*, 38–42.

89. Douglas John Hall, *Lighten Our Darkness* (Philadelphia: Westminster, 1976). This was an expansion of an earlier work: Douglas John Hall, *Hope Against Hope* (Tokyo: World Student Christian Federation, 1971).

90. Douglas John Hall, *Thinking the Faith: Christian Theology in a North American Context* (Minneapolis: Fortress Press, 1991); *Professing the Faith: Christian Theology in a North American Context* (Minneapolis: Fortress Press, 1993); *Confessing the Faith: Christian Theology in a North American Context* (Minneapolis: Fortress Press, 1996).

91. Hall, *Thinking the Faith*, 93–106.

92. Douglas John Hall, "The Theology of Hope in an Officially Optimistic Society," *Religion in Life* 40 (1971): 379.

93. Hall, *Lighten Our Darkness*, 35.

94. Douglas John Hall, *God and Human Suffering* (Minneapolis: Augsburg Publishing House, 1986), 54–56.

95. Ibid., 33.

96. Hall, *Thinking the Faith*, 198, 191.

97. Hall, *Bound and Free*, 71.

98. Hall, *Professing the Faith*, 255.

99. Hall, *Lighten Our Darkness*, 117.

100. Hall, *Thinking the Faith,* 207–35.

101. Hall, *Professing the Faith*, 147.

102. Ibid., 155.

103. Ibid., 58–61.

104. Ibid., 67; Hall, *Thinking the Faith*, 147–48.

105. Hall, *Professing the Faith*, 153.

106. For a survey of these, see Gerd Theissen, "The Ambivalence of Power in Early Christianity," *Power, Powerlessness, and the Divine*, ed. Cynthia Rigby (Atlanta: Scholars Press, 1997), 21–36.

107. This kind of dichotomy was critiqued in Paul Tillich, *Love, Power and Justice* (New York: Oxford University Press, 1954), 67–71.

108. Hall, *Professing the Faith*, 163.

109. Hall, *Lighten Our Darkness*, 149.

110. Hall, *Professing the Faith*, 380.

111. Ibid., 410–12.

112. Hall, *God and Human Suffering*, 100–4.

113. Ibid., 108–13; Douglas John Hall, *The Cross in Our Context* (Minneapolis: Fortress Press, 2003), 146.

114. Hall, *Professing the Faith,* 530.

115. "What happened to the dead body of Jesus? I am not prepared (with liberalism in its more radical expression) to say, 'Nothing—except the usual.' But neither am I prepared (with fundamentalism) to name the physical resurrection as one of the five fundamentals of faith. As I have said . . . if the resurrection of Jesus is unique, then to comprehend it is impossible, because comprehension of anything requires previous experience and comparison"; Hall, *Professing the Faith*, 388.

116. Hall sees this as in keeping with the dogma of perichoresis, that there is no absolute separation of the persons and work of Christ and the Spirit; ibid., 435.

117. Douglas John Hall, *Imaging God* (Grand Rapids: Eerdmans; New York: Friendship Press, 1986), 198.

118. "Government is by representation. . . . Mothers and fathers represent their children to teachers. . . . The idea of representation, in our social context, is not only an idea but a ubiquitous reality"; Hall, *Professing the Faith*, 507–8.

119. Ibid., 513.

120. Ibid.

121. Ibid., 523.

122. Hall refers to this appreciatively several times: *Lighten Our Darkness*, 212–13; *Professing the Faith*, 534–35, 545; *The Cross in Our Context*, 122.

123. Hall, *The Cross in Our Context*, 40.

124. Hall, *Thinking the Faith*, 223, 225–26.

125. Hall, *The Cross in Our Context*, 9.

126. Hall, *Confessing the Faith*, 133.

127. Hall, "Christianity and Canadian Contexts: Then and Now," 26–28; Hall, *The Cross in Our Context*, 221–30.

128. Hall, *Confessing the* Faith, 427.

129. Marilyn McCord Adams, "Love of Learning, Reality of God," in *God and the Philosophers*, ed. Thomas Morris (New York: Oxford University Press, 1994), 141–43.

130. Ibid., 146.

131. Ibid., 155.

132. Ibid., 157.

133. Marilyn McCord Adams, *Horrendous Evils and the Goodness of God* (Ithaca, N.Y.: Cornell University Press, 1999), 104.

134. Marilyn McCord Adams, "Chalcedonian Christology: A Christian Solution to the Problem of Evil," in *Philosophy and Theological Discourse*, ed. Stephen Davis (New York: St. Martin's, 1997), 195.

135. Ibid.

136. Marilyn McCord Adams, *Christ and Horrors: The Coherence of Christology* (New York: Cambridge University Press, 2006), 11.

137. Ibid., 17–20.

138. Ibid., 23. However, two pages later Adams criticizes postliberal theologians for attempting to sever critical dialogue between Christian theology and other disciplines, on the grounds that as truth is one, theology must be done in dialogue with other disciplines. Refusal to do so "flirts with anti-realism," ibid., 25. This critique can be turned back on her own rejection of the quest for the historical Jesus as a source for Christology. Her argument for this, that the criteria of the quest are

uncritically applied and that the Gospels are few in number and the wrong kind of document to provide historical evidence (ibid., 23), seems more an excuse for not engaging with the findings of the quest than the result of a respectful consideration of it.

139. Ibid., 13.

140. Adams, *Horrendous Evils and the Goodness of God*, 26.

141. Marilyn McCord Adams, "Evil and the God-Who-Does-Nothing-In-Particular," in *Religion and Morality*, ed. D. Z. Phillips (New York: St. Martin's, 1996), 112.

142. Adams, *Horrendous Evils and the Goodness of God*, 3, 14.

143. Ibid., 28.

144. Ibid., 82–83.

145. Ibid., 80.

146. Reinhold Niebuhr, *The Nature and Destiny of Man*, vol. 1, *Human Nature* (New York: Charles Scribner's Sons, 1941), 181–86.

147. Adams, *Horrendous Evils and the Goodness of God*, 95.

148. Adams, *Christ and Horrors*, 207.

149. Adams, "Chalcedonian Christology," 176.

150. Adams, *Christ and Horrors,* 47–48, 189.

151. Matthew 2:16-18.

152. Marilyn McCord Adams, "The Coherence of Christology: God, Enmattered and Enmattering," *The Princeton Seminary Bulletin* 26, no. 2 (New Series 2005): 163.

153. Adams, *Horrendous Evils and the Goodness of God*, 127.

154. Ibid., 162, 167.

155. John B. Cobb Jr., "Theodicy and Divine Omnipotence," in *Philosophy and Theological Discourse*, ed. Stephen Davis (New York: St. Martin's, 1997), 201.

156. Adams, *Christ and Horrors*, 191.

157. Ibid., 72–73.

158. Ibid., 79.

159. For Adams's explanation of this term, see ibid., 135–40.

160. Ibid., 2.

161. Adams does not speculate much on how this is communicated to those who have never heard of Christ.

162. Adams, *Christ and Horrors*, 149, 273. For Adams, in relation to God and the grandeur of creation, people never progress beyond an infant-like state and so need the constant help of God just as an infant needs a parent or nurse; Marilyn McCord Adams, "The Problem of Hell: A Problem of Evil for Christians," in *God and the Problem of Evil*, ed. William Rowe (Malden, Mass.: Blackwell, 2001), 292–94; Adams, *Christ and Horrors*, 168–69.

163. Marilyn McCord Adams, *Wrestling for Blessing* (London: Darton, Longman and Todd, 2005), 51–52.

164. Ibid., 64.

165. Adams, *Christ and Horrors*, 274.

166. Ibid., 308.

167. Ibid., 304–7.

168. Ibid., 306.
169. Ibid., 276–77.
170. Ibid., 306.
171. Ibid., 206.
172. Ibid., 212–13.
173. Ibid., 226.
174. Charles Taylor, *Sources of the Self* (Cambridge, Mass.: Harvard University Press, 1989), 519.

## Chapter Five

1. Yann Martel, *Life of Pi: A Novel* (Toronto: Knopf Canada, 2001).
2. Ibid., 99.
3. Ibid., 100.
4. S. Mark Heim, "Witness to Difference: Mission and the Religions in Post-Pluralist Perspective," in *News of Boundless Riches*, ed. Max Stackhouse and Lalsangkima Pachuau (Delhi: ISPCK/UTC/CTI, 2007), 1:96–97.
5. Harold Wells, *The Christic Center* (Maryknoll, NY: Orbis, 2004), 182–84.
6. However, Karl Barth leaned toward affirming that through Christ all will be saved, and the association of his name with exclusivism sometimes overlooks that late in his career, in his doctrine of the "other lights' alongside the one light of Jesus Christ" there was a new opening in his theology to other religions as a source of truth relative to but distinct from Jesus Christ; Hans Küng, *Theology for the Third Millennium* (New York: Doubleday, 1988), 279.
7. Jacques Dupuis notes that "Professor Panikkar's Christian name has been written as both 'Raimundo' and 'Raimon.' The latter is the version Panikkar personally uses today (1997)"; Jacques Dupuis, *Toward a Christian Theology of Religious Pluralism* (Maryknoll, N.Y.: Orbis, 1997), 149n18.
8. Serene Jones, *Feminist Theory and Christian Theology* (Minneapolis: Fortress Press, 2000), 135, 152, 170–72.
9. Raimundo Panikkar, *The Unknown Christ of Hinduism,* rev. and enlarged ed. (Maryknoll, N.Y.: Orbis, 1981).
10. Ewert Cousins, "Introduction: The Panikkar Symposium at Santa Barbara," *Cross Currents* 29, no. 2 (1979): 132.
11. Joseph Prabhu, "Lost in Translation: Panikkar's Intercultural Odyssey," in *The Intercultural Challenge of Raimon Panikkar*, ed. Joseph Prabhu (Maryknoll, N.Y.: Orbis, 1996), 2. Paul Knitter notes one change: In the first edition of *The Unknown Christ of Hinduism*, Panikkar described Christianity as "the end and plenitude of every religion." He had moved away from any claims for the finality of Christianity by the time the second edition came out; Paul Knitter, "Cosmic Confidence of Preferential Option? In Prabhu, *The Intercultural Challenge of Raimon Panikkar*, 181.
12. Panikkar insists on using the term *man* for humanity. His explanation for this is as follows: "Neither *purusa*, nor *anthropos*, nor *homo* (and Romance derivatives), nor *Mensch* in Indo-Europeans langagues, nor analogous words in other cultures, stand for the male alone. I would not want to give males the monopoly on humanness (from *homo*) nor would I want to contribute to the fragmentation of

'Man' (the knower) by accepting the fragmentation of knowledge when dealing with that being which stands between heaven and earth and, different from other entities, knows it.—No discrimination! As I have explained elsewhere, 'wo-man' can be a derogatory expression, for it betrays male domination (and 'feminine' submission)"; "Editor's Note," Raimundo Panikkar, "The Jordan, the Tiber, and the Ganges," in *The Myth of Christian Uniqueness*, ed. John Hick and Paul Knitter (Maryknoll, N.Y.: Orbis, 1987), 99. See also Raimundo Panikkar, "The Myth of Pluralism: The Tower of Babel—A Meditation on Non-Violence," *Cross Currents* 29, no. 2 (1979): 199. For a man intent on dialogue, Panikkar doesn't seem to be listening to women on this point.

13. Panikkar, *The Unknown Christ of Hinduism*, 25.

14. Raimon Panikkar, "A Self-Critical Dialogue," in Prabhu, *The Intercultural Challenge of Raimon Panikkar*, 287–89.

15. Panikkar defines "cosmovision" as "the vision we have of reality as it presents itself to us, as we see it in a vital relationship that constantly moves between objectivity and subjectivity"; Raimon Panikkar, *Christophany: The Fullness of Man* (Maryknoll, N.Y.: Orbis, 2004), 19.

16. Ibid.

17. Panikkar, "A Self-Critical Dialogue," 265.

18. Raimundo Panikkar, *The Intrareligious Dialogue* (New York: Paulist, 1978), 2.

19. Ibid., 57.

20. Raimundo Panikkar, *The Trinity and the Religious Experience of Man* (Maryknoll, N.Y.: Orbis, 1973), ix.

21. Raimundo Panikkar, "The Invisible Harmony: A Universal Theory of Religion or a Cosmic Confidence in Reality?" in *Toward a Universal Theology of Religion*, ed. Leonard Swidler (Maryknoll, N.Y.: Orbis, 1987), 136.

22. Panikkar, "The Jordan, the Tiber, and the Ganges," 102.

23. Panikkar, *The Unknown Christ of Hinduism*, 25.

24. John B. Cobb Jr., "Metaphysical Pluralism," in Prabhu, *The Intercultural Challenge of Raimon Panikkar*, 47–48.

25. Panikkar, *The Intrareligious Dialogue*, 21.

26. Cheriyan Menacherry, *Christ: The Mystery in History: A Critical Study on the Christology of Raymond Panikkar* (New York: Peter Lang, 1996), 118–20.

27. Panikkar, *The Trinity*, 46.

28. Ibid., 47. While Panikkar uses traditional trinitarian terms, in his view, only the Son is a person, and one has a personal relationship to God only in the Son; Ibid., 52.

29. Ibid., 63.

30. Panikkar, *Christophany*, 125.

31. Panikkar, *The Trinity*, 64.

32. Panikkar, *The Unknown Christ of Hinduism*, 58–61.

33. Ibid., 94.

34. Panikkar, "The Invisible Harmony," 144, 148.

35. Panikkar, *Christophany*, 86.

36. Ibid., 162.

37. Ibid., 84.

38. Ibid., 137.

39. Ibid., 135.

40. Ibid., 136. This idea that Jesus never experienced any frustration seems to clash with his lament over Jerusalem in Matt 23:37 and with the account of his inability to do any "deed of power" in Nazareth, in Mark 6:5.

41. Panikkar, *Christophany*, 137.

42. Ibid.

43. Ibid., 181–83.

44. Panikkar, *The Unknown Christ of Hinduism*, 69.

45. Panikkar, *Christophany*, 151.

46. Panikkar, "A Self-Critical Dialogue," 271.

47. Panikkar, *Christophany*, 162, 164.

48. Knitter, "Cosmic Confidence of Preferential Option?" 184–86. Rowan Williams evaluates Panikkar's ethical stance more positively; Rowan Williams, "Trinity and Pluralism," in *Christian Uniqueness Reconsidered*, ed. Gavin D'Costa (Maryknoll, N.Y.: Orbis, 1990), 11–14.

49. Panikkar, "A Self-Critical Dialogue," 261.

50. Ibid., 282–83.

51. Peter Slater, "Hindu and Christian Symbols in the Work of R. Panikkar," *Cross Currents* 29, no. 2 (1979): 174–76; R. Sahayadhas, "Perspectives in Christological Reconstructions: An Exploration of the Writings of Select Theologians," *Bangalore Theological Forum* 38, no. 2 (2006): 130.

52. Slater, "Hindu and Christian Symbols in the Work of R. Panikkar," 179.

53. Samuel George, review of *The Fullness of Man: A Christophany*, by Raimon Panikkar, in *Indian Theological Journal* 1, no. 2 (2007): 124.

54. "Christophany's transcendence of historical christology belongs to the cultural moment in which we live"; Panikkar, *Christophany*, 162.

55. At one point, Jürgen Moltmann argued that it must; Jürgen Moltmann, *The Crucified God* (London: SCM, 1974), 99.

56. George, review of *The Fullness of Man: A Christophany*, 124; Sahayadhas, "Perspectives in Christological Reconstructions," 130–31.

57. David Ray Griffin, "John B. Cobb Jr.: A Theological Biography," in *Theology and the University*, ed. David Ray Griffin and Joseph Hough Jr. (Albany: State University of New York Press, 1991), 225. Most of the following details of Cobb's biography are drawn from here. For Cobb's own autobiographical reflections, see John B. Cobb Jr., *Can Christ Become Good News Again?* (St. Louis: Chalice, 1991), 3–13.

58. Griffin, "John B. Cobb Jr.," 227.

59. Cobb, *Can Christ Become Good News Again?*, 8–9.

60. Griffin, "John B. Cobb Jr.," 229–34.

61. Cobb, *Can Christ Become Good News Again?*, 12; idem, "A Critical View of Inherited Theology," *The Christian Century* 20 (February 1980): 194.

62. John B. Cobb Jr., *The Structure of Christian Existence* (Philadelphia: Westminster, 1967), 40.

63. Ibid., 52.

64. Ibid., 112.

65. Ibid., 122–23.

66. Ibid., 144.

67. John B. Cobb Jr., *Christ in a Pluralistic Age* (Philadelphia: Westminster, 1975), 244.

68. Ibid., 181.

69. Ibid.

70. John B. Cobb Jr., *God and the World* (Philadelphia: Westminster, 1969), 45.

71. Ibid., 65, 82.

72. John B. Cobb Jr., *Liberal Christianity at the Crossroads* (Philadelphia: Westminster, 1973), 37.

73. Ibid., 39–40.

74. John B. Cobb Jr., "Barth and the Barthians: A Critical Appraisal," in *How Karl Barth Changed My Mind*, ed. Donald McKim (Grand Rapids: Eerdmans, 1986), 173–74.

75. John B. Cobb Jr., "A Whiteheadian Christology," in *Process Philosophy and Christian Thought*, ed. Delwin Brown, et al. (New York: Bobbs-Merrill, 1971), 395.

76. For Cobb's overview of God in a process perspective, see John B. Cobb Jr. and David Ray Griffin, *Process Theology: An Introductory Exposition* (Philadelphia: Westminster, 1976), 41–62.

77. Cobb, *Christ in a Pluralistic Age*, 69–70.

78. Alfred North Whitehead, *Process and Reality* (corrected edition), ed. David Ray Griffin and Donald Sherburne (New York: Free, 1978), 343–46.

79. Cobb, *Christ in a Pluralistic Age*, 72, 76.

80. Ibid., 87.

81. Ibid.

82. John B. Cobb Jr., "The Relativization of the Trinity," in *Trinity in Process*, ed. Joseph Bracken and Marjorie Suchocki (New York: Continuum, 1997), 10.

83. John B. Cobb Jr., "Christ beyond Creative Transformation," in *Encountering Jesus*, ed. Stephen Davis (Atlanta: John Knox, 1988), 156–57.

84. Cobb, *Christ in a Pluralistic Age*, 117–18.

85. Ibid., 183–84. Here Cobb overlooks the role that Jesus' resurrection played in establishing him as the center of this force field and avoids the difficulty of reconciling the New Testament proclamation of this as an interruption in history with Whitehead's philosophy.

86. Ibid., 131–32.

87. Ibid., 139.

88. Ibid., 139–40. According to Cobb, as this happened, "the 'I' in each moment is constituted as much in the subjective reception of the lure to self-actualization that is the call and presence of the Logos as it is in continuity with the person past. This structure of existence would be the incarnation of the Logo in the fullest meaning sense"; Ibid., 140.

89. Ibid., 142.

90. Ibid., 138.

91. Ibid., 142.

92. Ibid., 167. These are the two main contrasting traditions of christological thought underlying the Chalcedonian Definition. However, one might ask

whether Cobb has gotten to Chalcedon by way of bypassing Nicaea. The doctrine of the Trinity affirmed at the Council of Nicaea recognized that in Jesus Christ God had become present in history in a new way. God is not an element in the structure of creation but rather is transcendent to it and able to introduce a new possibility into it that did not previously exist. Cobb affirms a restricted version of this, but not the radical hope of a transformed creation in which sin and death are no more that Paul endorses. Parallel to this, while Cobb insists that recognizing Jesus as the Christ requires rethinking the attributes of God in light of this, particularly that of immutability, which patristic theologians continued to endorse, he refuses to go beyond the limits of Whitehead's concepts. While patristic theologians retained notions of divine immutability that clashed particularly with the suffering and death of Jesus, they did rethink the philosophical conceptualities they worked with more radically than Cobb in affirming the triune nature of God in light of Jesus Christ. For Cobb's limited endorsement of the doctrine of the Trinity, see Cobb, "The Relativization of the Trinity."

93. Cobb, *The Structure of Christian Existence*, 137–50.

94. Cobb, *Christ in a Pluralistic Age*, 22; *Liberal Christianity at the Crossroads*, 12.

95. Cobb, *Christ in a Pluralistic Age*, 22.

96. Cobb and Griffin, *Process Theology*, 106–7.

97. Cobb, *Can Christ Become Good News Again?*, 117.

98. John B. Cobb Jr., *Transforming Christianity and the World*, ed. and Introduction by Paul Knitter (Maryknoll, N.Y.: Orbis, 1999), 45.

99. Ibid., 60. This was a further application of his notion of the universality of Christ; Cobb, *Christ in a Pluralistic Age*, 21, 63. At this time, Cobb begins to supplement his use of Whitehead's concepts with the notions of internal and external history, developed in H. R. Niebuhr, *The Meaning of Revelation* (New York: Macmillan, 1941); Cobb, *Transforming Christianity and the World*, 80–82.

100. Ibid., 71.

101. Cobb and Griffin, *Process Theology*, 100.

102. Cobb, *Christ in a Pluralistic Age*, 80.

103. John B. Cobb Jr., *Becoming a Thinking Christian* (Nashville: Abingdon, 1993), 99.

104. Cobb, "Christ Beyond Creative Transformation," 157.

105. Cobb, *Can Christ Become Good News Again?*, 97–103.

106. Ibid., 94.

107. This dialectical relationship between the understanding of Jesus and its practical effects reflects the relationship in Cobb's thought between faith in Jesus Christ and speculative thought. He understands speculative thought to be continually open to revision in light of new knowledge and experiences. As this happens, one's understanding of Christ is also revised. Thus, while one believes in Jesus Christ and is guided by this, one's understanding of Christ is continually open to revision; John B. Cobb Jr., "Ally or Opponent? A Response to Stanley Hauerwas," *Theology Today* 51, no. 1 (1994): 572.

108. Cobb, "Christ Beyond Creative Transformation," 142.

109. Ibid., 143.

110. For instance, see John B. Cobb Jr., "American Imperialism," in *Resistance: The New Role of Progressive Christians*, ed. John B. Cobb Jr. (Louisville: Westminster John Knox, 2008), 115.

111. Ibid., 152–53.

112. Ibid., 153.

113. In a later essay on the Trinity, Cobb picks up on an instance where Whitehead does speak of God's consequent nature entering into history and relates it to experiences of the paranormal, religious ecstasy, and unusual guidance in life; Cobb, "The Relativization of the Trinity," 14–20.

114. Cobb, *Liberal Christianity at the Crossroads*, 45.

115. As Wolfhart Pannenberg noted, "In that he connects the figure of Jesus with Whitehead's philosophy through the concept of the logos, the universal cosmic significance of the history of Jesus becomes articulated in an imposing way. That must be the goal of all Christology. But perhaps Cobb, through the wholesale acceptance of Whitehead's natural philosophy, attains this goal too easily, without the difficult work of a critical transformation, in the light of the history of Jesus, of the foundations of the philosophical system from which he proceeds"; Wolfhart Pannenberg, "A Liberal Logos Christology," in *John Cobb's Theology In Process*, ed. David Ray Griffin and Thomas Altizer (Philadelphia: Westminster Press, 1977), 138. David Tracy also notes how process thought, for all its achievements, prevents the radical transcendence of God revealed in Jesus' resurrection from coming to expression; David Tracy, *On Naming the Present* (Maryknoll, N.Y.: Orbis, 1994), 40–43.

116. Ibid., 158, 172.

117. Cobb, "Christ beyond Creative Transformation," 154.

118. Robert Blair Kaiser, "Dupuis Profile," in *In Many and Diverse Ways*, ed. Daniel Kendall, et al. (Maryknoll, N.Y.: Orbis, 2003), 222.

119. Jacques Dupuis, *Jesus Christ and His Spirit: Theological Approaches* (Bangalore: Theological Publications in India, 1977); *Jesus Christ at the Encounter of World Religions* (Maryknoll, N.Y.: Orbis, 1991); *Who Do You Say That I Am?* (Maryknoll, N.Y.: Orbis, 1994); *Towards a Christian Theology of Religious Pluralism* (Maryknoll, N.Y.: Orbis, 1997); *Christianity and the Religions* (Maryknoll, N.Y.: Orbis, 2002).

120. Notification of the Congregation for the Doctrine of the Faith Regarding Jacques Dupuis's Book "Toward a Christian Theology of Religious Pluralism," January 24, 2001; http://www.vatican.va/roman_curia/congregations/cfaith/documents/rc_con_cfaith_doc_20010124_dupuis_en.html (accessed June 24, 2009). For discussions of the Congregation for the Doctrine of the Faith's investigation and conclusions, see Franz Cardinal König, "Let the Spirit Breathe," in Kendall, ed., *In Many and Diverse Ways*, 14–17; Gerald O'Collins, "Jacques Dupuis: His Person and Work," ibid., 18–29.

121. "Father Jacques Dupuis," *Times Online* January 12, 2005 (http://www.timesonline.co.uk/tol/comment/obituaries/article411125.ece [accessed June 24, 2009]).

122. Kaiser, "Dupuis Profile," 223.

123. Dupuis, *Jesus Christ at the Encounter of World Religions*, 116.

124. Dupuis, *Who Do You Say I Am?*, 10.

125. Paul Tillich, *Theology of Culture*, ed. Robert Kimball (New York: Oxford University Press, 1959), 42.

126. Dupuis, *Jesus Christ at the Encounter of World Religions*, 15–91.

127. Ibid., 9.

128. Ibid., 41, 45.

129. Ibid.

130. Ibid., 33.

131. Ibid., 85, 93.

132. Representative selections of this can be found in *Readings in Indian Christian Theology*, ed. R. S. Sugirtharajah and Cecil Hargreaves (London: SPCK, 1993), 1:73–125.

133. Dupuis, *Who Do You Say I Am?*, 78. Dupuis argues that this transposition happened without reduction (ibid., 78–82), but he also writes of "limitations and shortcomings" in the resulting christological dogma; ibid., 103.

134. Ibid., 102–7.

135. Dupuis, *Jesus Christ at the Encounter of World Religions*, 45

136. Even though this notion of immutability clashes with the gospel, it became an axiom of patristic Christology and theology; Jaroslav Pelikan, *The Christian Tradition*, vol. 1, *The Emergence of the Catholic Tradition (100–600)* (Chicago: University of Chicago Press, 1971), 229.

137. Dupuis, *Jesus Christ at the Encounter of World Religions*, 143–44.

138. Dupuis, *Towards a Christian Theology of Religious Pluralism*, 381.

139. Dupuis, *Jesus Christ at the Encounter of World Religions*, 42.

140. Gregory Baum, *The Credibility of the Church Today* (New York: Herder and Herder, 1968), 156–74.

141. Gregory Baum, "The Self-Understanding of the Roman Catholic Church at Vatican II," in *The Church in the Modern World*, ed. George Johnston and Wolfgang Roth (Toronto: Ryerson, 1967), 86–107.

142. Dupuis, *Jesus Christ at the Encounter of World Religions*, 5.

143. Ibid., 5–6.

144. Ibid., 34–35.

145. O'Collins, "Jacques Dupuis: His Person and Work," 25.

146. Dupuis, *Jesus Christ at the Encounter of World Religions*, 51.

147. Ibid., 62–63.

148. Dupuis, *Who Do You Say I Am?*, 42, 74–75.

149. Ibid., 53–54.

150. Ibid., 34.

151. Dupuis, *Jesus Christ at the Encounter of World Religions*, 142.

152. Dupuis, *Who Do You Say I Am?*, 55.

153. Dupuis, *Towards a Christian Theology of Religious Pluralism*, 283.

154. Dupuis, *Christianity and the Religions*, 42.

155. Dupuis, *Who Do You Say I Am?*, 36.

156. Ibid., 100.

157. Dupuis, *Jesus Christ at the Encounter of World Religions*, 33.

158. Dupuis, *Towards a Christian Theology of Religious Pluralism*, 223.

159. Dupuis, *Jesus Christ at the Encounter of World Religions*, 203; *Towards a Christian Religious Pluralism*, 249.

160. Dupuis, *Towards a Christian Theology of Religious Pluralism*, 298–99.

161. Ibid., 249–50. Dupuis describes three modes in which the Logos is present in history: in the saints, prophets, and scriptures of other religious traditions; in the scriptures and traditions of Judaism; and in the New Testament; Dupuis, *Jesus Christ at the Encounter of World Religions*, 174–77.

162. Dupuis, *Jesus Christ at the Encounter of World Religions*, 148.

163. Ibid., 151.

164. Dupuis, *Towards a Christian Theology of Religious Pluralism*, 283.

165. Ibid., 253, 277.

166. Ibid., 383.

167. Ibid., 209.

168. Cobb, *Transforming Christianity and the World*, 45.

169. Gregory Baum, *Man Becoming* (New York: Herder and Herder, 1970), 155.

170. Mark Kline Taylor, *Remembering Esperanza* (Maryknoll, N.Y.: Orbis, 1990), 175.

## Conclusion: Fifteen Christologies Later

1. Marilyn McCord Adams, *What Sort of Human Nature?* (Milwaukee: Marquette University Press, 1999), 69.

2. Don Schweitzer, "Theology, Ethics, and Deep Ecology," *The Ecumenist* 41, no. 3 (2004): 10–15.

3. Charles Taylor, *A Secular Age* (Cambridge, Mass.: Belknap Press of Harvard University, 2007), 695–700.

4. Paul Tillich, *Systematic Theology* (Chicago: University of Chicago Press, 1957), 2:155.

5. Douglas John Hall, *God and Human Suffering* (Minneapolis: Augsburg Publishing House, 1986), 99–101.

6. Peter Schmiechen comes to a similar conclusion, comparing a greater number of atonement theories. Peter Schmiechen, *Saving Power* (Grand Rapids: Eerdmans, 2005), 340.

7. Gregory Baum, *Religion and Alienation* (New York: Paulist, 1975), 218–19.

8. Charles Taylor, *Sources of the Self* (Cambridge, Mass.: Harvard University Press, 1989), 93.

9. Gregory Baum, "Cultural Causes for the Change of the God Question," in *New Questions on God: Concilium*, ed. Johann Baptist Metz (New York: Herder and Herder, 1972), 76:49–51.

10. Charles Taylor, *Sources of the Self: The Making of the Modern Identity* (Cambridge, Mass.: Harvard University Press, 1992), 215–18.

11. There is a critique of democracy in Jon Sobrino, *No Salvation outside the Poor* (Maryknoll, N.Y.: Orbis, 2008), 11–12.

12. This return of religion to the public sphere is studied in José Casanova, *Public Religions in the Modern World* (Chicago: University of Chicago Press, 1994).

13. Rudolf Bultmann, *The Gospel of John: A Commentary* (Philadelphia: Westminster, 1971), 46–47.

14. Serene Jones, *Feminist Theory and Christian Theology* (Minneapolis: Fortress Press, 2000), 169–76.

15. Mark Lewis Taylor, *Remembering Esperanza* (Maryknoll, N.Y.: Orbis, 1990), 175.

16. Ibid., 190.

17. H. Richard Niebuhr, *Christ and Culture* (New York: Harper and Row, 1951).

18. Ibid., 83.

19. Ibid., 65.

20. Ibid., 231.

21. For Schleiermacher's Christology, see Catherine Kelsey, *Thinking about Christ with Schleiermacher* (Louisville: Westminster John Knox, 2003).

22. John B. Cobb Jr., "Christ Beyond Creative Transformation," in *Encountering Jesus*, ed. Stephen Davis (Atlanta: John Knox, 1988), 150. Cobb argues that the need is not for a choice between a Christ of culture approach like his earlier one and a more socially radical one, but for a synthesis; ibid. In one sense, he is right in attempting to develop a more inclusive and thus more adequate position. But Niebuhr's point is that every choice excludes as well as includes, no matter how inclusive it tries to be. And no choice can include and integrate all that is worthy of inclusion.

23. Jürgen Moltmann, *God in Creation* (London: SCM, 1985), 31.

24. Roger Haight, *The Future of Christology* (New York: Continuum, 2005), 120.

25. Ibid., 122.

26. Robert Wuthnow, *Christianity in the 21st Century* (New York: Oxford University Press, 1993), 114–15.

27. Haight, *The Future of Christology*, 122.

28. John B. Cobb Jr., "Ally or Opponent? A Response to Stanley Hauerwas," *Theology Today* 51, no. 4 (1995): 571.

29. Ernst Bloch, *Heritage of Our Times* (Cambridge: Polity, 1991), 97–116.

30. Baum, *Religion and Alienation*, 257.

31. Don Schweitzer, "Gregory Baum on the Revelatory Work of the Holy Spirit," *Horizons* 24, no. 1 (1997): 73–88.

32. Martin Kähler, *The So-Called Historical Jesus and the Historic Biblical Christ*, ed. with an introduction by Carl Braaten (Philadelphia: Fortress Press, 1964), 61–62.

33. For an overview of this, see Roger Haight, *Jesus: Symbol of God* (Maryknoll, N.Y.: Orbis, 1999), 30–45.

34. Ibid., 479.

35. Jürgen Moltmann, *The Crucified God* (London: SCM, 1974), 200.

36. Don Schweitzer, "Karl Barth's Critique of Classical Theism," *Toronto Journal of Theology* 18, no. 2 (2002): 231–44.

37. Elizabeth Johnson, *She Who Is* (New York: Crossroad, 1993), 224–27.

38. Karl Barth, *Church Dogmatics* II/1, ed. G.W. Bromily and T. F. Torrance, (Edinburgh: T&T Clark, 1957), 303.

39. Moltmann, *The Crucified God*, 240–41.

40. John B. Cobb Jr., *Christ in a Pluralistic Age* (Philadelphia: Westminster, 1975), 244.

41. Taylor, *Remembering Esperanza*, 232.

42. Sallie McFague, *A New Climate for Theology* (Minneapolis: Fortress Press, 2008), 34, 171–72.

43. Hendrik Vroom, "On Being 'Reformed,' " *Reformed World* 58, no. 4 (2008): 202.

44. Sharon Betcher, *Spirit and the Politics of Disablement* (Minneapolis: Fortress Press, 2007), 68–89.

45. Wonhee Anne Joh, *Heart of the Cross: A Postcolonial Christology* (Louisville: Westminster John Knox, 2006).

46. Michael Welker, "Who Is Jesus Christ for Us Today?" *Harvard Theological Review* 95, no. 2 (2002): 129–46.

# INDEX

# Index

Jesus as the Christ, 2, 4, 11–12,
19–20, 25–27, 37–38, 43–45,
46, 48, 59–60, 65–66, 69, 78–80,
87–88, 93–95, 104–5, 109, 110–12,
119–21, 127–28
male gender of Jesus, 3, 39–40, 44,
68–69, 115
resurrection of, 2, 3, 9, 10, 12, 14, 15,
16, 22, 25, 27, 36, 39, 44, 50–51,
55–56, 59, 60, 61–62, 65, 69–70,
74, 76–77, 79, 80, 84, 87, 96, 106,
120, 139
and women, 3, 39–40, 44, 47–48, 62,
67–69, 74, 79
Joh, Wonhee Anne, 184n45
John Duns Scotus, 93, 128
Johnson, Elizabeth, 55–56, 66–70, 71,
137, 159n45, 163n27, 164n62, 166–
67nn104–26, 167n129, 183n37
Jones, Serene, 131, 167n114, 175n8,
183n14
Judaism, 23, 37, 66, 84, 88, 107, 113
justice, 3, 8, 20, 21, 37–39, 41–42, 44, 47,
52, 56, 61, 64, 67, 70, 79, 114, 128–29,
130

Kähler, Martin, 136, 183n32
Kaiser, Robert Blair, 180n118, 180n122
Käsemann, Ernst, 60
Kelsey, Catherine, 183n21
Knitter, Paul, 175n11, 177n48
König, Franz Cardinal, 180n120
Küng, Hans, 169n43, 175n6

liberation theology, 15, 16, 17, 38, 59,
62–64, 68, 75–76, 114, 115, 148
Loewe, William, 165n66
Logos Christology, 12–13, 26–27, 38, 79,
110–12, 113, 114, 115, 119–22, 149
Luciani, Rafael, 165n71

Macquarrie, John, 171n69
Marcus, Joel, 170n45
Marquez, Gaspar, 153n5, 153n6

Martel, Yann, 175n1
martyr (martyrdom), 65, 82, 114,
165n65
McDermott, John, 154n21, 154n25
McDougall, Joy Ann, 170n65
McFague, Sallie, 159n43, 184n42
McGovern, Arthur, 165n69
Meier, John, 66, 153n1, 166n98
Menacherry, Cheriyan, 176n26
Messiah, 37, 74, 79, 85
Metz, Johann Baptist, 17, 63, 149
modernity, 7, 10–11, 22–23, 70, 77, 84,
110, 118, 130, 132, 133, 134, 152
Moltmann, Jürgen, 17, 28, 63, 73, 75–82,
96, 133, 137, 138, 156n72, 162n120,
163n27, 163n31, 168–71nn8–82,
177n55, 183n23, 183n35, 184n39
Muck, Otto, 154n13

Nicaea, Council of, 2–3, 14, 19, 25, 27,
41, 58, 63–64, 117, 127, 137, 146
Niebuhr, Reinhold, 82, 89, 92, 174n46
Niebuhr, H. Richard, 132–33, 197n99,
183n17, 183n22
Noia, J. A. Di, 153n9
Noll, Mark, 172n87

O'Collins, Gerald, 180n120, 181n145
Oliver, Dianne, 155n45

Panikkar, Raimon (Raimundo), 99–100,
100–7, 123–24, 139, 175n7, 175n9–12,
176–77nn13–54
Pannenberg, Wolfhart, 4, 66, 108, 141,
157n105, 162n119, 163n27, 163n31,
180n115
Parker, Rebecca, 74, 168n6
patriarchy, 42, 43, 67, 159n28
Pelikan, Jaroslav, 154n29, 162n118,
181n136
Peukert, Helmut, 156n74
Pinnock, Sarah, 158n24
postmodern, 8, 23–25, 28, 29, 82, 109,
129, 132–34, 136, 138–39, 149

187